SCOTLAND – THE LAND AND THE WHISKY

SCOTLAND

THE LAND AND THE WHISKY

RODDY MARTINE

PHOTOGRAPHS BY

PATRICK DOUGLAS-HAMILTON

JOHN MURRAY IN ASSOCIATION WITH

THE KEEPERS OF THE QUAICH

First published in 1994 by John Murray (Publishers) Ltd.,
50 Albemarle Street, London W1X 4BD

A catalogue record for this book is available from the British Library
ISBN 0-7195-5700-3

Typeset in Monotype Joanna
Printed and bound in Italy by Graphicon, Vicenza

Designed by Peter Campbell

The publishers are grateful to the following for permission to reproduce additional illustrations:
John Murray Collection: p.23 (Walter Scott); Woodmansterne Ltd: p.23 (Walter Scott meeting Robert Burns);
Scottish National Portrait Gallery: p.28; The Bridgeman Art Library: pp. 26, 29, 62, 114-115, 128, 174, 194; The Victoria and Albert Museum: pp. 72, 126; Eric Thorburn: p.14 (all the quaichs except the bottom centre)

Maps by Peter Haillay

Frontispiece: pot-stills, Auchentoshan Distillery

CONTENTS

Acknowledgements 6 / Foreword 7 / The Glory that is Scotch 8

The Quaich 12 / The Keepers of the Quaich 13

THE LOWLANDS

1. The Borders, the Lothians and Fife 21 / 2. The Southwest 51

THE HIGHLANDS

3. The Southern Highlands 77 / 4. The Western Highlands 99

5. Grampian Region and the Eastern Highlands 127 / 6. Speyside 143

7. The Northern Highlands 165

THE ISLANDS

8. Islay, Jura, Mull and Skye 179 / 9. The Orkney Islands 199

THE DISTILLERIES

207

INDEX

ACKNOWLEDGEMENTS

Roddy Martine and Patrick Douglas-Hamilton would like to thank the management committee of The Keepers of the Quaich for making this book possible. Chairman: James Bruxner, Chairman, Justerini & Brooks Ltd; Treasurer: John Goodwin, Chairman, The Highland Distilleries Co plc; Members: Andrew Dewar-Durie, Managing Director, Allied Distillers Ltd; James Espey, President, The Chivas & Glenlivet Division, The Seagram Company; James Wolfe-Murray, Strategic Affairs Director, United Distillers; and Director: Gordon McIntosh.

The author and photographer would also like to thank the following for their invaluable advice and help in the preparation of this book: Karen Ambrose; Peter Arbuthnott; John Ashworth; Andy Barclay; Marcie J. Bell; Brian J. Bissett; Bill Bergius; Yvonne Brandon; Ken Buchanan; Mark Butterworth; George Cameron; Islay Campbell; Shena Campbell; Grant Carmichael; James Casey; Evan Cattenach; Ricky Christie; Dennis Clark; Frank Clarke; Gloria Clyde; Trevor Cowan; Angus Darroch; Lutz Deisinger; Peter Derbyshire; Campbell Evans; Peter Fairlie; Lyn Falconer; Elisa Ferbj; Matthew Gloag; Heather Graham; Charles Grant; David Grant; John Grant; Dr Sandy Grant Gordon; Dr Chris Greig; Gina Harley; Jenifer Hartman; Elspeth Henderson; Iain Henderson; Sheena Hilleary; Turnbull Hutton; Philippa Ireland; Brian and Oona Ivory; Fiona Jack; Nicola Jackman; Barrie M. Jackson; Tim Jackson; James Johnston; Susan Kilgour; Gillian Kirkwood; Mark Lawson; Ronnie Learmond; Colin Liddell; Harry Lindley; Jonathan Lyddon; Eddie MacAffer; Shirley McCaffray; Jim McColl; John S. McDonald; Jim McEwan; Alastair S. McIntosh; Charles MacLean; Hector MacLennan; Willie MacNeill; Iain MacPherson; James MacTaggart; David Mair; Alex Malcolm; Ian Matthew; T. Morris H. Miller; Wallace Milroy; Hugh Mitcalfe; Zoë Mizen; Georgina Murdoch; Brian Nodes; Ronald D. Oakes; Moyra Peffer; Bill Phillips; Jill Preston; Keith Rose; Jill Ross; Christopher Rowe; Keith and Suki Schelenberg; J. Patrick Scott; Estelle Scroggie; David Smith; Peter Smith; Rena Steel; the Hon James Stewart; James Stewart; Joe Stirling; Pauline Thomson; Janice Thomson; Jim Thurle; Brenda Walsh; Carol Anne Ward; John Watson; Jim Young.

A special thanks to Margaret McIntosh for her invaluable assistance in checking detail and fact, and to David Munro for producing the superlative colour prints from which the photographs in this book were reproduced.

FOREWORD

HIS GRACE THE DUKE OF ATHOLL

As Grand Master of The Keepers of the Quaich, I feel most honoured to have been asked to write the foreword to a volume such as this. It is superbly illustrated and full of stories. It goes into the history of Scotch whisky, telling how it reached its present plain with tales of illicit distilling, smuggling and how evasion of the exciseman evolved into a national pastime. How in 1823 legislation was passed to encourage the licensing of stills and how from this legislation have emerged the well-known (and not so well-known) names we know today.

When a new book about Scotland and Scotch whisky appears, it is always looked through with great attention to see if it comes up with a new idea, or anything which can be thought of in that way. This book is no exception, and I personally found that it was a very good way of tracing the enormous number of places where whisky is produced, in an enthralling way, and a way which has not been used before.

I commend this book to all of you who have an interest in Scotland and Scotch whisky. I am sure you will find it a welcome addition to your library, and I am also sure that it will provide you with hours of pleasurable reading.

7

THE GLORY THAT IS SCOTCH

This book is a celebration of Scotland and Scotch whisky – its oldest and most universally acclaimed product. It is the land itself, the water, the wind, the climate, even the people, which give Scotch whisky its unique quality. No attempt to manufacture the *uisgebeatha* anywhere else in the world – even using the same processes and ingredients – has been successful. The single malts, the de luxe and the blended whiskies of Scotland, each distinctive, individually reflect the character of the immediate landscape in which they were created; and by understanding the landscape one can more fully appreciate the different whiskies.

Scotch whisky is the largest selling 'single source' spirit in the world. Approximately 70 million cases are distributed annually throughout home and international markets. With annual earnings of about £2,000,000,000, the success of Scotch whisky is phenomenal. Its acknowledged health-giving properties together with its purity and excellence can undoubtedly claim to have brought prodigious benefits to mankind. It is world renowned and to anyone anywhere 'Scotch' can mean only one thing – Scotch whisky.

The process of distillation came to Scotland, it is believed, with the early Christian missionaries, followers of St Columba, although Neil Gunn, the Scottish novelist, places the discovery in Clan/Druid mythology. Others insist that the art originated in Ireland, also associated with Christianity, coinciding with the arrival of St Patrick in AD 461. Evidence suggests that distillation was known in England in the reign of Henry II in the twelfth century although the earliest actual reference to it in Scotland is in the Exchequer Rolls of 1494 which mention 'eight bolls of malt to Friar John Cor wherein to mak aqua vitae'. Although whisky was undoubtedly manufactured throughout medieval Scotland, this early mention was seized upon by the Scotch Whisky Association, the official trade association for the Scotch whisky industry, to make 1994 a year of celebration for the Spirit of Scotland.

For five hundred years scholars and authors, when reflecting on Scotland, have borne testimony to the remarkable properties of Scotland's national drink. Writing of the Isle of Lewis in 1695, Martin Martin, the MacLeod of MacLeod's factor on the Isle of Skye, comments that 'the air is temperately cold and moist, and for the corrective, the natives use a dose of trestarig or uisgebeatha'.

In his masterly work on Scotch whisky, Professor David Daiches writes that by the seventeenth century whisky was already established as the characteristic Highland spirit; that in the eighteenth century, in spite of continuous troubles with the excise after the failure of the 1745 Jacobite uprising, whisky distilling flourished in the Highlands and soon spread to the Lowlands.

By 1777 Edinburgh had eight licensed stills and, according to excise officers, four hundred illicit stills. Whisky drinking, however, was very much the indulgence of the lower orders. Toddy – whisky, sugar and hot water – was a common drink, whereas the great houses held claret and hock, possibly brandy, rum and port, in their cellars.

Research into household books by the 11th Earl of Elgin reveals that between 1759 and 1770 the 5th Earl and his wife purchased modest amounts of whisky for themselves, but mainly for making punch. However, for the working people of their estate, it was a very different matter.

In the eighteenth and nineteenth centuries the Elgins' Broomhall estate purchased malt and grain whisky in bulk for estate employees. From 1824 there are book entries of a village shop, run by the estate, where employees were allowed credit. The entry on 7 February 1824 reveals that the estate bought from William Young & Co of Grange a hogshead of grain at 100 degrees proof at five shillings and four pence per gallon and a hogshead at 100 degrees proof malt at six shillings and four pence per gallon. On 28 January 1825 the purchase is recorded from James Haig & Sons of Edinburgh of four casks containing 134 gallons, 199 gallons, 130 gallons and 124 gallons, 587 gallons of proof malt in all. With such evidence it was possible for the present Lord Elgin to calculate that over the average number of male employees on the Broomhall Estate, each male drank six bottles of proof whisky per week.

In his treatise on the Scots, Iain Finlayson comments: 'Temperance, if not a typically Scottish virtue, was a magic word among the nineteenth century reformers. In the early years of the nineteenth century, the Scots certainly merited their reputation as hard and consistent drinkers; viciousness, however, was not part of their motive – rather, the Scots used drink as an aid to conviviality, and the occasions of compliment and kindness were many and varied.'

In the Highlands whisky rapidly acquired significant ritual associations. For example, it became customary to give new-born infants a spooonful to welcome them into the world, and it was the standard drink at funerals. David Daiches tells the story of the little girl whose aunt was gravely ill. When Sir Archibald Geikie inquired as to the old lady's health, the niece replied: 'Ay, she's no deid yet; but we've gotten in the whisky for the funeral.'

With the Industrial Revolution came engineering and the railways. Distilleries were streamlined but still largely owned and controlled by the families who had founded them. An accelerating demand for the product created a speculative boom among the Victorian investors of the 1890s – distilleries had shown a good return on investment and, as a result, a large number of new brand names appeared. Within ten years the market had become flooded, causing many distilleries to change hands. Some survived and prospered; others disappeared without trace. Overall, ownership of the Scotch whisky industry in Scotland was to change dramatically after 1887, the year in which Alfred Barnard compiled his authoritative book *The Whisky Distilleries of the United Kingdom.*

The production of grain whisky, dramatically different from malt whisky in its distillation process and taste, led to the revolutionary discovery of the art of blending in the second half of the nineteenth century. This was to add an entirely new dimension to the concept. Lowland Scotland rapidly developed as the traditional home of grain whisky and over the years, thirty or more grain distilleries became active. Today there are seven massive grain distilleries operational in Scotland, with 95 per cent of their production going into Scotch blends.

By the middle of the twentieth century, Scotch whisky, as a result of the overseas marketing initiatives of several key companies, had become Scotland's largest net export earner, and today accounts for more than 80 per cent by value of exports of all alcoholic drinks from the United Kingdom. With the approach of a new millennium, however, hitherto untouched markets have sprung up around the world opening up new opportunities for the industry.

This book sets out to pay rightful tribute to the single malts of Scotland which capture the imagination, and to show the unique land of Scotland from which they have been created. Scotland can be both stunningly beautiful as well as daunting and harsh, with a history that fully reflects this. Above all it is the water that runs off the mountains in rivers and burns to the lochs and sea, together with the peat, that gives whisky its distinctive quality.

No longer are Scotland's distilleries largely inaccessible; no more are the magical malts of Scotland a connoisseur's secret. Nowadays, the general public is being actively encouraged to experiment; to understand the difference between a blended whisky and a single malt; to appreciate the regional variations, to learn the difference between a Lowland, a Highland, a Speyside, an Islay and an Orkney malt.

Not so very long ago it would have been easier for the average individual to enter the vaults of a bank than to gain access to the still-house of a distillery. Then came the Speyside Whisky Trail introducing distilleries to tourism in 1982. The pioneers were William Grant & Sons with their imaginative facilities at the Glenfiddich Distillery which today accommodates 135,000 visitors each year. Other companies responded with similar attractions and, most recently, United Distillers have invested in five specialised distillery visitor centres. A range of single malts hitherto unavailable to the general public began to appear in hotel bars, pubs and on the shelves of Off-Licences.

Although many distilleries are today controlled by the large, powerful conglomerates, many of the original whisky families remain, either working within the ownership company – familiar surnames such as Haig, Dewar, Lang, Mackinlay,

Mackenzie, Teacher, Bergius and Gloag – or fiercely retaining their independence, such as the Grants and Gordons of William Grant & Sons, the Grants of J. & G. Grant, the Morrisons of Morrison Bowmore Distillers, the Macdonalds of Macdonald Martin, the Wrights of Springbank, the Christies of Speyside and the MacKinnons of Drambuie.

Following takeovers, some family members have even branched out to start up on their own; others, new to the industry, have started from scratch. For example, in Edinburgh, in 1993, James Walker, the young great-grandson of Archibald Walker, owner of distilleries in Limerick, Liverpool and on Clydeside, revived the family's Adelphi Distillery label which dates from 1826, and Sir Iain Noble, the merchant banker based on the Isle of Skye, launched his own blended and vatted labels. Harold Currie, formerly with Chivas Brothers, has been spearheading the first legal distillery for over 150 years on the Isle of Arran. Taking water from the Eason Biorach, near Lochranza, the first bottled Isle of Arran single malt is scheduled for marketing in January 2001.

'The traditional produce of Scotland – porridge, oatcakes, haggis and whisky – have one thing in common,' once observed Sir Nicholas Fairbairn of Fordel, painter, wit and former Solicitor General for Scotland. 'They derive from grain and bits of beast you cannot sell. Scotland, being a poor place, the Scots have developed these things

The Earl and Countess of Elgin at Broomhall

10

through peasant necessity and have since transformed them into a fantasy.' As the full potential of Scotch whisky – the brands, the subtle variations, the rituals associated with its consumption – comes to be better known around the world, so too will be enhanced an awareness of its land of origin.

Writing of Scotland, the land of his birth, R.H. Bruce Lockhart, politician, diplomat, author, one of the most distinguished Scotsmen of the first half of the twentieth century, had the following observation to make of his fellow Scots: 'Whisky has made us what we are . . . It is our release from materialism, and I often think that without it we should have been so irritatingly efficient that a worse persecution than the Hebrews ever suffered would have been our fate.'

On a stormy winter's night, warmed by his fire in the great hall at Broomhall, Lord Elgin occasionally takes pleasure in a tour of Scotland. As the wind, rain and snow obscure the surrounding landscape of the Kingdom of Fife, it is customary for him to inspect his collection of malt whiskies. As he selects a malt, it carries him in spirit to its place of origin and so he embarks upon his journey. 'Sometimes I like the solace of Morayshire,' he says. 'On other occasions I prefer the vigour of the Western Isles or the fire of Orkney. In this way I can travel around Scotland without leaving the comfort of my armchair.'

THE QUAICH

The quaich, the ancient drinking vessel of the Scots, takes its name from the Gaelic 'cuach' meaning 'cup'. The most widely used of these early drinking vessels were made of wood, and were wide and shallow in shape, their size depending on their purpose. The typical quaich has two handles, is well proportioned and often carved. By the late seventeenth century quaichs began to be made in bone, pewter, silver and gold.

Pewter quaich, late seventeenth century

A quaich dated 1925 made of plane carved with Celtic ornamentation

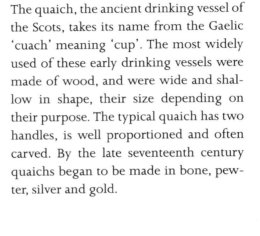

Silver mounted quaich of wooden staves commemorating the wedding in 1678 of John Campbell to Mary, daughter of the Marquess of Argyll

Bonnie Prince Charlie's quaich, presented by him to Mrs Stewart of Stenton in 1745

Quaich of The Brotherhood of Scotch Whisky Tasters

THE KEEPERS OF THE QUAICH

The Keepers of the Quaich is an exclusive, non-profit making, international society founded by the leading Scotch whisky distillers to honour those around the world who have recognised the nobility of Scotch whisky by working with it, or writing and speaking about it. The organisation includes as its members leading representatives of the Scotch whisky industry and those who have contributed to the successful marketing of Scotch whisky in countries across the world, together with noted Scotch whisky connoisseurs and characters. All have one fundamental link – a love of Scotland and Scotch whisky.

In establishing The Keepers of the Quaich, the Scotch whisky industry pooled its enormous resources and strength to build on the image and prestige of Scotch whisky at home and abroad. As a Scotch whisky institution, it is intended that charitable donations will, from time to time, be made to worthwhile causes benefiting Scotland and its people. The Society's mission statement declares that the intention is to advance the standing and prosperity of one of Britain's premier export industries and to make more widely known its uniqueness, traditions, quality, and benefits to the community it serves, both at home and in the markets of the world. Membership, by invitation only, must be approved by a management committee representing the five founding companies.

The Keepers of the Quaich banquets take place

The Society's Grand Quaich

at Blair Castle, registered headquarters of the Society, twice a year. Against a backdrop of some of Scotland's finest scenery, the best of Scotland is on show – a superb dinner drawn from Scotland's larder, accompanied by the very best of Scotch whiskies and traditional Scottish entertainment. At the start of the proceedings, a formal induction ceremony honours those who have been of outstanding service to the industry. Each new member is presented with a small quaich and a medal by the Grand Master, who is appointed on an annual basis. The implications thereafter, as with the Chevaliers de Tastevin in Burgundy and the Commanderie du Bontemps de Médoc et des Graves in Bordeaux, are that, for the first time, the many integral parts and outposts of the industry are being bonded together with a sense of overall destiny and place.

To this end the Society has carefully selected its patrons from among the great Scottish families whose histories date back to the beginning of the

Scottish race. They are the 24th Earl of Erroll, Mac Garadh Mor, Hereditary Lord High Constable of Scotland, Chief of Clan Hay; the 12th Duke of Argyll, Mac Cailein Mor, Chief of Clan Campbell; the 10th Duke of Atholl, Chief of Clan Murray; the 11th Earl of Elgin & 15th Earl of Kincardine KT, 37th Chief of the name of Bruce; and the 8th Earl of Mansfield and Mansfield, Hereditary Keeper of Lochmaben Castle. Two outstanding figures from the industry, Sir Iain Tennant KT, a former Chairman of Seagram Distillers, and Lord Macfarlane of Bearsden, Chairman of United Distillers, complete the impressive line-up.

The Grand Quaich of The Keepers of the Quaich, measuring 24 inches across and specially made for the Society, is a magnificent example of contemporary silversmithing. Made from sterling silver and carrying the Edinburgh hallmark, the Quaich, with its unique base of ten-year-old burr elm, sits at the centre of Society ceremonies. Keepers take particular pride in the fact that the Lord Lyon, King of Arms, granted an heraldic achievement comprising a shield, crest and coat-of-arms. The society motto, also bestowed by the Lord Lyon himself, is 'Uisgebeatha Gu Brath', which is the Gaelic for 'Water of Life Forever'.

The Keepers of the Quaich also have their own tartan: based on a design of the 1700s, the colours represent the main constituents of Scotch whisky: blue for water, gold for barley and brown for peat.

MEMBER COMPANIES OF THE KEEPERS OF THE QUAICH

Founding Partners
Allied Distillers Ltd
Justerini & Brooks Ltd
The Highland Distilleries Co plc and
Robertson & Baxter Ltd
United Distillers plc
The Chivas & Glenlivet Group

Corporate Members
Berry Brothers & Rudd Ltd
Burn Stewart Distillers plc
Campbell Distillers Ltd
J. & G. Grant Distillers
William Grant & Sons Ltd
The Invergordon Distillers Ltd
Inver House Distillers Ltd

William Lawson Distillers Ltd
Macallan-Glenlivet plc
Macdonald Martin Distilleries plc
Morrison Bowmore Distillers Ltd
The North British Distillery Co Ltd
Tomatin Distillery Co Ltd
Whyte & Mackay Group plc

The Keepers of the Quaich banquet at Blair Castle

SCOTLAND

THE LAND AND THE WHISKY

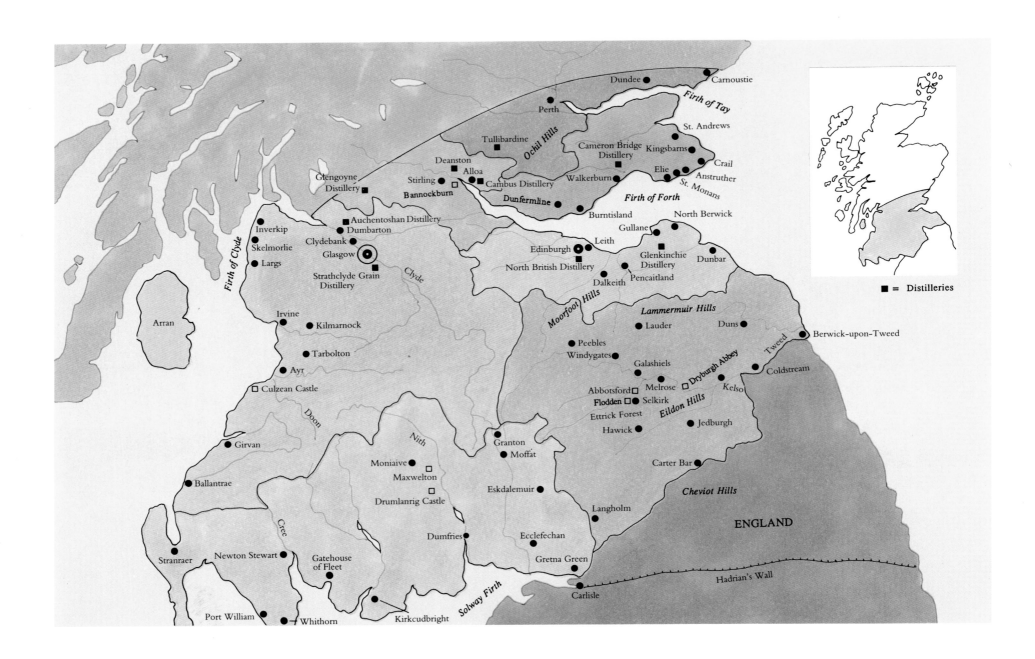

Dundee • Carnoustie
Firth of Tay
Perth • St. Andrews
Tullibardine ■ Ochil Hills Cameron Bridge Kingsbarns
Deanston Distillery Crail
Glengoyne ■ Alloa Elie Anstruther
Distillery Stirling ■ Cambus Distillery Walkerburn St. Monans
Bannockburn Firth of Forth
Dunfermline •
Burntisland North Berwick
Auchentoshan Distillery Gullane
Inverkip Dumbarton Leith Dunbar
Skelmorlie Clydebank Edinburgh ⊙ Glenkinchie ■
Largs Glasgow ◉ North British Distillery Distillery
Strathclyde Grain Dalkeith Pencaitland
Firth of Clyde Distillery Clyde
Moorfoot Hills Lammermuir Hills
Arran Irvine Lauder Duns
Kilmarnock Berwick-upon-Tweed
Peebles Tweed
Tarbolton Windygates Galashiels Dryburgh Abbey
Ayr Abbotsford Melrose Coldstream
Culzean Castle Doon Flodden Selkirk Kelso
Ettrick Forest Eildon Hills
Girvan Hawick Jedburgh
Nith
Ballantrae Granton Carter Bar
Moniaive Moffat
Maxwelton Cheviot Hills
Drumlanrig Castle Eskdalemuir
Cree Langholm ENGLAND
Dumfries Ecclefechan
Stranraer Newton Stewart Gatehouse Gretna Green
of Fleet Hadrian's Wall
Port William Whithorn Kirkcudbright Solway Firth Carlisle

■ = Distilleries

THE LOWLANDS

Berwick upon Tweed — gateway to the Lowlands

THE BORDERS, THE LOTHIANS AND FIFE

THE SOUTHWEST

THE LOWLANDS

The Scottish nation, which came together between the sixth and the fourteenth centuries, absorbed several races in the process of creating what has come to be regarded by many as the pure Scot, if indeed there can be said to be such a thing. To begin with there was the Anglo-Saxon kingdom of Bernicia which stretched from the River Tyne to the Firth of Forth with its fortification of Dun Eideann. In the early seventh century Bernicia amalgamated with Deira, the territory around Humberside with York as its capital, to form Northumbria, and the language of that region was a form of English which later came to be known as Lallans. Until 971, the region of Strathclyde, extending south from the Clyde to encompass Cumberland and Westmorland, was held by Britons who spoke a Cumbrian dialect akin to Welsh. In the southwest corner, Galloway was dominated by Gaelic-speaking Picts.

Early Scots were a Celtic people who invaded the western coast of northern Britain, a region known as Alba, landing on the shores of Argyllshire, which they named Dalriada. These Scots had travelled over the sea from Ireland and, previously, as suggested by evidence, from the Middle East. Long before their incursion, the inhabitants of Alba's northern territories were known as the Picts

or Picti because they painted their bodies, and their language was 'pictorial'. Through colonisation over the centuries, and because they had no written language with which to record what was happening to them, they simply disappeared.

In the eleventh century came the Saxon refugees from the Norman William the Conqueror's invasion of England. In the following century Norman families were imported by David I to assist him with his government. It may seem improbable in the present age, but from the tenth to the twelfth century, Scotland was the place in Europe where the younger sons of English and continental families came to seek advancement from the Scottish king, to acquire lands and to breed new dynasties. The clans of the north, in their true and unique Highland context, did not come about in most cases until King Robert I of Scotland, himself of Norman descent and a cousin of the King of England, had beaten back an English invasion in 1314, unifying the majority of interests in Scotland against English imperialism. This gave Scotland its first triumphant sense of identity as a nation, despite the fact that the majority of its leading nobles were of Norman blood, and that in the far north, Caithness, Sutherland, Orkney and Shetland, and the Hebrides were under Viking control until as late as 1266.

In the centuries that followed there was much

coming and going. Scotland has always been a great coloniser, but has itself been systematically colonised. This came about through the Auld Alliance, when Louis XII of France decreed that all Scots were entitled to the privileges of French nationality, and then through trade with the Low Countries – Holland, Belgium and North Germany. Lithuanians and Italians appeared in the second half of the nineteenth century, Polish refugees arrived during the Second World War, and, more recently Scotland has become home to many Indian, Pakistani and Chinese immigrants.

It can be seen, therefore, that Scotland's Lowlands – the Border Country – added to the old Strathclyde Kingdom, provide a very different historic entity to the Gaelic-speaking communities north of the Highland line. And there are distinctly different cultural characteristics north and south, east and west in Scotland. It was much later, in the nineteenth century, essentially through the mass immigration from the glens and Northern Ireland that, despite Glasgow's southerly location, its character evolved as more Highland than Lowland.

Geographically, the Lowlands of Scotland, incorporating Edinburgh and Glasgow, comprise one tenth of the land area and today accommodate three quarters of Scotland's total population. Agriculture continues as the mainstay of the economy, but new technology, textile and tweed manufacture, light industry and computer developments have made massive inroads, supplanting the coal, steel and heavy engineering of the Victorian era.

To begin with, however, the story of the Borders was largely that of defence. Scottish kings appointed their Wardens of the March, officers of the Crown whose task it was to maintain law and order. The border with England was ill defined, the area being known as The Debatable Land, a locality for skirmishes, raiding parties back-and-forth and cattle reiving. From Berwick-upon-Tweed, on the eastern seaboard, to Dumfriesshire, spanning the northern shore of the Solway Firth, families such as Douglas, Home, Scott, Kerr, Armstrong, Elliott, Maxwell and Johnstone did as they pleased, contemptuous of authority, all too conscious of their importance as a human shield against the threat of English invasion.

Fortified keeps and peel towers sprang up along the river banks – Neidpath, Horsburgh, Elibank, Cardrona, Newark, Smailholm – strategic watchtowers. With rich farmland, undulating and variable, the Borders prospered through being well defended, yet accessible. To begin with, Edinburgh, where the Court was located, was within easy riding distance. Later, when James VI headed south to London, the Borders was as close as it was possible to get to the Court in London without being in England.

Thus the majority of the great and powerful families of Scotland clustered tightly into this one region: the Scotts (dukes of Buccleuch) at Bowhill and Dalkeith; the Douglases (dukes of Queensberry) at Drumlanrig; the Hamiltons (earls of Angus and dukes of Hamilton) at Hamilton Palace (demolished in 1927); the Kerrs (dukes of Roxburghe) at Floors, and many others. These great Lowland families, preoccupied with amassing land and wealth and building their fine palaces, easily distanced themselves from the remote, internecine traumas of the Highlands. To the Lowland Whig, the territory north and west of Perth remained alien territory. In W.H. Murray's account of the life and times of Rob Roy MacGregor, he refers to the civic hostility meted out in the 1680s towards clansmen arriving in Glasgow for the winter mart. In the same way that the majority of Lowlanders would have condoned the brutal act of Glencoe in 1692, their response to Prince Charles Edward Stuart's arrival half a century later at the head of an army of unruly Highland 'savages' was predictably one of suspicion and mistrust. While readily winning the hearts of the ladies of Edinburgh, the Bonnie Prince fatally failed to sustain the approval of the majority of their menfolk. Thus Culloden, the final conflict of the Jacobite cause, was a Highland battle fought by ill-equipped Highlanders against the full might of the House of Hanover. The silent majority of the Lowland community chose to look the other way.

With the relative prosperity of the Lowland Scots, at no time was there among farmers either a significant necessity or idiosyncratic urge to manufacture whisky. Those who required whisky were usually able to purchase sufficient quantities and its legality was of little concern. Despite a proliferation of illicit stills in and around the centres of population, distilling remained very much a rural Highlands and Islands preoccupation. There are several obvious reasons for this. First, tenant farmers in the Highlands, being more impoverished than their southern counterparts, found distilling a lucrative sideline. Secondly, remoteness from centres of legislation made such activities almost impossible to police. Thirdly, the northern landscape with an abundance of peat deposits, barley, and a constant supply of mountain water, spontaneously provided all the necessary ingredients for the production process. Also to be taken into account is the harsh climate and the genuine warmth that a tot of the *uisgebeatha* brings to the common man. Scotch whisky was to develop into a connoisseur's delight, but it began as a poor man's pleasure.

CHAPTER ONE: THE BORDERS, THE LOTHIANS AND FIFE

The Lammermuirs in summer

The Borders of Scotland represent a compromise. Not so remote as the Highlands, the undulating terrain still encompasses that sense of freedom brought on by open spaces, a landscape of fast flowing rivers and rolling farmland. It is rich country, near enough to two great cities, yet neglected so often by those bound for the legendary glens and bens and lochs of the north.

From the Borders crossing of the Cheviot Hills at Carter Bar there is a fine prospect of all five of the old Borders counties: Dumfriesshire, Roxburghshire, Selkirkshire, Peebles-shire and Berwickshire. Across the grassy ridges of Roxburgh there is a glimpse of the Eildons, and to the north can be seen the Moorfoots with the shadowed ripple of the Lammermuirs beyond. To the west are the tops of Tweedsmuir as Peebles-shire meets Dumfriesshire. Once over Carter Bar, the initial impression may be of bleak, unpopulated landscape, dotted with sheep, but as Jedburgh, in the gentle valley of the Jed Water, comes into sight, the surroundings become increasingly wooded and more welcoming.

The red sandstone Jedburgh Abbey was founded in 1138 by David I for Augustinian canons from Beauvais in France, but since the years have brought many sackings and rebuildings, only ruins remain. In 1516, Mary Queen of Scots passed this way to open the Justice Eyres and to visit her lover and future husband, Lord Bothwell, at Hermitage Castle. To the west is Hawick, where the River Teviot meets the Slitrig Water, and here the Scottish textile industry has its largest Borders centre. In June, Hawick celebrates one of the oldest annual Common Ridings to commemorate the Hornshole Skirmish, when a party of local youths routed English raiders and captured the Abbot of Hexham's standard. Wilton Lodge, ancestral home of the Langlands family, houses the Hawick Museum and Art Gallery, and with song and verse and tales of reivers and grim peel towers, reveals why Borderers are so fiercely proud of their heritage.

Selkirk is another ancient royal burgh which overlooks the Yarrow Valley, and annually commemorates a Common Riding tradition that after the Battle of Flodden in 1513 only one man out of eighty of those who went off to war returned. Mungo Park, the explorer of Africa, was born at Foulshields here in 1771, and his statue stands in the High Street.

To the north, towards Dalkeith and Edinburgh, is Lauder where the Maitland family have held land for centuries. William Maitland was secretary to Mary Queen of Scots, and a nephew was created 1st Earl of Lauderdale in 1642. In 1660, the 1st and only Duke of Lauderdale, Secretary of State for Scotland in 1660, instructed the architect Sir William Bruce to build on to the old Maitland family castle at Lauder, creating the imposing mass which today reflects the magnificent baroque taste of that time. Thirlestane Castle is the home of Lauderdale's descendant, the Hon Gerald Maitland Carew, and on display in the castle are exhibits

illustrating various aspects of Borders country life, traditions, folklore and land-use.

In the history of the Borders there are three literary giants whose ever-present shadows have moulded a prevailing image of Scotland: Sir Walter Scott, James Hogg, the Ettrick Shepherd, and, in this century, Hugh MacDiarmid. MacDiarmid's *A Drunk Man Looks at the Thistle*, published in 1926, is a burning nationalistic analysis of the Scottish predicament, a self-inflicted sense of failure in the context of a greater England, deeply pessimistic.

Walter Scott was born into middle-class Edinburgh in 1771, the son of a lawyer. A sickly child, his summer holidays were passed at his grandfather's farm at Sandyknowe, near Smailholm – to a boy infinitely more appealing – and here he discovered the inspiration for the greater part of his creative output. As a teenager, in the drawing room society of Edinburgh, he once encountered Robert Burns, a meeting of no significance to the bard, but one which Scott would remember all his life.

Following in his father's footsteps, Scott was destined for a career in the law which was to elevate him ultimately to the rank of sheriff. But from an early age he chose to lead a double life. This involved venturing forth into the deepest folds of the countryside to study the manners of the people of the land and document their stories and oral traditions – even the exploits of witches, ghosts and fairies were revelations as far as he was concerned. Every river, valley and stream, castle

Flycasting on the Teviot

and keep, he came to know as if he had personally shared its history. In this way, Scott was able to capture and bring to life through his prose and poems a Scotland beyond living memory.

Exploring Liddesdale on horseback gave him the material for his *Minstrelsy of the Scottish Border* (1802). In the Highlands he visited survivors of Culloden and listened to their tales of the old Highland way of life. One such encounter, at Dunnottar in Kincardineshire, was with Robert Paterson (on whom *Old Mortality* was modelled). A native of Balmaclellan in Kirkcudbrightshire, this ancient stone-

The meeting of Robert Burns and the young Walter Scott in Sciennes House, Edinburgh (from the painting by Hardie)

Sir Walter Scott who transformed the world's view of Scotland (portrait by Stewart Newton)

mason had dedicated his long life to cleaning and restoring the gravestones of Covenanting martyrs slaughtered during the 'Killing Times' of the seventeenth century. These meetings, often by chance, formed the substance of Scott's wealth of ballad and prose material. From them he created the popular historic novel, an accessible characterisation of Scotland's past which was to have enormous influence in shaping people's ideas of Scotland, both at home and abroad.

In his paper on 'The Romantic Movement and the study of history', Lord Dacre points out that Scott was the foremost creator of the new romanticism which was to change the character of historical study. And for Thomas Carlyle, another Scottish author, it was Scott who first showed 'the old life of men resuscitated for us ... Not as dead tradition but as palpable presence, the past stood before us'. The Wizard of the North, insisted Carlyle, showed that 'the bygone ages of history were actually filled by living men, not by protocols, state-papers, controversies and abstractions of men'.

23

Abbotsford, the Borders home of Sir Walter Scott

Sir Walter Scott's favourite view of the Tweed and the Eildon Hills

A military review on the occasion of the visit of George IV to Edinburgh in 1822 (John Wilson Ewbank)

Scott's first literary work was published when he was just twenty-five. Success followed rapidly. His output was prodigious, but in mid-career, having ill-advisedly financed his brother and a friend in a publishing venture, he found himself bankrupt. Worse still, on the fruits of earlier success, he had already committed himself to building his romantically self-indulgent mansion, Abbotsford, near Melrose. Such was the esteem and affection in which he was held that so many of his friends and contemporaries should have instantly rallied to his aid, met the outstanding costs and the mansion was handed over to him as an appreciation of his services from a grateful nation.

Abbotsford, on the site of an old farmhouse called Cartleyhole, remains the shrine of Scott's imagination. It was designed for him by William Atkinson, using features from many older vernacular buildings. The result was a mock-Tudor baronial extravaganza of turrets and gables, a forerunner to the late nineteenth-century fad for Scottish baronial. Today the house is lived in by Sir Walter's great-great-great granddaughter and is open to the public. On display are Scott memorabilia including a small travelling quaich once owned by Prince Charles Edward Stuart. The story goes that this was presented to the Prince by a supporter mindful of the Young Pretender's safety. In a typically suspicious Scottish manner, the base is made of glass so that 'he who quaffed might keep an eye on the dirk [dagger] hand of his companion'.

In 1822 all Scotland was gripped with great excitement at the prospect of a reigning British monarch setting foot on Scottish soil for the first time since Charles I's visit of 1633. And who better was there to mastermind the pageantry and pomp than Sir Walter Scott. George IV's visit took place in August, and it marked a dramatic upsurge in Scottish national pride and far beyond Scotland inspired a romantic view of all things Scottish. When the king attended an evening reception at Holyroodhouse, the entire company, from all over Scotland, dressed themselves in fanciful tartan costume, reflecting a largely forgotten and somewhat imaginary age which Walter Scott was in no small way responsible for creating. The publicity surrounding the visit, coupled with David Wilkie's splendid portrait of a plump George IV in kilt and tartan doublet, established an image of Scotland that has endured to this day. In a future generation, Queen Victoria would again set the seal of approval on heather and tartan, and Sir Walter Scott would largely be held responsible.

There is one other interesting aspect of George IV's visit: he is recorded as having acquired his liking for Glenlivet in the company of Scott. It should, however, be remembered that the product then was essentially illegal, it being two years before the Glenlivet Distillery became licensed. Notwithstanding, at dinner at Dalkeith Palace and elsewhere, a liberal supply was made available to His Majesty by John Grant of Rothiemurchus, a merchant from Dundee, and others, and quantities were consumed mixed with oatmeal and honey in the guise of Athole brose.

Sir Walter Scott died ten years later in 1832 and lies buried at Dryburgh Abbey, founded in 1159 for Premonstratensian monks on the left bank of the Tweed, close to Melrose. He is in good company with Hugo de Morville, Constable of Scotland in the twelfth century, and Field Marshal Earl Haig. In 1834 the 12th Earl of Buchan erected a statue to commemorate Sir William Wallace, and this stands nearby overlooking the river.

Border legend has it that King Arthur and his knights sleep under the Eildon Hills, and that one day they will ride again. There is also a tradition that these three hills were once as one but were split into three by the twelfth-century Border wizard Michael Scott. In dividing the Eildons, Michael Scott, it is said, sought employment for the devil. Dominating the local landscape, there is a magical quality about the Eildons. From the highest summit (1385 ft), Sir Walter Scott observed that he could 'point out forty-two places famous in war and verse'.

Border mill towns – grey chimneys, narrow streets – deflect attention to the glorious scenery that surrounds them. Galashiels is one such busy manufacturing town which grew out of the nineteenth-century textile mills. Nearby, in 1537, a troop of English soldiers was surprised by a party of local youths after picking wild plums, and all were killed. From this event Galashiels took its slogan 'Wild Plums', and each year this event is celebrated by the Braw Lads' Gathering in which the townsfolk re-enact their history.

From Galashiels along the twisting banks of the

River Tweed, beloved by fishermen, there is a sense of leisure in the spread of the landscape, sloping, gentle and wooded. The tiny mill towns of Clovenfords, Walkerburn and Innerleithen could hardly be described as beauty spots, but they do sustain a character of their own, and their Tweedside settings create a special attraction. From the top of Dunslair Heights, approached on foot from Innerleithen, the view becomes a sea of rolling hills as far as the eye can see. As is the case throughout the Borders, it is continually the unexpected that captures the imagination, and explorers can find innumerable gems hidden away in the narrow roads which weave through the Moorfoot, Lowther and Tinto hills.

At Tweedsmuir, towards the Devil's Beef Tub and Moffat, a steep and narrow road climbs into the spectacular lonely hills, skirting the man-made reservoirs of Tala and Megget. Its destination is Cappercleuch on the western shore of St Mary's Loch. Beyond, to the south, lies the Loch of the Lowes and the waterfall known as the Grey Mare's Tail, identified in Scottish Arthurian legend as the hiding place of the Holy Grail. On all sides converges the richly planted Ettrick Forest.

At the north end of St Mary's Loch is the old St Mary's Kirk and the ruins of Dryhope Tower, rebuilt in the seventeenth century and said to have been the birthplace in the seventeenth century of Mary Scott, the 'Flower of Yarrow', who married 'Auld Watt of Harden' from whom Sir Walter Scott proudly claimed descent.

The village of Ettrick lies on the Ettrick Water

James Hogg, the Ettrick Shepherd

north of Eskdalemuir. It is famous for its associations with James Hogg, that other literary giant from the Borders, the classic poor shepherd boy made good. Without any formal education, through his narrative poetry, Hogg provided Scotland with some of its richest reflective stories and ballads. Born in 1770 near the parish church of Ettrick in Selkirkshire, his family came of a long line of shepherds. As a boy, Hogg himself tended sheep, and avidly read books on loan from his master's library. His inventiveness was fired from an early age by tales from his mother's oral tradition. In 1802, an encounter with Walter Scott led to his

writings being recommended to Constable, the publishers. Before long he had an established name.

It was *The Queen's Wake* (1813), that established his reputation. Lord Byron recommended it to John Murray, his London-based publisher, who brought out an English edition. Before that he had dedicated his 1810 collection of songs *The Forest Minstrel* to the Countess of Dalkeith (later Duchess of Buccleuch), and on her deathbed in 1820 she asked her husband to help him. As a result, the 5th Duke of Buccleuch made over the lease for life of a farm at Altrive, now Edinhope, where Hogg was to spend the remainder of his life. Married, with a well-stocked farm, Hogg continued to contribute to the celebrated *Blackwood's Magazine*, winning more popular acclaim. But it was from his stay in Edinburgh that he evolved the extraordinary *Private Memoires And Confessions Of A Justified Sinner*, a haunting tale of split-personality and betrayal, published in 1824. He died in 1835, ever remembered as Borderland's great peasant poet.

On St Mary's Loch still stands the celebrated coaching inn known as Tibbie Shiel, named after the lady proprietress of Hogg's time. Hogg and Scott and their literary friends would meet here regularly, and it is likely that in such convivial company Hogg may first have reflected on the benefits of *uisgebeatha*. 'Give me the real Glenlivet, and I well believe I could mak' drinking toddy out o' seawater,' he wrote. 'The Human mind never tires o' Glenlivet, ony mair than o' caller air. If a body

Facing: salmon fishing beneath the Eildon Hills (Charles Landseer)

could just find oot the exact proper proportion and quantity that ought to be drunk every day, and keep to that, I verily tro that he might live forever, without dying at a', and that doctors and kirkyards would go oot o' fashion.'

For many Scots the Border region spiritually starts at Flodden, albeit that melancholy site is situated three miles south of Coldstream, and in England. Here, on 19 September 1513, nine thousand Scots, the flower of Scotland's manhood, including their king, James IV, lay dead after a two-hour battle against the army of Henry VIII of England.

James was a much loved king, having travelled in disguise amongst his subjects throughout his kingdom to learn first hand of their grievances. His soldiers came from throughout Scotland, a force estimated at over 30,000 led by fifteen earls, twenty barons and hundreds of knights. Not one Scottish family was untouched by the disastrous outcome of the Battle of Flodden.

> Their King, their lords, their mightiest low,
> They melted from the field as snow,
> Where streams are swoln and south winds blow,
> Dissolves in silent dew,
> Tweed's echoes heard the ceaseless plash,
> While many a broken band,
> Disorder'd through her currents dash,
> To gain the Scottish land;
> To town and tower, to down and dale,
> To tell red Flodden's dismal tale,
> And raise the universal wail.
> Tradition, legend, tune and song,

_____

Dryburgh Abbey, last resting place of Sir Walter Scott

> Shall many an age that wail prolong:
> Still from the sire the son shall hear
> Of the stern strife, and carnage drear,
> Of Flodden's fatal field,
> Where shiver'd was fair Scotland's spear,
> And broken was her shield!

Sir Walter Scott, *Marmion*

Many Scots refused to believe that their king was dead. If he was, why would Henry have failed to press home his advantage and invade Scotland? A myth sprang up that James had departed on a pilgrimage to Jerusalem and would one day return, the 'Once and Future King'.

Coldstream, on the Border, is a pleasant, peaceful place of one main street, two fine churches with clock steeples and a town house. Close by are the gates to The Hirsel, home of the earls of Home, a great Border family dating from the twelfth century. In more recent times, in 1963, the 14th Earl of Home renounced his title to become British prime minister.

West from Coldstream is Kelso, the capital of Borders towns. Floors Castle, home of the 10th Duke of Roxburghe, is located on one side, and the twelfth-century Kelso Abbey on the other. Kelso Abbey was the largest of the Borders abbeys, but in 1545 was used as a stronghold against the Earl of Hertford's English invasion. The hundred defendants, including the monks, were ruthlessly slaughtered and the abbey destroyed.

Some 400 yards from Floors Castle, designed by William Adam in 1721, with nineteenth-century dramatisation by William Playfair, stands a holly

tree marked with a white post. On this spot in 1460 King James II of Scotland was accidentally blown up and killed by an exploding cannon while laying siege to Roxburghe Castle, the remaining earthworks of which can be seen at a distance to the southwest.

From Coldstream, the road twists and turns northeast towards Duns, believed to have been the birthplace of Duns Scotus (1266–1308), a Franciscan who became a leading divine and one of the greatest of medieval philosophers. Throughout this region there are countless great mansions, manors, and Border strongholds. At Duns there are two: Duns Castle, originally an ancient tower house acquired by the Hay family, with additions by Gillespie Graham, and Manderston House, built for Sir James Miller, son of Sir William Miller of Leith, who had amassed a great fortune through trading with Russia.

Another great Berwickshire house, west of Berwick-upon-Tweed, is Paxton, built between 1756 and 1772 by Patrick Home as a suitable home for his intended German bride, Charlotte de Brandt, a natural daughter of Frederick the Great. Berwick-upon-Tweed, on the east coast, has the misfortune of just being over the border in England, although between the twelfth and sixteenth centuries it changed hands thirteen times, eventually becoming independent of both England and Scotland in recent times.

The road north along this coastline passes St Abbs and Coldingham with the Lammermuirs to the distant west. Dunbar, with its seventeenth-century town house, is a popular holiday resort, and has regularly boasted more sunshine hours than anywhere else in Britain. Towards North Berwick, the Bass Rock, rising 312 ft steeply out of the sea and now a bird sanctuary, comes into view. In the mid-seventeenth century it was employed as a prison for Covenanters. Inland to the west, the Lammermuir Hills spill at a leisurely pace from Berwickshire into East Lothian. The whole of the eastern Border country was once shaken by strong volcanic forces, and the rounded hills and deep, winding pastoral valleys of the Lammermuirs, entirely devoid of rugged grandeur, are a reminder of this. In effect, as the name suggests, these are higher moors, rather than hills. On this wide stretch of relatively empty country, each year, on the Glorious Twelfth of August, when the purple heather sets off the green of the bracken, the guns come out. As a habitat for the red grouse, the Lammermuirs rank among the finest in Scotland.

The earliest record of this particular species of bird, the *Lagopus scoticus*, being pursued in Scotland comes from Caithness in the year 1157. Generally red grouse are found wherever there are heather-clad moors, but only in the United Kingdom. Undoubtedly there are related species such as the willow grouse in Europe, Asia and North America, but the red grouse has remained staunchly indigenous to Britain. In recent years the effect of late summers on the growth of heather, the natural habitat of the young birds, has to some extent caused a fall in the grouse population, but the ritu-

Grouse shooting on the Lammermuirs: a bird successfully retrieved

alised sport and challenge involved in shooting them remains as popular as ever.

From North Berwick to Prestonpans, along the estuary of the Firth of Forth, the East Lothian coastline features a string of picturesque villages in close proximity to sandy beaches and popular golf courses, notably at Gullane. Dirleton has a castle dating from 1225, destroyed in 1625 by Oliver Cromwell. In later years this village offered a safe landing for smugglers. Ships from continental Europe could lie off the mouth of the Forth and glide in on the night tide when the hurried exchange of gold for cloth, tobacco and spirits would take place.

Saxon settlers are said to have given the name to the market town of Haddington which, by the twelfth century, had become Scotland's third town. William the Lion built a palace here where Alexander I was born in 1198. William's mother, Ada, founded an abbey for Cistercian nuns nearby. In the following century Franciscan monks built a church of unsurpassed beauty which came to be known as the Lamp of the Lothian. Destroyed several times by invading English armies, St Mary's Church has resolutely survived. Two miles to the south is Lennoxlove, formerly called Lethington, headquarters of William Maitland, Mary Queen of Scots' secretary. The name Lennoxlove commemorates 'La Belle Stuart', the doctor's daughter much admired by Charles II and who, in 1667, eloped with Charles Stuart, Duke of Richmond and Lennox. The house, which incorporates a fifteenth-century tower, was built by Lord Blantyre in the eighteenth century, and is the home of the 15th Duke of Hamilton, Hereditary Keeper of Holyroodhouse, the Queen's official residence in Scotland.

The red laterite soil of East Lothian has always made it prime farmland. In the early eighteenth century, at Ormiston, to the west of the county, lived John Cockburn, founder of the Society of Improvers of Knowledge of Agriculture. This enlightened association introduced the turnip and the potato, imported experts from far and wide to give advice, and began an agriculture revolution which changed the landscape of Scotland.

In the next door village to Ormiston, the brothers John and George Rate farmed the adjoining lands of Milton, Lempock Wells and Peaston Bank.

In 1837 they were recorded as being licence holders of the Glenkinchie Distillery at Pencaitland, where they grew and malted their own barley, mashed it with the soft water of the Kinchie Burn, which flows from the Lammermuir Hills into the River Tyne, and distilled it to make a distinctive Lowland malt whisky. With the end of their tenure, the manufacturing of whisky stopped, influenced by a fall in demand. For a period of over twenty-five years the premises were used as a sawmill, then were reinstated as a distillery, and by 1914 had become one of five Lowland malt whisky distilleries controlled by Scottish Malt Distillers. Of these, Glenkinchie alone survives.

In 1968 the floor maltings at Glenkinchie were closed, but the discarded equipment now forms the nucleus of the collection of the Museum of Malt Whisky Production. This has as its prize exhibit a model of a Highland malt whisky distillery, part of the Scotch Whisky Exhibit at the British Empire Exhibition at Wembley in 1924. Glenkinchie retains a close relationship with the local community and for some years it was famous for its side activity of breeding horses and cattle.

Each of Scotland's distilleries has its own unique personality, but generally the process of manufacturing Scotch whisky follows a prescribed pattern involving steeping, germinating, kilning, milling, mashing, fermentation, distillation, cask filling and maturation. In a typical, traditional distillery, barley is soaked (steeped) in water for

The Glenkinchie Distillery served by the soft water of the Kinchie Burn

Facing: germinating barley   *Above: the receiving room*

two or three days, then cast over the concrete floor of the maltings where it starts to germinate. The rate of germination is controlled by turning the barley at regular intervals and after about six or seven days, when the germination has developed far enough, the green malt, as it is now called, is placed in a kiln. The kiln floor is perforated, allowing hot air and smoke from a peat furnace underneath to percolate through the grain bed. Normally a proportion of the kiln fuel would be peat as the smoke from it adds flavour to the end product.

Laying out malt

Turning malt

Top left: cutting peat for the furnace.   Bottom left: spreading malt on to the kiln floor.   Above: the kiln room.

The mill room

Facing: the grist in the mash

After drying, the finished malt is put into sacks or wooden bins and allowed to 'rest' for a few weeks prior to mashing. The next stage is to crush the malt to form a meal, 'grist', which resembles a coarse flour. The grinding is carried out between two pairs of steel rollers and when crushed the grist is transferred to a grist hopper.

At this stage two essential ingredients of malt whisky come together. Grist is mixed with hot water in the mash tun, a large, circular metal vessel. The mixture is stirred by revolving rakes and a sweet liquid known as wort is drained off through perforated floor plates and pumped through a cooler into a fermentation vessel known as a wash-back. There are still sugars in the husks left behind at this stage, so a second, third and sometimes fourth input of water takes place (sparging), to extract them. The remaining husks, known as

draff, are removed and usually sold to local farms as cattle food.

Wort is held in washbacks which are normally made of pine or larch. A measured amount of yeast is added causing the wort to froth and bubble into barm. After a couple more days the fermentation turns the wort into a weak form of alcohol, creamy brown in colour, known as wash, and it is from this that the spirit which becomes malt whisky is created. Wash from the washback is pumped to the wash charger, an intermediate holding vessel.

Pot-stills resemble vast copper kettles. The basic shape of these has remained unchanged since

Above: fuelling the peat furnace

Below: the tun room (model)

Left: mash house (model). Above, top: still house (model). Bottom: interior of pot-still showing heaters. Facing: checking the pot-stills

Scotch whisky was first manufactured although no two distilleries have identical pot-stills. Shape, undoubtedly, does influence the character of the end-product. Small, tubby stills produce dense, oily spirits; the spirit from tall stills is fresh and light in character.

Having flowed into the wash-still, the wash is heated until it turns into vapour which then rises up the still. The alcohol and water in the vapour are condensed into liquid by being passed through what is known as the worm, a spiral copper tube immersed in a vat of cold water. Thus alcohol is separated from the wash and leaves the waste products in the still. The condensed, cooled liquid is known as low wines and is collected in the low wines receiver from which it runs into the spirit-still, ready for the second distillation. The low wines are once again heated to the point of separation and the alcoholic vapours condensed and cooled whereupon the spirit is run off. All the low wines and spirit run through the spirit sample safe which is operated by the stillman. All spirit is dutiable and is required by Customs and Excise to be kept under lock and key. As the low wines pass through the sample safe, the stillman assesses the quality by measuring temperature and strength. The strength is determined by using a hydrometer which floats in a testing jar within the safe. The spirit from the distillation in the spirit-still is split into three parts, the 'middle cut' or 'heart of the run' being the required strength and quality for malt whisky. The first and final parts of the run, representing the larger proportion of the run, are

Production quality and alcohol content are controlled by spirit safes in the still room

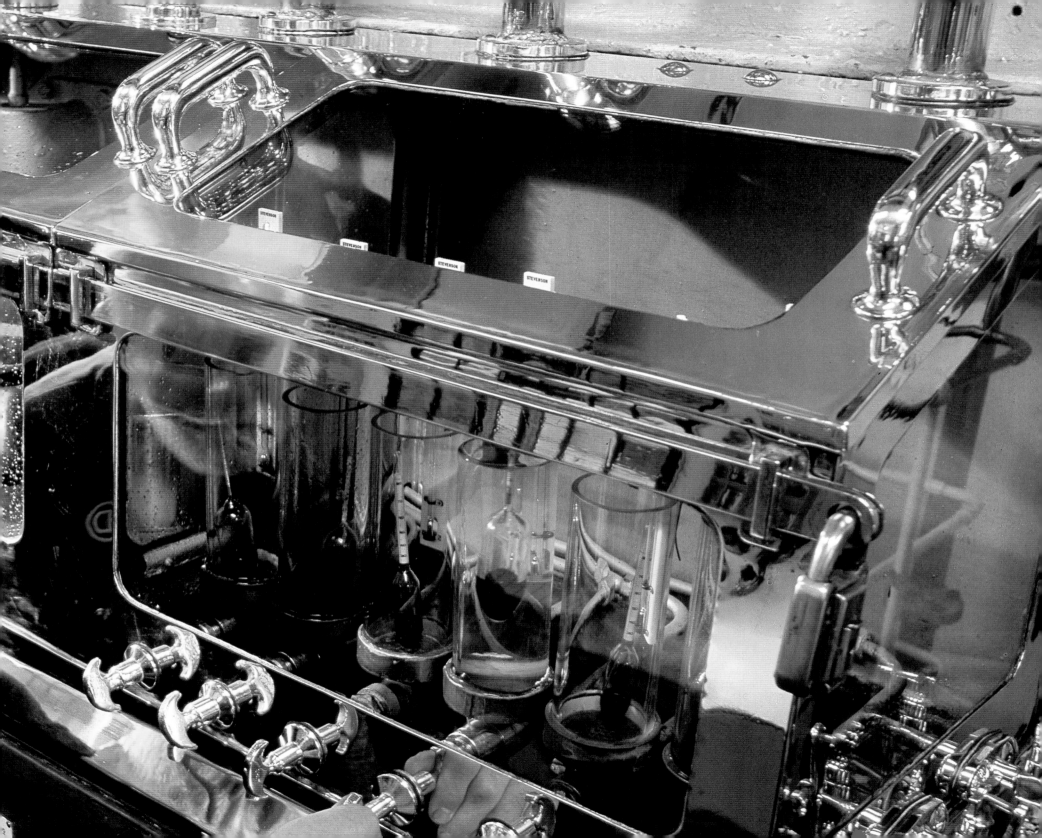

Condensing worm (model)

Spirit safe and receiver room (model)

Spirit store (model)

directed back into the low wines vessel for redistillation. Most distillers operate a double distillation system: one distillation in a wash-still followed by one distillation in a spirit-still. At Auchentoshan Distillery in Clydebank, however, a triple distillation system is used. The 'middle cut' is routed into the intermediate spirit receiver, an oak vessel which holds the spirit until full, and then it is pumped to the spirit receiver in the filling store.

At this stage the spirit is clear in colour and the strength is around 70–75 per cent alcohol by volume (123° to 131° proof). The strong spirit is

then reduced to maturation strength, normally about 64 per cent alcohol by volume (112° proof) by the addition of water. This may be the same water as used for mashing, but not necessarily so. Casks are weighed before and after filling. Cask weight can then be deducted from the filled weight to calculate individual weights and the quantity of spirit since every cask is manufactured by hand and thus different in size. Casks are made from top quality oak and may have been used previously for maturing sherry in Spain or American bourbon whiskey. From the wood of these casks

comes the spirit's eventual colour.

The final phase is the maturation. Casks are marked and stored in a warehouse, where by law they are left undisturbed for a minimum of three years. Only after that period may casks be removed for blending purposes; the ageing for single malts before bottling varies depending upon the policy of the individual distilleries.

Fringing the Firth of Forth, Edinburgh, the capital of Scotland, is often shrouded in a coastal mist

Facing: casks awaiting filling

known as the North Sea haar. For a thousand years there has been a fortress on a rock, and from this dominant position Edinburgh Castle has witnessed most great events in a restless history.

In the seventh century a king of Northumbria called Edwin took possession of whatever fortification existed at that time, and thus this came to be known as Edwin's Burgh. In the eleventh century, however, it was Queen Margaret, the saintly second wife of King Malcolm III, who first saw the full potential of Edinburgh. This remarkable woman, a Saxon princess and granddaughter of the English King Edmund Ironside, had fled to Scotland with the Norman invasion of England in 1066.

Capturing the heart of the king, she introduced new ideas into government and replaced the ancient Celtic faith of the people with the Roman religion. Although King Malcolm held court at Dunfermline, across the Firth of Forth in the Kingdom of Fife, in 1076 Margaret built her little chapel of worship on the highest point of Edinburgh Castle rock. From then on the city began to develop along and below the spine of rock which runs east towards the parkland where, after her death, Margaret's son, King David I, erected the Abbey of the Holy Rood in her memory.

Originally the palace which grew up on this spot was no more than a guest house for the abbey. In 1544, at the time of the Earl of Hertford's invasion, it was a high, turreted building, and it is no wonder that Mary Queen of Scots found it cold and gloomy when she took up residence in 1561.

The murder of her private secretary, David Rizzio, followed by the intrigue which led to the blowing up of her husband, Lord Darnley, at the adjacent Kirk o' Field, can hardly have left her with fond memories of the place.

After the Reformation Charles II, determined to rebuild Holyroodhouse as a suitable royal residence, commissioned Sir William Bruce as architect. Queen Victoria first visited Holyrood in 1842 and was disturbed by the squalor of the High Street. Serious restoration, however, began in 1911 when King George V and Queen Mary took up residence on an annual basis, a tradition the Queen retains to this day. The road from Edinburgh Castle to Holyrood Park is known as the Royal Mile. Here is the High Kirk of St Giles where, in the sixteenth century, the reformer John Knox railed against Catholicism in the person of Mary Queen of Scots.

In the eighteenth century, while the overcrowded Old Town had become the haunt for every kind of vice, the city worthies of Edinburgh turned their eyes to the lush fields to the north, a pleasant meadowland sloping towards the Firth of Forth. Here they commissioned the young architect James Craig to build a Georgian New Town, the envy of all Europe for its quality and grace, and, not least, for the intellects of its inhabitants: one could expect to encounter within the one square mile, and in one day, such luminaries as the philosopher David Hume, the economist Adam Smith, the chemist James Black and the mathematician John Playfair, not to mention Sir Walter Scott.

The outward appearance of Edinburgh has survived remarkably unscathed.

There is an old Edinburgh maxim that 'one is either in a profession or one does something in Leith', Edinburgh's port on the Firth of Forth. Professional, respectable Edinburgh preferred to keep commerce at a distance. Leith, which lies less than a mile from the fringe of Edinburgh's New Town, was only officially incorporated into the city as late as 1929.

One prime source for astute Scottish investment over the past two centuries has been the liquor trade, and intuitive Edinburgh-based financial institutions have always known a good thing when they saw one. Like Glasgow, Edinburgh too produced its share of whisky barons, enterprising men who saw and exploited the potential for distilling and blending spirits. Through the creation of marketing companies they were, in several cases, to acquire significant wealth enabling both social and political influence.

Up until 1860, the manufacture of malt whisky was essentially a small-scale operation, malt whisky being limited in its appeal. The most significant development in terms of mass markets, however, was the production of grain spirit, manufactured from a mixture of barley and other cereals. Dramatically different from malt whisky in its distillation and taste, grain whisky will on average represent around 60 per cent of most bottles of blended whisky.

_____

Facing: sunset catches the ruins of St Anthony's Chapel, Holyrood Park

Whisky blending vats at Invergordon's Leith plant

Grain whisky is created by converting cereal starch into sugar which is then transformed into alcohol through a process of fermentation and distillation. In 1827–8, the most prominent distiller in Scotland, Robert Stein, took out patents for a still which was heated internally by steam, instead of by an external furnace, and which distilled whisky in one continuous operation, unlike the traditional pot-still which had to be filled, emptied and filled again. Stein carried out some of his trials at Kirkliston Distillery, owned by Andrew Stein & Co, where one of his stills was working before 1829; another was installed by a cousin, John Haig, at Cameron Bridge Distillery in 1827. But it was Aeneas Coffey, a Dublin-based exciseman, who in 1830 was shrewd enough to further adapt, patent and market the idea, and with 'Coffey's Continuous Patent' stills it suddenly became possible to produce a light, palatable whisky fast and economically.

Grain whisky is produced under the same definition as malt whisky, in that only malted barley, whole grain and yeast may be used in its manufacture. Whole grain (maize or wheat) is cooked under pressure before being added to previously milled malt in a mash tun, where conversion of the starch in both the malt and other cereals takes place. The resultant wort-sugar solution is cooled and pumped to washbacks where, by the addition of yeast, fermentation takes place.

The fermented wort (wash) is then pumped to distillation columns (the Coffey stills). Distillation of the wash is a continuous process, the spirit produced being put into casks and matured in the same way as malt whisky. Because very large volumes are involved, grain distilleries have substantial by-product plants which recover approximately 30 per cent of the original grain as animal feed. The carbon dioxide discharged during fermentation is generally recovered and sold as liquid CO_2.

Thus grain whisky could be manufactured cheaply and in bulk, and it was Andrew Usher, a whisky merchant of Edinburgh, who first experimented with a selection of two or three malts and two or three grains and created a blend with popular appeal. The idea caught on rapidly and before long all of his competitors were experimenting with blends. Many of the household names in Scotch whisky today, some comprising a mix of up to fifty different malt and grain whiskies, date from this period. And nowadays virtually all grain whisky is supplied direct to the blenders. In 1877, the objective of six prominent grain whisky distillers to amalgamate into the Distillers Company Limited (DCL), was simply to prevent over-production and to agree on cost structures. A giant was being formed, and by 1885, after the Caledonian Distillery had joined DCL, the company accounted for 75 per cent of grain whisky output in Scotland. In the first quarter of the twentieth century the DCL consortium mushroomed. This was achieved under the guidance of Andrew Drysdale and William Ross, the latter earning the title of 'The Great Amalgamator'. It was through his initiatives that John Haig & Company was acquired in 1919, Macdonald & Greenlees in 1926, White Horse Distillers in 1927, and Sanderson, owners of the celebrated VAT 69, in 1937.

In 1878 James Martin, a whisky traveller, set up business in Broughton Street, just inside the New Town. Six years later he moved his company to Leith and went into partnership with Edward Macdonald who, on Martin's death in 1899, persuaded his brother Daniel to join the partnership. In the meantime, in 1893, a third Macdonald brother, Roderick, with Alexander Muir, his brother-in-law, had set up his own business, Macdonald & Muir, also in Leith. Very soon they were joined by his sons Roderic (known as Eric)

Preparation for bottling at Invergordon's Leith plant

and Alexander. In 1912, Macdonald and Muir acquired James Martin & Co for the then large sum of £375,000. Brand names included Martin's VVO, Royal Abbey, House of Lords and Perfection. Uncle Edward decided to emigrate to the USA, and Uncle Daniel emigrated to South Africa.

Still prospering in 1918, Macdonald & Muir

bought over the wine merchants Charles Muirhead and the Glenmorangie Distillery on the Dornoch Firth at Tain. The Glen Moray-Glenlivet Distillery was bought in 1920, and in 1921 Nicol Anderson & Co was purchased, with brands such as Souter Johnnie, Old Oak Tree, Dunvegan and Baillie Nicol Jarvie. Today Macdonald Martin Distilleries, the

Whisky bottling at Invergordon's Leith plant

parent company, remains a family-owned business which operates with professional management. David Macdonald, the chairman, is a grandson of Roderick Macdonald, the founder.

Invergordon Distillers, with headquarters in Salamander Place, Leith, came into being in 1959 with the incorporation of a company to build and operate a grain distillery at Invergordon on the Cromarty Firth. In 1988 four directors, headed by Charles Craig, then Chairman, staged a management buyout. There followed a stock exchange flotation. In 1993 Invergordon was acquired by the Glasgow-based Whyte & Mackay Group.

In 1885 the whisky blending boom was in full surge and Edinburgh had the largest patent still for grain in Europe. But since the monopoly was held by the – even then – giant Distillers Company, blenders and brand owners were becoming in-

Lord and Lady Macfarlane at home

David Macdonald with his daughters Fiona and Alison

ceeded in raising the necessary capital to build The North British Distillery at Gorgie.

In those days the site could not have been better located for communications. The buildings formed an island with a nexus of three railway lines: the Wester Dalry branch of the Caledonian line connected Edinburgh's Caledonian Station with Glasgow; the Granton and Leith branch of the same line connected Leith, principal grain port of Scotland, with Carlisle and the south; and the Edinburgh Suburban and South Side Junction railway made a sweep around the city to merge with the North British lines to Berwick-upon-Tweed.

Over the past century The North British Distillery has successfully weathered the ups and downs of the industry. In 1970 the 250,000,000th proof gallon of North British whisky was distilled and now lies in the directors' dining room at Gorgie. In 1989 John A. R. Macphail CBE, the North British Distillery's longest serving chairman, and former chairman of the Scotch Whisky Association, became the first Grand Master of The Keepers of the Quaich. The current chairman of the North British Distillery is James Bruxner, also chairman of The Keepers of the Quaich.

To the west of Leith, where the River Almond flows into the Firth of Forth, is Cramond, where the Romans built an extensive encampment. Cramond became a popular haunt for smugglers in the seventeenth and eighteenth centuries, the white-washed, cottage-style houses reminiscent of those found across the water in the coastal villages of Fife. On the west bank of the Almond is the Dalmeny Estate, owned by the 7th Earl of Rosebery whose home, Dalmeny House, features Goya tapestries and a fine collection of Napoleonic memorabilia.

Tradition has it that St Margaret, queen to King Malcolm III, instituted the ferry crossing here to travel to and from her husband's court at Dunferm-

creasingly uncomfortable about the fluctuations in price and quality. Before long a group of non-aligned trade in Edinburgh and Glasgow made a decision to do something about it. Led by Andrew Usher, a board comprising John M. Crabbie and William Sanderson of Leith, Alexander Murdoch, John Somerville and James McLennan, all of Glasgow, and George Robertson of Edinburgh, suc-

line, in the Kingdom of Fife, hence the name 'Queensferry'. The spectacular Forth Bridge, opening up the north for rail travel, dates from 1890, and an equally impressive road bridge was built in 1960.

To the west of South Queensferry is Hopetoun House, seat of the 4th Marquess of Linlithgow. His ancestor, the 1st Earl of Hopetoun, commissioned Sir William Bruce to build him a stately home at the end of the seventeenth century. Thereafter William Adam and his sons, John and Robert, all contributed to create this masterpiece.

From South Queensferry the Forth estuary stretches west in view of the ruined palace of Linlithgow, where Mary Queen of Scots was born in 1542. At Alloa, on the northern Clackmannanshire side of the Firth of Forth, is the great Cambus Grain Distillery.

The Kingdom of Fife, which occupies the east coast bulge of land between the firths of Forth and Tay, has resolutely maintained its independent personality since the days when kings sat in Dunfermline town, where David I built an abbey in memory of his mother, St Margaret.

Throughout the centuries the Bruces of Clackmannan, a family from whom King Robert Bruce himself descended, have played a consistently significant role in Scottish public life. In the early nineteenth century it was the 7th Earl of Elgin, a noted archaeologist, who brought the so-called Elgin marbles to Britain from Greece; the 8th Earl served as Governor General of Jamaica from 1842 to 1846, as Governor General of Canada from 1847 to 1854, then as Governor General of India from 1860 to 1863; the 9th Earl served as Viceroy of India from 1894 to 1899.

The 11th Earl of Elgin & Kincardine KT, 37th Chief of the House of Bruce, whose home is Broomhall on the outskirts of Dunfermline in Fife, is a patron and a former Grand Master of The Keepers of the Quaich. He has twice held the royal appointment of Lord High Commissioner to the General Assembly of the Church of Scotland and his distinguished involvements in Scottish affairs are such as to fill several paragraphs in reference books. At The Keepers of the Quaich banquets he was responsible for introducing the rousing song 'Scotland Yet', a celebration of Sir Walter Scott's rediscovery of the Honours of Scotland in 1822.

With the opening of the Forth Road Bridge in 1960, Fife instantly become more accessible. Punctuating the coastline around to St Andrews are the picturesque former fishing ports of Elie, St Monans, Pittenweem, Anstruther, Crail and Kingsbarns. Near Windygates, on the River Leven, is the Cameron Bridge Distillery. Founded by John Haig in 1823 and licensed in 1824, it began by producing Lowland malt whisky in pot-stills. Following the relaxation of the Corn Laws, John Haig began to produce grain whisky and in 1877 Cameron Bridge and five other grain distilleries combined to form the Distillers Company.

Since the earliest days, whisky from Cameron Bridge has been in 'chief demand' in Fife, and 7500 cases of 'Old Cameron Brig' grain whisky produced each year are sold in the region. Legend has it that the bones of the apostle St Andrew, Scotland's patron saint, were brought to the Kingdom of Fife in the seventh century by the Greek monk St Regulus under the protection of King Nectan, king of the Picts. The town of St Andrews which sprang up on the spot where St Regulus landed also became the home of Scotland's first university, founded in 1410 and formally recognised by the Pope three years later.

CHAPTER TWO: THE SOUTHWEST

Otter statue in memory of Gavin Maxwell above Monreith Bay

Today those travelling up the west coast of England speed over the Scottish Border and north through Gretna Green towards Glasgow and the Highlands. They are often unaware that they are bypassing one of Scotland's most beguiling regions. Should they decide to turn to the west, they will find themselves among the hills of Queensberry and Green Lowther. Alongside the great expanse of the Solway Estuary the farmland is rich and varied, the climate always mild.

The ancient tribes of Selgovae, the Dalriads, the Romans, the Picts and the Scots each left their mark on this region, now known as Dumfries and Galloway. Later came Norman landowners, the Comyns, the Bruces, and the Maxwells ranking among the most powerful families in Scotland. In the sixteenth century the Armstrongs and the Johnstones established themselves in their scattered tower houses, violently at odds with each other, the stealing of each other's cattle becoming a way of life. As in all such rural areas the personalities of these families indelibly moulded the character of the countryside.

Most significant were the Bruces who built Lochmaben Castle in the thirteenth century. This great fortress was to change hands many times between England and Scotland in the relentless internecine struggle for political precedence. At one time it served as the headquarters of the mighty earls of Douglas. Today the site remains impressive, although the ruins are largely the result of vandalism, not warfare.

Dumfries and Galloway cover 2459 square miles. The population is scattered, since much of the territory is mountain and moor, with the majority of inhabitants living along the coastal lowlands.

In the north of this region lies Moffat, famous for weavers, toffee, and its wells which, in the late eighteenth century, acquired a reputation for curative properties. Moffat's economy is based on farming, and particularly on sheep, which are scattered like flies on the undulating hillsides. This was the heart of Covenanting country. During the 'Killing Times' of the seventeenth century, when thousands were persecuted for allegiance to the Presbyterian doctrine as the sole religion of Scotland, resistance was largely rural. North of Moffat is the Devil's Beef Tub, an extraordinary natural gulley in the landscape where stolen cattle were regularly hidden. On the edge of this great hollow, as the

land slopes out of sight, stands a melancholy stone marking the execution by Douglas Dragoons in 1685 of one John Hunter, condemned for his faith.

A short distance cross-country to the west is Sanquhar, which boasts the oldest post office in Scotland (1763), and nearby is Drumlanrig, the monumental castellated home built by the Douglas family who became dukes of Queensberry. On receiving the final bill for the building work, the 1st Duke was so horrified at the expense that he spent only one night in the castle. Today, however, it is the home of his descendant, the 9th Duke of Buccleuch and 11th Duke of Queensberry, Chief of the name of Scott.

The Royal Burgh of Dumfries was created by King William I and was once a port. The channel of the River Nith on which it perches serviced ships from the Solway Firth, but the high and ebb tides were so extreme that it was never a success and in time the Nith was allowed to silt up. Dumfries, however, has always prospered as an agricultural centre. Horse and hiring fairs were held on the Whitesands, and there have been markets here for eight hundred years. In 1745 Prince Charles Edward Stuart, the Young Pretender, passed through with his army on its march to Derby, but found little support. Incensed by the apathy of the burghers, he fined the town £2000 and one thousand pairs of shoes.

On the banks of the River Nith at Whitesands can be seen the stone bridge which dates from 1350. The Lady Devorgilla, widow of John Balliol, founder of the Oxford College, built an earlier

wooden bridge joining the two towns of Maxweltown and Dumfries. This warm and tranquil area has always had appeal for artists and writers. For Robert Burns, the move from Edinburgh was for practical reasons. Despite the widespread popularity of his poetry he needed money, and in 1788, following his marriage to Jean Armour, he succeeded in acquiring the lease of a farm at Ellisland on the River Nith, above Dumfries, where he built a cottage with his own hands. Farming also failed to make him rich, so Burns soon found himself earning a living in a way which he must have found highly compromising.

> The Deil cam fiddlin thro' the town,
> And danc'd awa wi' th' Exciseman.

These lines were, in fact, composed in the course of one night in 1790 when Burns himself had become employed as an exciseman. He and colleagues had been watching a smack on the Solway Firth suspected of smuggling and, while one of their party went in search of help, the bard came up with a song to amuse his friends. Burns' thoughts on his employment must have been ambivalent, but there can be no doubt that he was kept busy. For the excisemen of that time, the Solway was one of the most difficult of Scotland's coastlines to police, with extensive smuggling of every kind of contraband.

Fame had come too early for the ploughman

Facing: the Devil's Beef Tub in the Tweedsmuir Hills, once the hideout of the cattle reivers

poet. In 1791, disenchanted with publishers, a failure as a farmer, he repaired to Mill Vennel (now Burns Street) in Dumfries. In the taverns he drank heavily, espousing the aims of the French Revolution and thus alienating many of his supporters. 'Whisky and Freedom gang thegither.' 'Tak aff your dram' might well have been Burns' retort.

> O Whisky! Soul o plays and pranks!
> Accept a bardie's grateful thanks!
> When wanting thee, what tuneless cranks
> Are my poor verses.

Ironically, by 1795, he had turned patriot again, but too late for any purposeful use and to win back the friends he had lost. In July of that year, at his house in Dumfries, at the age of thirty-seven, he died of endocarditis. Five years earlier he had penned *Tam O'Shanter*, expounding the philosophy that 'Wi uisgebeatha we'll face the Devil!'

It is a melancholy story, but not without virtue. Burns' down-to-earth, satirical, even sentimental, words have found a lasting place in literature, and his interpretation of the Scottish folk tradition represents everything that is best about Scotland. Burns' identity with the common man meant that as Scots emigrated to the New World, his poems and songs travelled with them, finding their way into many languages and giving Burns his immortality. Each year on January 25th, the date of Burns' birth, ritual dinners are held nationwide to honour his name. Cock-a-leekie soup, haggis, neeps, tatties and Athole brose are consumed in quantity,

The River Nith at Dumfries, and 'Devorgilla's bridge' built in 1350

accompanied by toasts and speeches in celebration of the Immortal Memory. As with the Ayrshire cottage in which he was born, the Dumfries house in which he died and the tavern in which he met his friends are places of pilgrimage for his admirers, and his statue stands in front of Greyfriars Church.

From early times Dumfries, and indeed the entire length of the Solway coast, with its remote inlets, harbours, and sparsely populated communities, was an obvious focus for smuggling. Goods could be transported rapidly inland and distributed to the centres of population through the network of hill tracks and roads leading north and south. In some cases kegs of whisky might find their way overland from the Highlands but, often as not, were landed along the southwest coast having been shipped out of some secret location on the northeastern seaboard.

It was also relatively easy for overseas shipping to slip into Scottish coastal waters undetected, unload and load up with cargo, then cruise silently west towards Ireland or south towards the ports of England, notably Liverpool and London, then France. Hestan Island, off Auchencairn, inspired 'The Isle of Rathan' in S.S. Crocket's stirring book on smugglers, *The Raiders*, and no less than three secret caverns have been identified as having been used to store contraband goods. In 1711 the Collector of Dumfries reported that a tide-watcher named Young had heard of suspicious goings-on, and had hurried, early in the morning, to Glenhowan where he learned from a fisherman that Morrow of Hidwood, a notorious native smuggler,

had returned home with a sizeable cargo. Accompanied by the parish constable, Young proceeded to Morrow's house where they seized a large haul of tobacco and spirits. They were preparing to leave when, suddenly, as if from nowhere, a 'multitude of women' set upon them. The unfortunate Young was soundly beaten and trussed-up.

On eventually being released, the disconsolate exciseman reported to headquarters where he was immediately despatched back to the scene of the outrage with a force of ten men, whereupon they were promptly set upon by yet another force of women, wives of local fishermen and farmworkers, this time armed with clubs and pitchforks. In the understandably indignant report of this affair to Edinburgh, much emphasis was laid on the impunity with which the law had been defied and its representatives maltreated. A troop of dragoons was hastily sent to round up the women and bring them to trial. Witnesses in the case professed such malice against the accused that the charges were 'politically' dismissed.

Customs warehouses were often broken into and their contents carried off. In 1711, in Kirkcudbright, a gang assaulted the officer in charge and rifled the premises; a similar break-in was effected in Dumfries by means of false keys whilst a few years later magistrates and collectors were seized in order that a gang of smugglers might intercept four confiscated casks of brandy forwarded from Annan. The on-going battle between smuggler and

The statue of Robert Burns in front of Greyfriars Church in Dumfries

gauger continued throughout the eighteenth century, but whisky smuggling was to reach its peak in Solway waters in the early nineteenth century, around the time of the Napoleonic wars, when crippling taxes drove a large proportion of whisky production underground. Many landowners, apart from being enthusiastic about the product, encouraged the practice in order to maximise their rents. Even after 1823, when a licence fee of £10 could purchase legality, many Highlanders resented the imposition and scorned their neighbours who complied with the law.

Along the Solway lush green farmland blends into dense forests and there are stretches of sand punctuated with small harbours idyllic for sailing. For the horticulturalist, there are splendid gardens, notably at Threave, where the National Trust for Scotland runs a training school. Threave was a Douglas stronghold built by Archibald the Grim, 3rd Earl of Douglas, in the fourteenth century. Nearby is Caerlaverock, one time fortress of the Maxwell earls of Nithsdale, now a nature sanctuary where, in winter, thousands of wildfowl, including barnacle geese, take refuge.

Thomas Carlyle, 'prophet in the guise of a man of letters', was born in the village of Ecclefechan in 1795, and the poet Hugh MacDiarmid was born at Langholm in 1892. At Maxwelton House, by the River Cairn, 18 miles northwest of Dumfries at Moniaive, a young Jacobite, William Douglas, composed the words of one of Scotland's most haunting love songs:

Whithorn Priory where Christianity first touched mainland Scotland

Maxwelton Braes are bonny
They're a' clad ower wi' dew,
Where I and Annie Laurie
Made up the promise true.
Made up the promise true
That ne'er forget will I,
An' for bonny Annie Laurie
I'd lay down my head and die.

Alas, the young Douglas was forced to flee to Europe and Bonny Annie Laurie married another.

Near Gatehouse of Fleet, in close proximity to two small chambered cairns dating from the Neolithic period (2000 BC), is a remarkable cave described by Sir Walter Scott in his novel *Guy Mannering*. Scott's smuggler Hatteraich was fictitious, but the cave was probably that used by Jack Yawkins, the notorious eighteenth-century smuggler.

On the River Cree is Newton Stewart, a market town once famous for its woollen mills, and serving as the eastern gate to this glorious southwest corner of Scotland. It was on the Baldoon Sands at Wigtown Bay that Dunbar of Baldoon, husband of 'Lucia de Lammermuir' was trampled to death by the devil.

Strategically placed between the bays of Luce and Wigtown is Whithorn. This Anglo-Saxon name meaning 'White House', describes the monastery founded here by St Ninian at the time of the collapse of the Roman Empire. It is the oldest of mainland British Christian sites, dating from around AD 397, and recent excavations have unearthed vital clues to the existence of a later, far more magnificent Christian church of possibly the mid seventh century.

Along the south and west coast around Luce Bay there are fine views out to the Irish Sea and Atlantic Ocean. Above Monreith Bay, on the east coast of Luce Bay, the statue of a small bronze otter has been erected in memory of Gavin Maxwell, the author of *Ring of Bright Water* and many other books,

Left: the lonely coast of the
Solway Firth near Dumfries —
haunt of smugglers' and curse
of excisemen

Right: Hestan Island,
the smugglers' haunt of
S.S. Crocket's The Raiders
on the Solway Firth

including *The House at Elrig*, in which he recalls his Galloway childhood. Nearby Port William is a small fishing village with a harbour founded towards the end of the eighteenth century and on one occasion the exciseman from Wigtown, with twenty-five soldiers, challenged a heavily armed brig offshore. The captain instantly threatened to fire a 22-gun broadside and to land one hundred armed men. On the other hand, if the troops withdrew, he would present them with thirty kegs of spirits when he was ready to set sail. Needless to say the excisemen withdrew and later collected the booty.

From Stranraer, at the head of Loch Ryan, the road runs north to Ballantrae, an attractive seaside town associated with Robert Louis Stevenson's novel *The Master of Ballantrae*, although this was not

the setting he used in the plot. All around this area are ruined Clan Kennedy strongholds: Ardstinchar, Kirkhill and Knockdolian. Three miles to the north at Bennane Head on the coast is Sawney Bean's Cave, home in the sixteenth century to a large and notorious family of cannibals whose practice it was to seize passers-by and eat them. Spare limbs were pickled and kept in a store cupboard. Nobody knows exactly how many innocent travellers met this grisly end. Finally, when somebody did manage to escape, King James VI personally supervised the arrest and execution of the entire family.

Girvan, to the north, is a popular summer holiday resort and it was here, in 1968, that William Grant & Sons, encouraged by the escalating popularity of Grant's Scotch whisky in its

Left: the dark grains plant at Girvan Distillery built by William Grant & Sons in 1968   Above: The Kennedy coat of arms at Culzean Castle

triangular bottle, chose to build the most modern grain distillery in Europe.

Further north along the coast, defiant, spectacular, the great castle of Culzean presides in clifftop majesty over the Firth of Clyde. Built in the late eighteenth century by Robert Adam, this most splendid of Scottish dwellings occupies the site of an ancient fortified house dating from three hundred years earlier. Adam's achievement was to transform a strategically placed fortalice into a palace to symbolise the achievement of the

Kennedys of Carrick who established themselves as the most powerful family in the southwest of Scotland. Today Culzean Castle is 'the jewel in the crown of the National Trust for Scotland', who took it over in 1945. The following year, in recognition of his services to Britain during the Second World War, President Eisenhower of America was presented with the lifetime use of an apartment within the castle, and an exhibition occupying these rooms traces his career and his association with Scotland.

From the start the Kennedys were covetous of land, and as their power grew so did their acreage. Prior to living at Culzean, their seat had been Maybole Castle, nine miles southwest of Ayr, close to the thirteenth-century Cluniac abbey of Crossraguel. In 1570, intent on acquiring abbey lands, the 4th Earl of Cassilis had the unfortunate Commendator roasted over an open fire.

Culzean Castle is a dramatic contrast to the humble cottage built at Alloway by William Burns, and where his son Robert was born on 25 January 1759. Here the poet lived for the first seven years of his life before the family moved to a farm at Mount Oliphant, two and a half miles to the southeast. Burns introduced Alloway Kirk into his poem *Tam O'Shanter*, and today the village is full of reminders of his presence.

Ayrshire abounds with memories of Burns' short life. The Tam O'Shanter Museum in Ayr once was a brewhouse to which Douglas Graham of Shanter Farm supplied malt grain. The bard's first edition of poems was published at Kilmarnock and a statue of him by John Wilson stands in Kay Park. At Mauchline is the Burns House Museum, on the upper floor of which is the room he took for Jean Armour in 1788. Eight years earlier, at Tarbolton, Burns founded a literary and debating society which became known as the Bachelors' Club. At Kirkoswald, where Burns went to study surveying, the National Trust for Scotland has Souter Johnnie's Cottage. Mauchline Churchyard is the scene of 'The Holy Fair', and four of the poet's daughters are buried here. Poosie Nansie's ale

A Christmas view of Glasgow City Chambers

house, which inspired 'The Jolly Beggars', is still in use today.

In August 1839 the 13th Earl of Eglinton, inspired by the colourful romance of Scotland's distant past, held a lavish medieval jousting tournament at Eglinton Castle which made him the most popular peer in Scotland and impoverished him for life. Leading families from all over Britain took part, encased in suits of armour and providing a dazzling spectacle for the watching crowds. All that

remains of Eglinton Castle is a tower.

For centuries the seaboard of Ayrshire was a land of fisherfolk and seafarers, where smugglers, in unity with their brethren on the Solway, cocked a snook at generations of powerless excisemen. In the seventeenth century the prevalence of smuggling on the Ayrshire coast can be measured by the contemporary estimate that in the vicinity of Irvine, in one year, £20,000 worth of goods were landed on the beaches and shores illegally. The legislation by the Scots parliament to restrict the importation of foodstuffs, notably salt, merely encouraged the traffic with Ireland. Whisky from the Highlands found its way ashore in large quantities at such locations as Saltcoats.

Largs played its role in Scotland's history in 1263, when King Haakon of Norway invaded with a fleet of 160 longships carrying 20,000 Viking warriors. In October a fierce storm blew them ashore at Largs where Alexander III and his army were waiting. The Vikings were fiercely repulsed and scattered, although both sides later claimed victory. King Haakon died on Orkney two months later and, as a result, Scotland was to acquire the Hebrides and the Isle of Man.

From Largs past Skelmorlie and Inverkip, there are fine views across the silvery Firth of Clyde towards the Isle of Bute and Dunoon on Cowal. Rounding the headland, there are glimpses of Holy Loch, Loch Long and Gare Loch.

To the southeast is Paisley, now largely an industrial suburb of Glasgow, but in the twelfth century an abbey was founded there. On the outskirts is

Elderslie, traditionally the birthplace in 1270 of William Wallace, Scotland's great hero of the Wars of Independence. Nobody has better defined the spirit of Scottish resistance to English domination than Wallace. Captured and taken to London, condemned to death, humiliated and dragged through the streets to Smithfield to be hanged, drawn and quartered, Sir William remained defiant to the end. The barbarous manner of his death ignited a flame of fury in Scottish hearts which culminated eight years later with the decimation of the English army on the field of Bannockburn.

The region known as Strathclyde is dominated by the City of Glasgow which sprawls across the narrows of the River Clyde. This royal burgh of 1454 prospered as a Lowland city, largely untouched by the dynastic turbulence which, for the most part, took place to the north and east. In 1746 Bonnie Prince Charlie passed this way on his northerly retreat from Derby. As at Dumfries, on his way south, he levied a toll, greatly resented at the time, but later reimbursed as a sop from the Hanoverian Whig government in London.

Making use of Glasgow's prime situation on the Clyde estuary, Glaswegian merchants at first profited from importing tobacco from the New World. The cotton trade followed, and before long Glasgow emerged as the shipbuilding centre of the world, attracting hoards of immigrant workers from the Highlands and Northern Ireland.

Facing: Port Glasgow, evening, on the River Clyde, early nineteenth century (Samuel Bough)

Before this great population influx from the Highlands, Glasgow, already one of the ten largest towns in Britain although smaller than Edinburgh, was essentially a Lowland city. Indeed, a university, the second oldest in Scotland, had been founded by Pope Nicholas V in 1451. Apart from their different origins, the Gael and the Lowlander spoke different tongues. City dwellers mistrusted the clansmen from the north and rarely ventured into their territory since, to the north, roads, as such, were virtually non-existent. Highlander and Lowlander came into contact with each other infrequently, mostly through the autumn markets when the folk of the glens would travel south, by sea or track, to stock up with provisions for the winter, bartering with their surplus corn, poultry, butter and whisky.

It was in the nineteenth century that Glasgow truly flourished. The 'dear green place', deriving its name from the Celtic 'Gleschu', became recognised as the commercial centre of Scotland and as an outward manifestation of this, constructed palatial office buildings, banks and civic headquarters. A prime example of the prosperity of this era is Glasgow City Chambers with its magnificent marble staircase and murals. In the late nineteenth century the work of the architect and artist Charles Rennie Mackintosh, such as the Glasgow School of Art of 1897, was to exert a radical influence on European design movements, despite the initial outraged response to his work in Glasgow. In this Victorian age Glasgow reigned supreme, the envy of the Empire, and with the city's new-found

affluence emerged the whisky barons.

In 1820 a grocery business was purchased by the trustees of John Walker, a minor. On coming of age, Walker took control of his inheritance, but it remained a retail business until the 1850s when his son Alexander, who had been trained in the office of a Glasgow whisky merchant, took over the family business and began to specialise in Scotch whisky.

After Alexander's death in 1889, his sons, George and Alec, continued to expand the company. The Johnnie Walker trademark – the striding man – was introduced in 1909. Soon Johnnie Walker's Red and Black labels had gained the world recognition that they retain today.

Another world-famous brand, White Horse, also has its roots in Glasgow. In 1845 James Logan Mackie went into partnership with Alexander Graham, a Glasgow wines and spirit merchant, and agent for the Lagavulin Distillery on Islay, then owned by his brother.

When Graham retired in 1850 Mackie took over the Glasgow business, and eleven years later merged the Mackie and Graham family interests under J.L. Mackie & Co. Mackie's nephew, Peter, had been taken into the firm and astutely came to the conclusion that the immediate future of Scotch whisky lay in blends. In 1890 White Horse was launched. When the screw top bottle was introduced in 1926, prior to the merger with the Distillers Company, sales of the brand doubled within six months.

Sir Peter Mackie goes down in history as one of

the great, indomitable characters of the Scotch whisky industry. Annual General Meetings became a platform for his strongly held opinions concerning the state of the whisky industry, the nation, and, especially, the British Empire. 'Restless Peter', as he was referred to by his staff, was a rich man, owning 12,000 acres in Ayrshire and Argyllshire. Other pet enthusiasms included the manufacture of feeding-cake for farm animals, also of concrete slabs and partitions, the weaving of Highland tweed, the distribution of carragheen moss, and BBM (Bran, Bone and Muscle), flour mixed according to a secret recipe by machinery under the boardroom floor, and which every member of Mackie's staff was expected to use at home.

By 1887 the Greenlees Brothers, based in Glasgow, were large-scale blenders, also describing themselves as whisky distillers. They had a licence for two distilleries at Campbeltown, their place of origin. From their London offices they monopolised London's pub trade with their Lorne Scotch Whisky – at least until James Buchanan began selling a branded Scotch whisky blended to appeal to the English palate at the top end of the market. Originally sold as the Buchanan Blend, Buchanan's product came in a distinctive black bottle with a white label, and before long Buchanan became exclusive supplier to the House of Commons. By 1900 the company's main line was Black & White, with Buchanans being the name of the de luxe.

By the early nineteenth century the Greenlees Brothers had introduced the de luxe brand, Old Parr, and had merged with Alexander & Macdonald

Auchentoshan Distillery at Clydebank

Rolling casks from the cooperage at Auchentoshan

of Leith. The distiller Sir James Calder had been a partner in the company since 1895. In 1919 Calder combined the two companies with long-established blenders William Williams & Son of Aberdeen, and in 1925 this company was sold to the Distillers Company.

In the early 1850s William Robertson, an ambitious Fifer, came to Glasgow to seek his fortune. To begin with he worked for Lade's, a wine and spirit company. Soon after founding his own business he promoted his clerk, John Baxter, to a full partnership. Robertson & Baxter was founded in 1860 with the agencies for two whisky distilleries, Henkes' gin, and so little capital that in their first year they bought only one hundred cases of gin and one cask, and forty cases of claret.

In the 1870s and 1880s whisky accounted for approximately one third of Robertson & Baxter's total stock in their Glasgow warehouses. But in 1885 Robertson was involved in the formation of the North British Distillery Co Ltd in Edinburgh. Two years later the Highland Distilleries Company was first floated, with Robertson a key figure in the consortium based at Robertson & Baxter's West Nile Street offices.

Highland Distilleries was initially formed to take over the Rothes-Glenlivet and Bunnahabhain distilleries. In the first year of trading alone, 174,988 gallons of Highland's whisky were marketed.

Facing: a view across to the eastern banks of Loch Lomond with the snow-capped peak of Ben Lomond in the distance

A famous Glasgow name in today's Allied Distillers portfolio is that of William Teacher who, in 1830, established himself as a modest grocer in the city. Teacher was a classic example of the Victorian entrepreneur whose hard-nosed business sense earned him the nickname of 'Old Thorough'. Success came rapidly when he began selling his Teacher's Highland Cream blend through twenty or more public houses or 'Dram Shops', as they came to be known. In 1899 the company expanded to build the Ardmore Distillery in Aberdeenshire while the bottling and blending operation remained in Glasgow. The company's head office was for many years at 14 St Enoch Square, but since 1991 has been at Dumbarton. Allied's impressive Strathclyde Grain Distillery, commissioned in 1928 for Scottish Grain Distillers, is located close to Glasgow Green, in the heart of the city.

In 1898 control of the business passed to William Curtis Teacher, grandson of the founder, William Bergius, his cousin, and Robert Hart. A popular innovation in 1913 was William Bergius' 'self opening' bottle, in which a stopper replaced the traditional cork.

In 1875 William Scott, sole partner in Allan & Poynter and Scott & Steel, which owned warehouses, recruited two young men, James Whyte and Charles Mackay. When Scott died in 1881 Whyte and Mackay decided to bid for the wines and spirits part of Scott's business and by 1882 they were bottling and blending whisky from premises in Robertson Street. At this time it was fashionable for every licensed grocer, hotel and

public house to sell its own blend, occasionally unique, but more often standard blends individually bottled. In 1896 Whyte and Mackay took offices in Wellington Street and began to market their own 'Special Reserve' brand, a blend of thirty-five different malt and grain whiskies, which by 1911 was selling as far afield as Australia. Today the Whyte & Mackay brand is exported to over one hundred countries throughout the world.

Despite the Second World War bombing of Clydebank, the decline of shipbuilding on the Clyde, and the inner-city planning ravages of the 1950s, Glasgow remains Scotland's great merchant city. Much fine Victorian architecture survives alongside new additions such as Barry Gasson's 1983 building in Pollok Park for the Burrell Collection. After the 1988 British Garden Festival, and the choice of Glasgow as the 1990 European City of Culture, Glasgow has once more emerged as a self-assured, stylish and innovative metropolis.

At Port Dundas in the north of the city, situated at the junction of the Forth and Clyde and Monkton Canals, United Distillers has the smaller of its two large grain distilleries.

Clydebank, down the Clyde towards Dumbarton, had consisted of rich farmland until 1871 when James and George Thomson arrived from Govan. The following year they launched their first

This 50-foot waterfall supplies Glengoyne Distillery, Scotland's southernmost Highland malt distillery

Facing: the 'Scotch Watch' at Dumbarton

ship. Twenty-seven years later their business was acquired by John Brown & Co and this giant shipbuilding yard was to witness the launching of such famous liners as the *Lusitania*, the *Queen Mary*, the *Queen Elizabeth*, and the QE2.

Also at Clydebank is the Auchentoshan Distillery, founded around 1800. Auchentoshan is the only distillery in Scotland to use a triple-distillation process. The triple-distillation process involves three pot-stills instead of the usual two, and the spirit consequently undergoes a third distillation before passing through the spirit sample safe.

Further west on the northern banks of the Clyde, in close proximity to the southern swell of Loch Lomond, stands Dumbarton, once the capital of the British kingdom of Strathclyde. The 'Fort of the Britons', known by the Irish as Dun Bretann, was built on a twin-peaked rock located on the northern shore at the mouth of the River Clyde – the rock continues to dominate the coastline.

Dumbarton is the headquarters of Allied Distillers, also the location of the second of the company's great grain distilleries. The storage of vast quantities of maturing whisky demands elaborate security and Allied has adopted an unusual approach to this problem. Taking a lead from the Roman legions of long ago, a solution was found in 1959 with the employment of the 'Scotch Watch', a one-hundred-and-fifty-strong gaggle of white geese. To the intruder they present a formida-

The gate motif at Glengoyne Distillery

ble obstacle. Raising a terrifying noise when disturbed, they have clear eyesight, acute hearing, and are easier to look after than guard dogs. They also keep the grass cut during the summer months. The company has adopted the image of a goose as their official logo.

To the north the road along the eastern banks of bonnie Loch Lomond is the natural passageway to the West Highlands. Ben Lomond, the most southerly peak in Scotland over 3000 ft high, looms above the eastern shores. In centuries past the clans Buchanan, Colquhoun and MacFarlane would be constantly in a state of emnity towards each other, each separately threatened by the Children of the Mist, the cattle raiders of Clan Gregor from Craigroyston, and the wild northeast glens of Gyle, Dochart, Orchy and Lyon.

At Dumgoyne, in the Blane Valley to the southeast of Loch Lomond, under the Campsie Fells, is the Glengoyne Distillery, dating from 1833, although distillation was certainly practised in the area long before. Local tradition has it that young maidens of the neighbourhood would regularly smuggle containers of whisky hidden under their skirts to sell in Glasgow, a day away on foot across the Kilpatrick Hills.

At Glengoyne only naturally malted barley is used. The taste is untainted by peat smoke, thus making this Scotland's only unpeated malt. The distillery is the southernmost of the Highland malt whisky distilleries, and the name is believed to translate from the Gaelic 'wild goose'. Water is drawn from a 50-foot waterfall, and there is an attractive timber chalet-like visitor centre which overlooks a man-made loch.

Facing: the blender smells or 'noses' the different whiskies

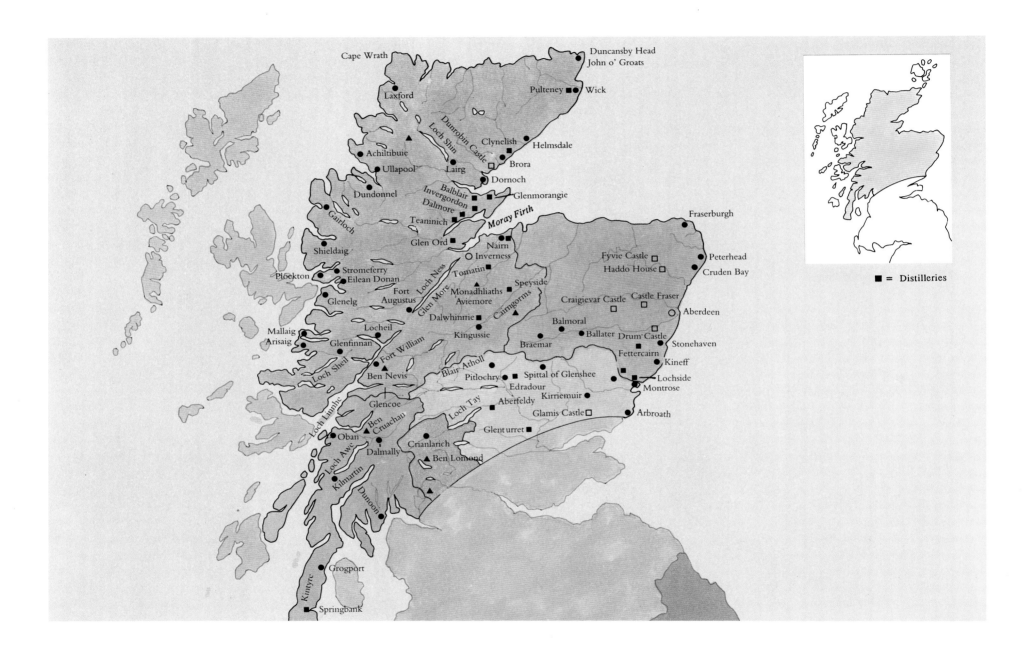

Cape Wrath

Duncansby Head
John o' Groats

Laxford

Pulteney ■ Wick

Dunrobin Castle
Loch Shin

Clynelish ■
Helmsdale

Achiltibuie

Ullapool

Lairg

Brora □

Dornoch

Dundonnel

Balblair
Invergordon ■
Dalmore ■

Glenmorangie

Teaninich ■

Gairloch

Moray Firth

Glen Ord ■

Shieldaig

Nairn

Fraserburgh

Plockton

Inverness ○

Stromeferry
Eilean Donan

Tomatin ▲

Fyvie Castle □
Haddo House □

Peterhead

Cruden Bay

Glenelg

Loch Ness

Speyside

Craigievar Castle □

Castle Fraser □

Fort
Augustus

Glen More
Monadhliaths
Aviemore

Cairngorms

Aberdeen ○

Mallaig
Arisaig

Locheil

Dalwhinnie ■

Balmoral

Braemar

Ballater

Drum Castle □

Stonehaven

Glenfinnan

Kingussie

Fettercairn ■

Kineff

Loch Sheil

Fort William

Blair Atholl

Ben Nevis ▲

Pitlochry ■

Spittal of Glenshee

Lochside
Montrose

Edradour

Kirriemuir

Glencoe

Aberfeldy

Glamis Castle □

Arbroath

Loch Tay

Loch Linnhe

Ben
Cruachan ▲

Glenturret ■

Oban

Dalmally

Loch Awe

Crianlarich

Kilmartin

Ben Lomond ▲

Dunoon

Grogport

Kintyre

Springbank ■

■ = Distilleries

THE HIGHLANDS

The Bay of Glenelg from the Isle of Skye

THE SOUTHERN HIGHLANDS — THE WESTERN HIGHLANDS

GRAMPIAN REGION AND THE EASTERN HIGHLANDS

SPEYSIDE — THE NORTHERN HIGHLANDS

An Illicit Whisky Still in the
Highlands (*Edwin Landseer*)

THE HIGHLANDS

The Highlands of Scotland comprise a vast region of wild and awe-inspiring beauty where, up until two hundred years ago, a burgeoning population scraped a meagre living. The Highland landscape consists of a dissected plateau of ancient crystalline rocks formed into glens and lochs carved by the action of ice and mountain torrents. The result is a wide area of irregularly distributed mountain ranges, Monadhliath, Grampian and Cairngorm, whose summits all rise to about the same height above sea level.

It is generally agreed that the Highland Line (dividing the Highlands from the Lowlands) follows a range of hills – the Campsie Fells and the Ochils – from north of Glasgow, east overreaching the old castle of Stirling towards Perth and through Strathmore. Prior to the building of the military roads in the eighteenth century, the region north of this line was largely inaccessible and travel was both arduous and dangerous. Yet communities thrived in the hidden-away straths, forming themselves into clans with their own tribal allegiances and a universal disregard for the outsider. For generations, Highlander and Lowlander had little or nothing in common.

At first it was the cattle trade with its drove roads to the fairs of the south which provided a life-line; then came General Wade with his thoroughfare through the Great Glen. Towards the end of the nineteenth century the Highlands were further opened up by the railway, and now motorways are pushing north.

Long before this however, in 1745, the arrival from France of Bonnie Prince Charlie aspiring to reinstate the Royal House of Stuart (the 'Kings across the Water'), in place of his Hanoverian cousins, was to have far-reaching and devastating implications for the future of the traditional, clan-based Highland way of life.

Highlanders, with their own deeply entrenched concept of clan allegiance, had been consistent supporters of the House of Stuart. Furthermore, the concept of the House of Hanover had been alien from the start. Highland chiefs were nevertheless divided, some playing safe by fielding sons on both sides.

The decimation that followed the Jacobite defeat at Culloden Moor in 1746 made few allowances. To begin with, the estates of Charles Edward Stuart's 'Jacobite' sympathisers were annexed. Tenants were either hounded out or chose to leave of their own accord, the majority finding their way to Glasgow. The wretched state of the Highlands, ravaged by the Hanoverian army, with rising rents and falling cattle prices, offered little encouragement for those who cherished a peaceful existence, let alone those whose dreams had been shattered.

The harvest failures and famines of 1771 and 1782 further increased the flow of emigrants to the New World. At Westminster the case for a sheep-based Highland economy was strongly advocated, landowners being given instruction on how to make their estates economically viable. Clearly an alternative to the old Highland way of life would have to be imposed if the Highlands were ever to be of value to anybody. Thus the policy of selective clearances was introduced.

The 2nd Marquess of Stafford, an English-born Liberal politician, had married Elizabeth, Countess of Sutherland in her own right. This striking lady, as her portrait testifies, was heiress to Dunrobin Castle at Golspie, and Scotland's largest landowner, although much of her territory consisted of mountain and uncultivatable moor. Stafford, created 1st Duke of Sutherland six months before his death in 1833, is usually cited as the worst offender in the sad saga of the Highland Clearances. The methods of eviction were undoubtedly vicious and brutal and were enforced by those in Stafford's employment. However, there are points in Stafford's defence. He was genuinely concerned that the tenants on his wife's estates were living in conditions of primitive and abject poverty, as was most of the population of the Highlands, and also that the Highland crofting communities were generally in a state of extreme deprivation; families were undernourished, barely managing to survive on a barren landscape in a harsh climate. Stafford's remedy was to remove his wife's tenantry from the interior acres of her land to the seaboard areas where various kinds of alternative employment were introduced. Given the bitterness created among the tenantry, who found their traditional way of life being destroyed overnight, it is not surprising that Stafford's grand design failed.

The legacy of the Clearances was that vast areas of the Highlands were depleted of their indigenous population, fulfilling a seventeenth-century prophecy of Coinneach Odhar, a native of Ross-shire, more commonly known as the Brahan Seer: 'The ancient proprietors of the soil shall give place to strange merchant proprietors and the whole highlands become one huge deer forest. The people will emigrate to islands now unknown, but which shall yet be discovered in the boundless oceans.'

Between 1815 and 1838, twenty-two thousand Scots arrived in Nova Scotia. There was further evacuation after the crop failure of 1846 and by the 1850s emigrants were finding their way to Canada, New Zealand and Australia. Over a period of eighty years the Gaelic-speaking population of the Highlands dropped by over 66 per cent.

A glance at the story of Canada gives an impression of the impact of this mass emigration. In Nova Scotia, even today, it is possible to tell a person's Scottish origins, even their town or village, from their name. Among the settlers who arrived in the 1790s were Ballantynes, Camerons, Living-stones, MacDonalds, MacEarchans, Macleans and MacNeils. Their numbers were augmented in the early nineteenth century by hundreds more, many of whom occupied the fertile valleys. Place names such as Morar, Keppoch, Lochaber and Eigg Mountain reflect the origins of these people.

Given the hard lot of the Highlander, which drove so many to emigrate, it is not surprising that solace should be sought in a brew of their own creation, serving not only to comfort the body, but also to heighten the senses. 'The northern nations,' wrote James Boswell, 'are more addicted to the use of strong liquors than the southern, in order to supply by art and want of that genial warmth of blood the sun produces.'

As early as 1597 whisky distillation had become so common that the Scottish parliament passed an act restricting the practice to the upper classes alone. This had little effect on the crofters, artisans, farmers and weavers for whom whisky production had proved a lucrative sideline, and they continued to supply local communities regardless. Excise duty was introduced by the Scottish parliament in 1644, the duty fixed at 2s 8d per Scots pint (approximately one third of a gallon) of aqua vitae or other strong liquor. The introduction of this taxation simply added to the long and colourful tradition of smuggling, and inevitably the practice of home-distilling continued to mushroom with small stills producing smooth malt whiskies, and the large-scale legal producers, spirit for the London market. It may be that Coinneach Odhar also foresaw this when he prophesied that:

'The time will come when dram shops will be so plentiful that one may be seen at the head of every plough furrow.'

The Treaty of Union between Scotland and England of 1707 trod carefully when it came to legislating against whisky manufacture: while a tax on malt was introduced in England, Scotland was exempt. This point of difference was regarded as having such importance that the Articles of Union highlighted the provision that malt should not be taxed in Scotland.

In 1713, when the Government did decide to extend the English tax to Scotland, it was met with immediate and massive opposition. It failed to be put into effect and the government retreated. In 1725, when Sir Robert Walpole successfully imposed such a tax, there was again an uproar culminating in what became known as the Malt Tax Riots. In Edinburgh these climaxed with the Porteous Affair, when the unfortunate Captain Porteous, a member of the City Guard, was lynched.

The reaction to this legislation was a widespread outbreak of whisky smuggling, which was actually encouraged by many of the larger landowners. Whisky smugglers were not considered to be petty crooks or criminals. Invariably they were individuals of high standing in the community, often wealthy, generally influential. Of excisemen, the enforcers of the legislation, even the law-abiding Dr Samuel Johnson was moved to comment that they were 'wretches, hired by those to whom excise is paid'.

Highland cattle by Loch etive

The prohibition of small-scale distilling during the wars which followed the French Revolution of 1789 continued to drive the industry underground. The Small Stills Act of 1816 which licensed stills with a minimum capacity of 40 gallons was marginally successful in reducing the smuggling trade, but in 1820, according to an Inland Revenue report, 'illicit distilling had become so widespread that half the spirits actually consumed were supplied by smugglers'.

In 1823 a more liberal act was passed, and within a few years the number of licensed distilleries had grown from a dozen to over three hundred. It should be noted, however, that most of these were located either on the edge of the Highlands or in the Lowlands. By law, a distiller with stills of over 500 gallons capacity could apply for a licence on payment of £10. Distilleries were also obliged to house a resident exciseman. Up until this time, virtually every Highland household had had its own still. The Statistical Account for Scotland of 1798 observed that for the majority of people working on the land, distilling was almost the only method for converting victual into cash for the payment of rent and servants. The Illicit Distillation (Scotland) Act of 1823, in a bid to encourage the taking out of licences for legitimate distilleries, made a still of under forty gallons illegal.

Such legislation was much condemned and William Larkin in his *Sketch of a Tour in the Highlands of Scotland* (1818) , had confirmed this. ' Whisky is to the full as much a staple commodity as black cattle, sheep and wool,' he wrote, '. . . and the smuggling of whisky is the only resource for the regular payment of their rents. The heavy duties on homemade spirits having debased the quality, while it has raised the price, the superiority of the smuggled article is so palpable that the demand for it is universal.'

Penalties were now defined for all offences connected with illicit distilling. Fines of £200 were stipulated in cases where persons were found in possession of unmarked stills, in use or not. The removal of spirits from one place to another, unless with a permit, also carried a penalty of £200. Despite this, illicit distilling was to continue for many years. Illegal stills were regularly discovered in the most unlikely places – land-locked caves on the west coast from Ballantrae to Plockton and caverns under the Free Tron Kirk in Edinburgh's High Street.

In his *Reminiscences of My Life in the Highlands* (1883), Joseph Mitchell, senior Highlands Road Inspector, describes how, in the course of his duties, he had once encountered, in Glen Moriston, a band of smugglers with a string of twenty-five horses each loaded with two kegs of whisky. So widespread and so profitable was the trade, records A.R.B. Haldane in his *New Ways through the Glens*, that more than one contemporary writer considered that the making of the improved Parliamentary roads in the late eighteenth century to replace the ancient drove roads had checked emigration by unintentionally facilitating the import of barley from the Lowlands, and the subsequent disposal of the home-brewed spirit.

This disposal amounted to an often farcical cat-and-mouse game played out in the most unlikely locations between smugglers and excisemen. A typical story concerns a party of gaugers (itinerant excisemen who measured containers and content) in Ross-shire. Having taken possession of a large cask of whisky, they removed it to a nearby inn for safekeeping. Not to be outwitted, the smugglers gained entry to the cellar below and bored through the ceiling into the cask to drain off the contents.

Dr John Mackenzie of Eileanach, a Justice of the Peace for the county of Ross, quoted by his nephew Osgood Mackenzie in *A Hundred Years in the Highlands*, gives an amusing account of an arrest:

On the way to Wyvis by a country road, the cutter policemen observed a grain or two of barley, then some more, and at length a continuous stream of grain, which had evidently dropped from a hole in a sack carried on a cart or horse. In due time the grain ceased opposite a steep heather-clad hillock close to the road. A poke from their wicked iron-pointed sticks showed them that the heather belonged to a pile of blocks of turf nicely arranged, and when these were pulled down, lo and behold! there was the door to a hillock cave in which malt was being nicely made. In the absence of the maltster, one of the cutter-men got into the cave, while his comrade built up the turf neatly again as if no one had touched it, and then hid himself behind a heather knoll ready to pounce out when required.

Soon after this the maltster came up the road, stopped at the hillock, pulled down the turf and got in, all but his feet. In a second these were flourishing in the air, while fearful shouts came from the cave, and in minutes out came the maltster, coatless, and away he ran down the road like mad, while his opponent emerged from the cave with the coat in his hand. He and his comrade ran after the maltster and caught him in his house. One can easily imagine the maltster's thoughts when, sure that all was safe as usual, he was grappled by two hands the moment he came into the cave. He admitted he *knew* it must be Satan who seized him.

CHAPTER THREE: THE SOUTHERN HIGHLANDS

Blair Castle, headquarters of The Keepers of the Quaich, catching the sunlight against the wooded slopes of the Grampian Mountains

The region known as Tayside encompasses rich, rather grand countryside at the heart of the map of Scotland. To the west lie the towns of Auchterarder, Crieff and Comrie, where the river flows from gentle Loch Earn. Between Strathearn and Strathallan sits the Gleneagles Hotel, host to the Scottish Open, among other notable golfing tournaments, on its famous King's and Monarch's courses. Since it first opened in July 1924, the Gleneagles Hotel, with its spectacular surroundings, has ranked among the best-known leisure retreats in Europe.

In close proximity to the hotel complex, at Blackford, nestling into the slopes of the Ochil Hills, is the Tullibardine Distillery, opened for business in 1949, and which takes its name from the nearby wooded moor. Water is drawn from a spring which once fed the first public brewery in Scotland, on record in 1488 for having produced a special brew for the Scone coronation of King James IV.

Loch Turret, 3000 ft above sea level

The little town of Crieff, on the River Earn, has important historical significance as one of the great tryst locations for the 'lifeblood' cattle droves of the sixteenth and seventeenth centuries. Cattle were then the staple trade and wealth of the Highlands; every year as many as 15,000 head would be driven across the most inaccessible country from the remotest glens and islands to be sold to buyers from the south. Crieff, as far as most of these Lowland and English merchants were concerned, was the last outpost of civilisation. At the foot of the hills, it was nevertheless a natural mar-

Facing: the Glenturret Distillery at Crieff

ket at the gateway between two worlds: the Highlands and Lowlands of Scotland.

Situated two miles northwest of Crieff, the Glenturret Distillery is the oldest in Scotland. There are records of a distillery in the neighbourhood in 1717, and some of the existing buildings date from 1775. The present-day distillery was revived in 1959 by James Fairlie, a Scottish businessman. The distillery draws its water from the Turret burn rising in Benchonzie and Loch Turret, 3000 ft above sea level, and where the winter snow remains until the end of June. The distillery's sheltered location is attributed to its having been originally run by smugglers, the site, conveniently sloping towards the river, selected as an ideal lookout post.

In recent years Glenturret's most famous inhabitant was Towser, the distillery cat and mouse-catcher, who lived in the still house for almost twenty-four years. In the course of her career, Towser reputedly caught 28,899 mice, qualifying for listing in the Guinness Book of Records as World Mousing Champion. Although Amber, her more diffident successor, carries on the tradition, Towser has proved a hard act to follow.

Northwest of the town of Stirling, across Strathallan, is Doune, where the ancient ruined castle, part of the Moray Estates, was built in the fourteenth century by Robert Stewart, Duke of Albany, Regent of Scotland and brother of the Wolf of Badenoch. Here, also located on the River Teith, is the Deanston Distillery. Originally built as a cotton mill in 1785 by Sir Richard Arkwright, it was con-

verted as recently as 1960.

Ten miles southeast of Doune Scottish kings felt safe in their castle on a rock at Stirling. Strategically situated, on the site of a Roman fort, the castle and town stand between a one-time marshy plain and a logical gateway to the Highlands, skirted by the Trossachs and the Ochils. On 23 June 1314, to the south of the castle, just beyond cannon shot, the great, decisive battle of the Wars of Independence took place on the bog land surrounding the

Amber, the Glenturret cat

Stirling Castle, sentinel to the Highlands

Bannock Burn. English horsemen, crowded together and floundering in the muddy ground, found themselves at the mercy of Robert the Bruce's pikemen. A rout turned into a headlong flight. The freedom of Scotland from English domination was won, at least until King Robert I's death on 7 June 1329.

The City of Perth, which may have been founded by the Roman Agricola in AD 83, has an ideal location at the meeting point of tracks and passes from the mountains. Straddling the broad, fast-flowing River Tay, Perth was a popular meeting place, so favoured by James I that it seemed destined to become the capital of Scotland. However, his murder at the royal lodgings of Blackfriar's Monastery on the night of 26 February 1437 soon put paid to any ambitions the town might have had in that direction. Edinburgh Castle, high on its impressive rock, within a mile from the Palace of Holyroodhouse, became the logical royal domicile in times of strife.

Thomas Sandeman, a relative of the Oporto family, opened a wines and spirits business in Perth in 1825. The company's traveller, Arthur Bell, became a partner in 1851. Fascinated by the art of blending, Bell was to make this the basis of the company's business. As sole partner from 1865 until 1895, he was adamant that quality was all, never advertising or using brand names. When he died in 1900 the company was bottling and selling three brands. The 'Scotch Fir' label was registered in 1897, depicting a Scottish country view with river, road and mountain, but curiously without a single tree. A second label, 'Colleen Brand', was registered shortly afterwards for an Irish whiskey, and the label for 'Skerryvore' Old Scotch whisky shows a moonlit lighthouse, rocks and sea. The famous Bell's label depicting a kilted curler was not to appear on the company's bottles until 1904.

Arthur's son, A.K. Bell, retained his father's belief that 'safe is sure', but the company did acquire its first blending and bottling plant in the 1920s, followed by its first distilleries in 1933. After A.K. Bell's death in 1942, the company remained with the family, trading mainly in the United Kingdom. Then, from 1958, a period of enormous expansion took place, largely pioneered by W. G. Farquharson and later the chief executive Raymond Miguel. Arthur Bell and Son joined Guinness in 1985.

Another notable Perth family is that of Gloag, who set up a grocery business at 24 Atholl Street in the early 1800s. In 1842, when Queen Victoria and Prince Albert attended a banquet in the city, Matthew Gloag supplied the wines. Matthew's son, William B. Gloag, was a great wine connoisseur who also appreciated his whisky, describing it as 'exhilarating, invaluable in repairing the exhausted forces of nature'. It was his nephew Matthew, however, who developed the blend that would appeal to the growing numbers of sporting gentlemen lured, by the influence of the royal family at

Balmoral, to the Northeast Highlands. In 1896 he chose the aptly named 'Grouse Brand', and his daughter Philippa sketched the Red Grouse (*Lagopus scoticus*) label which was to become its trademark.

The Earl and Countess of Mansfield at Scone Palace

So popular did this blend become that it was renamed The Famous Grouse.

The development of whisky bottling meant that Gloag's were able to promote their sales further afield, and by the mid 1920s whisky had come to dominate the firm's trade. At that time whisky producers were becoming concerned about the advent of Prohibition in the USA, and the serious threat this posed to exports. The resourceful Willie Gloag countered with a successful sales drive to

neighbouring countries such as those in the West Indies. With the repeal of Prohibition in the USA in 1933, so active did the export trade become that three years later the company found it necessary to open a bonded warehouse in Perth, in Kinnoull Street. A family tradition has now survived for six generations, continued today by Matthew I. Gloag.

At the Augustinian abbey at Scone, north of Perth, the kings of Scotland were required from ancient times to take part in the traditional coronation ceremony, performed on Moot Hill, a grassy mound within sight of the main entrance of present-day Scone Palace. The Stone of Destiny, the *Lia-Fail*, the very rock upon which the biblical Jacob is said to have rested his head on the occasion of his encounter with the angel at Bethel, was brought to Scone in the ninth century by King Kenneth MacAlpine, conqueror of the Picts, in his attempt to unify Scotland. Kenneth was crowned King of Picts and Scots in AD 843.

After his invasion in 1296, the English King Edward I had the stone removed to Westminster Abbey in London, where it remains to this day. Coronations of Scottish kings continued at Scone regardless, notably that of Charles II in 1631, and, three centuries before, the frantic enthronement of Robert Bruce, hotfoot from Dumfries and the slaying of John Comyn, his rival.

Based on the original abbot's house of the Augustinian monastery, enlarged and embellished in 1802, Scone Palace is the home of the 8th Earl and Countess of Mansfield and Mansfield, the dual

earldoms deriving from a rather complicated arrangement dating from the eighteenth century. The fortunes of this particular branch of Clan Murray prospered in the seventeenth century when Sir David Murray, Sheriff of Perth, saved the life of King James VI at the time of the Gowrie Conspiracy.

In 1582, while still a juvenile, James was seized by William Ruthven, Earl of Gowrie, and a group of Scottish nobles who held him prisoner for their own ends. A year later, aided by Murray and others, the young king escaped, and those who had supported him were generously rewarded to the detriment of Gowrie and friends. Gowrie lands were attainted and mostly given to Sir David Murray who became Master of the Horse. When the king moved to London in 1605 Murray was created 1st Lord Scone, later 1st Viscount Stormont. Two centuries later the brother of the 6th Viscount was created 1st Earl of Mansfield in recognition of his contribution to the English legal system – he served as Lord Chief Justice of England, virtually creating the commercial law of Great Britain and the USA.

As the owner of Scone Palace, the present Earl occupies the primary role of First Crown Estate Commissioner. He is responsible for administering the Crown land and properties first put into public trusteeship in the reign of George III, relieving the Head of State from the burden of financing the Royal Navy. In return the monarch was granted the

The Victorian rail bridge over the River Tay which replaced the one destroyed in the freak storm of 1877

The Fettercairn Distillery near Montrose

Civil List to cover the expenses of State, and this arrangement has lasted until the present day, being ratified by successive kings and queens within six months of their ascending the throne.

Within Scone Palace are fine collections of French furniture, ivories, sixteenth-century needlework and porcelain. The estate hosts regular race meetings, an annual game conservancy Scottish fair, polo tournaments and carriage driving competitions, popular with HRH the Duke of Edinburgh.

Towards the mouth of the River Tay, on a clear day, when sunlight glints on panes of glass, the high-rise blocks of Dundee resemble those of some citadel of the Côte d'Azur. When crossing the Tay Road Bridge for the first time it is hard not to think of that terrible night in 1877 when the old rail bridge was swept away in a storm, carrying helpless passengers of a train in transit to their deaths in the cold, dark waters. Dundee, which celebrated its 800th anniversary in 1991, is a university town existing in tandem with a range of light industry – timber, jute, light engineering and computer components. Alexander Stewart's whisky merchant business started here in Castle Street in 1831. Before long, he was involved with blending malts and grain to meet the demands of that time. His family continued to run the business until the

Glamis Castle, ancestral home of the Earls of Strathmore and Kinghorne

1920s, and thereafter a public limited company was formed, later joining Allied Lyons in 1968. Blends had included Royal Stewart, a twelve-years-old de luxe, packed in a bag liveried in Stewart tartan. The company's best-known brand, however, is Cream of the Barley.

Along the coastline from Dundee lie residential Broughty Ferry, Carnoustie with its famous golf club, then Arbroath, where the Stone of Destiny, removed from Westminster Abbey in 1951 by Scottish Nationalist students, was finally recovered. The name may be familiar, possibly because of the 1320 Declaration to the Pope signed by the Scottish clergy and barons in support of Robert the Bruce: ' For so long as but one hundred of us shall remain alive we shall never consent to bow beneath the yoke of English domination'. Most likely the association is from 'Arbroath smokies', unsplit smoked haddock, the strong and fragrant smell of which can be sensed as you approach the town.

The Abbey of Arbroath, founded by William the Lion in 1178, is dedicated to the memory of St Thomas à Becket, murdered in Canterbury in 1170. Subsequent Scottish monarchs made generous endowments, helping the burgh to grow from fishing village to trading port.

Further up the coast, at the mouth of the River

South Esk, is Montrose where the Fettercairn Distillery is reputed to have been founded in 1824. The inland hills around Cairn o' Mount once hid the original distillery of Fettercairn, but the present location is in the Howe o' the Mearns, not far from the Glen of North Esk. The Lochside Distillery, also situated in Montrose, was once the well-known James Deuchar Brewery, becoming a distillery in 1957. For those who choose to take the road inland, a short journey brings you to Forfar, a grey county town providing a centre for the rural community of the glens of Angus. Behind a great wall are the moody turrets of Glamis Castle, home of the earls of Strathmore and Kinghorne, the childhood home of Her Majesty Queen Elizabeth the Queen Mother. The castle is said to have been built originally on the top of nearby Hunter's Hill, inhabited by fairies who, every night, would scatter the building stones. Construction work was rapidly moved to the castle's present-day low-lying position.

In the eleventh century Glamis was used by Scottish kings as a hunting lodge, but in 1372 it formed part of a dowry gift to Sir John Lyon on his marriage to Princess Joanna, daughter of King Robert II. Mention Glamis Castle, and it conjures up images of William Shakespeare's Scottish play, *Macbeth*, an early laird playing cards with the devil, and the legend of a secret room wherein was kept a deformed being. Despite a reputation for being the most haunted house in Scotland, its warm

An etching of snow on the slopes of Glenshee

sandstone makes it a welcoming place, one of Scotland's grander, more lived-in ancestral homes. And as with others of Scotland's great houses, Glamis is associated with two whisky labels: Glamis Castle Reserve, a twelve-years-old blend, and Strathmore, a fifteen-years-old blend, both supplied by the Speyside Distillery Company at Drumguish.

Although the Queen Mother was not herself born at Glamis, it was her decision that her youngest daughter should be. Princess Margaret Rose became the first Royal baby in direct line to the throne of Britain to be born in Scotland for over three hundred years.

To the north, the twisting township of Kirriemuir, featuring in the title of a bawdy Scots ballad, is perhaps best known as the birthplace of Sir James Barrie, the playwright. Barrie's parental home, a humble cottage, is maintained by the National Trust for Scotland, and a statue of his creation, Peter Pan, is located on an exit street taking traffic northeast to Brechin and Montrose.

At Brechin, the Glencadam Distillery was built early in the nineteenth century, and takes its water from Moorfoot Loch. Bought by Ballantine's and managed by Stewart & Son of Dundee, the distillery was extensively modernised in 1959, and the malt is a major component of the Ballantine blends.

Stretching west, like the fingers of a hand, are the glens of Angus: Glenesk, Glen Mark, Glen Clova, Glen Prosen and Glenisla. Scenically this territory is beautiful, sparsely populated, rich in farmland. The roads twist like narrow veins through

The Glencadam Distillery

open moor and thickly wooded forests. One of the last wolves in Britain was killed here; in ancient days they were legion.

The hills of Glenesk, Glen Clova and Glenisla, however, remain full of wildcat, ptarmigan, red grouse, wild goats and deer. This is Clan Ogilvy and MacThomas country. In the seventeenth century, McComie Mor, 7th Chief of MacThomas, fought with the Marquis of Montrose and became a legend in Glenisla. A great athlete, a giant, he would wander from the Highland games field to visit the Crooked Loch where a mermaid would come out of the water to sit beside him. Clan MacThomas entered into a fatal feud with their kinfolk, the Farquharsons, who lived at Broughderig in Glenshee and, after a series of misfortunes, culminating in a financial dispute with the Ogilvy family, scattered from the glen. Each August they return, from the far corners of the world, in the company of their chief, Andrew MacThomas of

Finegand, McComie Mor, a London-based banker. For an hour they gather on the Cockstane, a mound close to the Spittal of Glenshee, and, after a brief ceremony led by the chief's personal piper, they march to take part in the annual Strathardle Highland Games.

About eight miles from Airlie Castle, ancient home of the Ogilvy Clan, is Cortachy Castle, home of the 13th Earl and Countess of Airlie. Gillibride, second son of Ghillechriost, Earl of Angus, received the barony of Ogilvy in the Parish of Glamis around the year 1163. The family prospered when Sir James Ogilvy, Scottish Ambassador to Denmark, was created 1st Lord Ogilvy of Airlie in 1491. Another James, 7th Lord, a supporter of Charles I, was created 1st Earl of Airlie in 1639. In 1962, the Hon Angus Ogilvy, second son of the 12th Earl of Airlie, married Princess Alexandra, daughter of the late Prince George, Duke of Kent and Princess Marina, Duchess of Kent. His brother, the 13th Earl of Airlie, is Lord Chamberlain of Her Majesty's Household. At the foot of the hill Glen Clova meets Glen Prosen, and it was in a bungalow in this latter glen that Captain Scott and Edward Wilson discussed and planned their ill-fated journey to the South Pole in 1912. In 1914 Scott's ship, the *Discovery*, was recovered from the ice and, in 1986, it was returned to the Dundee shipyard in which it was built and where it has become a notable tourist attraction.

The road up Glenisla passes Castle Forter, once

Facing: Cam an Tuire near Spittal of Glenshee

Blairgowrie highland games: throwing the hammer

Tossing the caber

The Edradour Distillery at Pitlochry

Pretender, while Farquharson of Invercauld joined the Young Pretender at Perth, although later transferred his allegiance to the Government, claiming he had been pressured to support the Prince by his feudal superior, the disgraced Earl of Mar. Invercauld's daughter, Anne, wife of Mackintosh of Mackintosh, was to restore the Farquharson's

another Ogilvy stronghold, and shortly meets the Blairgowrie to Braemar road through Glenshee, opening out to the west, with spectacular views across Shee Water which flows through the glen. From Spittal of Glenshee the road continues to climb until it reaches a bowl in the mountains where, in winter, the snow-blanketed slopes are thronged with skiers.

This is Farquharson country, settled by descendants of Farquhar, son of Alexander Ciar, 3rd Shaw of Rothiemurchus in Strathspey. Many Farquharsons fought for the Jacobite cause within and outside the Clan Chattan Confederation. Farquharson of Inverey, for example, gave support to the Old

honour by scattering English troops with a few of her father's men, enabling Bonnie Prince Charlie, yet again, to evade capture.

Each September, at the Blairgowrie Highland Games, the White Cockade Society, led by the Laird of Ardblair, re-enacts such skirmishes and scuffles of Scotland's turbulent history. Red-bearded, magnificently kilted for everyday wear, Laurence Blair Oliphant, his wife, son and two daughters live at Ardblair Castle, which has been the family home for over six hundred years.

On the far side of Strathardle to the west, Pitlochry, an attractive holiday town, provides a first-class festival theatre founded in 1951. The Hydro

Electric Dam and Fish Ladder, with an observation chamber, enables visitors to watch thousands of salmon being lifted annually as they travel up river.

Edradour Distillery, resembling a picturesque toy-town distillery, is tucked into the hills to the east. Built in 1825, this is the smallest distillery in Scotland, producing in a year what many distilleries produce in a week, and that remains the company policy of Campbell Distillers who own Edradour. Campbell Distillers dates back to 1879 through S. Campbell & Co, who purchased the Speyside Aberlour-Glenlivet Distillery Company in 1845. Since 1974 it has been owned by Pernod-Ricard, continental Europe's largest wine and spirits company. The Clan Campbell association has

Cluanie Water flowing to Loch Cluanie between Strathtay and Strathardle in the heart of Clan Macpherson territory

The White Cockade Society at Blairgowrie

Distillery still stands a great oak tree, which in 1746 played a significant part in the exploits of Robertson of Faskally, a local Clan Donnachaidh laird from Atholl. Fleeing from the Duke of Cumberland's troops at Culloden Moor, the Robertson chieftain took cover among its welcoming branches, remaining undiscovered while the search of the countryside continued. Taking refuge thereafter in the neighbouring farmhouse at Allt Dour, cold and disheartened, it is said he took a glass or two of the local distillation, a fond memory to carry with him into exile in France.

Robertson of Faskally's tree at Blair Athol Distillery

been fully developed with Clan Campbell whisky, the company's principal blend. The Duke of Argyll's involvement has also led to the successful European launch of 'The Noble Scotch Whisky'.

Situated in Pitlochry itself is the Blair Athol Distillery, established in 1798. The founders, John Stewart and Robert Robertson, named it 'Aldour', after the Allt Dour, Burn of the Otter, which flows through the grounds. In 1826 the distillery was licensed to Alexander Connacher, who leased the property from the Duke of Atholl, and he and his family were in control for the following thirty years until the distillery was taken over and enlarged by P. Mackenzie & Company.

In an enclosure across the road from Blair Athol

Laurence Blair Oliphant, Laird of Ardblair

Over to the west, towards Loch Tay, is the market town of Aberfeldy where the distillery produces a sweet, perfumed malt, not unlike a liqueur. In 1896 John Dewar & Sons, whisky blenders of Perth, took a feu of twelve acres from the last Marquess of Breadalbane, at this time proprietor of the magnificent Taymouth Castle, set back in the woods fronting the shores of Loch Tay. William of Orange entrusted John Campbell, 1st Earl of Breadalbane, with bringing Jacobite chiefs to terms with his accession to the throne after the revolution, and the flight overseas of King James VII and II. Highland chiefs were called upon to

Facing: Queen Victoria's favourite view of Loch Tummel

Pot-stills at Aberfeldy Distillery

swear allegiance to William and his queen. Albeit the word travelled slowly, and any indolence to co-operate could almost certainly be attributed to a natural lethargy prevalent in the Gaelic-speaking communities. It was pure bad luck, therefore, that the ageing Chief of the MacIain MacDonalds failed to reach Fort William in time to sign the necessary papers before the required date. The fact that the Government deemed it necessary to create an example underlined its insecurity.

Quartered in 1692 in the humble dwellings of the MacIain MacDonalds, the Glenlyon Campbells rose up, under government orders, in the middle of a winter's night to murder those who had been giving them food and shelter, thus causing one of the greatest atrocities of their time: the Massacre of Glencoe. Breadalbane was roundly held to blame, but the soldiers were essentially obeying instructions originating from John Dalrymple, Master of Stair, joint Secretary of State for Scotland. Henceforth, the lozenges represented in the arms of the Dalrymple family became synonymous with the Nine of Diamonds, the 'curse of Scotland'. Whether simple, evil connivance, or over-zealous soldiery, the Highlands have neither forgotten nor forgiven this ultimate example of the abuse of hospitality.

It is doubtful if the 1st Earl of Breadalbane was overly concerned by his local unpopularity. By this stage in his fortunes he could ride from the east end of Loch Tay to the coast of Argyll without leaving Campbell land. Successive earls became ambassadors to Copenhagen and St Petersburg, Lords of the Admiralty and Major Generals, and it was to Taymouth Castle, home of the Breadalbanes, that Queen Victoria and Prince Albert came on their first visit to Scotland in September 1842, forging their determination to acquire a Highland home of their own. Magnificent Taymouth Castle and all the Breadalbane Perthshire lands have now been sold.

Because the main railway line from Perth ran through the town, John Dewar built his distillery at Aberfeldy. The Pitilie Burn, which had supplied an illicit distillery of that name until 1867, provided the water source. The founder of the Dewar whisky dynasty was born, son of a crofter, two miles from Aberfeldy, on land held by the Menzies Clan of Castle Menzies. For a period he joined his elder brother's joinery business in Aberfeldy, but soon moved to Perth when offered a job in a relative's wine and spirit business. This is where he found his true vocation.

In 1846 he set himself up as a wine and spirit merchant. By 1870 he was receiving orders from Inverness in the north and Edinburgh in the south. The business expanded and, as a matter of course, John's two sons, John Alexander and Tommy, were brought into the company, renamed John Dewar & Sons Ltd. In 1887 the first London office was opened. John Alexander, an influential figure in Scottish life, was created 1st Lord Forteviot; Tommy, in turn, was created 1st Lord Dewar. Entre-

Roofs, Aberfeldy Distillery

River Tummel at Dowally in Strathtay

preneur, public servant, big game hunter, author, connoisseur and wit, there are many anecdotes surrounding the life of Tommy, 1st and, to date, only Lord Dewar. Once, confronted by a particularly grand lady who informed him of her name, adding, 'with a hyphen', he responded with: 'My name is Dewar, with a syphon'. Tommy Dewar's philosophy, as he toured the world appointing agents in twenty-six countries, was further indicated by the genial message printed on his business card: 'I have given up lending money for

some time. But I don't mind having a drink. Make it a Dewar's'.

In June 1917, for the war effort, the British Government instructed that all malt distilleries should close to conserve barley for foodstuffs. Two years of production thereafter were lost which resulted in serious post-war whisky shortages.

Between 1919 and 1923 Dewar's was able to acquire sole interests in seven malt whisky distilleries. In 1925 Dewar's, with John Walker & Sons and James Buchanan & Co, amalgamated with the

Distillers Company, a strategy to ensure that all parties were guaranteed adequate supplies of malt and grain whiskies. Today this has become United Distillers.

A more recent acquisition at Aberfeldy Distillery is an acreage of land where the management, encouraging a colony of red squirrels to breed, has created a nature trail along the Pitilie Burn.

Following the road north from Pitlochry, Blair Castle can be seen gleaming white against the green and thickly wooded slopes of the Grampian mountains. Prominently situated in the 135,000 acres of the Blair Atholl estates, the castle is the magnificent ancestral home of the dukes of Atholl. It is also the headquarters of The Keepers of the Quaich. In 1746 Blair was the last castle in Britain to withstand a siege. Although dating back to 1296, much of what we see today dates from the eighteenth century.

A tall, imposing figure, the 10th Duke of Atholl, chief of Clan Murray, inherited the dukedom in 1957 at the age of twenty-five, from his third cousin. He has since devoted his energies to admin-

istering his estate alongside fulfilling his role as the Chairman of Westminster Press, a commitment he retired from in 1993. Whenever he is in residence at Blair Castle his personal standard flies from the ramparts of Comyn's Tower.

The Duke of Atholl enjoys the privilege of being the only British citizen permitted to have his own private army, recruited from local landowners and Atholl estate employees. The history of this prestigious and exclusive unit is unusual. There was an Atholl brigade in the army of Prince Charles Edward Stuart in 1746, but the official

The band of the Atholl Highlanders at Blair Castle

Menzies Castle, the Clan Menzies headquarters near Aberfeldy

Dalwhinnie Distillery close to where the Highland drove roads converged to travel south to Crieff and beyond

beginning of the Duke's legions was in 1778, when the 4th Duke raised a regiment known as the 77th of Foot (Atholl Highlanders) for Home Service only. When they were ordered to board a ship at Portsmouth for service in America, they refused to embark and so were marched back to Berwick and disbanded.

It was in 1839 that the Atholl Highlanders took their present form when they accompanied Lord Glenlyon, later 6th Duke of Atholl, to the celebrated medieval, and rain-soaked, Eglinton Tournament organised at his Ayrshire home by the 13th Earl of Eglinton. After Queen Victoria stayed at Blair Castle in 1844 she presented them with colours and awarded them the right to bear arms, although they are, however, restricted to two artillery pieces.

West of Blair Castle, the main road continues northwest up Glen Garry before sweeping round to the northeast towards Inverness and the Moray Firth. Over Drumochter, before entering Glen Truim, at the foot of Meall Cruaidh to the west, the Dalwhinnie Distillery, deriving its name from the Gaelic word for 'meeting place', stands out against the mountain slope. In ancient days cattle drovers from the far north would gather here to fraternise with those who had crossed the Monadhliath Mountains from the west, resting and imbibing before ascending the Pass of Drumochter on their way to the cattle fairs of the south. As often as not, supplies of whisky, illicit, of their own creation, accompanied the sturdy participants in this 'rude and primeval' traffic.

They came from far and wide: they poured down from Caithness and Cromarty; from the Outer Hebrides – Lewis and Harris and the Uists – a typical route was across Skye, fording the kyle at Glenelg on the mainland, then over the switchback hills to Glen Garry. Trickling down the west coast,

97

herds divided off at Spean Bridge, east and west around Ben Nevis, both routes equally hazardous, prior to forging on through Glencoe and across the misty, marshy wasteland of Rannoch Moor. Thereafter lay the choice of Glen Lyon or Glen Dochart to take them to Loch Tay and Strathearn.

Droving to the trysts of Dumbarton, Crieff and Stirling would begin as early as June. The month of October, when the cattle were in their best condition – although smaller, leaner beasts than we are accustomed to seeing today – was the time for the great tryst at Crieff. Cows in the late seventeenth century fetched between 15s and one pound sterling; on a comparative note, a bottle of whisky in the year 1700 was priced at 6d.

At Dalwhinnie, around 1730, General Wade built his military road through the Central Highlands, forking west to Fort Augustus and leading north to Inverness. A section of this original road, now unused except by distillery transport, can still be seen immediately north of the distillery burn, beside the 'old A9'.

Across country to the west, past Loch Laggan and through Glen Spean, the traveller enters Glen More nan Alba, known as the Great Glen. Extending 60 miles northeast and southwest, sea to sea, from Inverness to Loch Linnhe at Fort William, this vast, natural fault encompasses Loch Ness, Loch Oich and Loch Lochy and includes the remarkable Caledonian Canal, built under the supervision of Thomas Telford and opened to traffic in 1822.

At a height of 1073 ft above sea level, originally called the Strathspey Distillery, Dalwhinnie, at the top of Loch Ericht, has access to abundant, cold and uncontaminated mountain water close to its source in Lochan an Doire-uaine. The supply flows underground for some distance before forming the Allt an t-Sluic Burn which feeds the distillery. The surrounding land, uncultivated and uninhabited, provides ample reserves of peat. In severe winters Dalwhinnie is often snowbound. Angus MacDonald, a former distillery manager, can recall the snowdrifts of 1937, over 20 feet high. The distillery is Station 0582 of the Meteorological Office and keeps a daily record of maximum and minimum temperatures, hours of sunshine, wind speed and snow depth.

Five miles east of Kingussie, at Drumguish, on the River Tromie as it enters the Spey, near the Forest of Gaick, is the Speyside Distillery, Scotland's second smallest distillery. In the 1970s George Christie, a whisky blender of some repute, who founded the Speyside Distilleries Group in the 1950s, commissioned Alex Fairlie, a specialist in dry stone dyking, to build him a distillery on the site of an old barley mill. Stone by stone, Fairlie completed his work by 1990 but, despite this, the Speyside Distillery has the appearance of having been there for a very long time.

Moving east, the road travels through Macpherson and Clan Chattan country to Aviemore, an all-purpose holiday resort which includes the Cairngorm Whisky Centre. Founded by Frank Clarke in 1980, this small whisky Mecca boasts one of the largest collections of malt whiskies and miniatures to be found in the world.

Situated at the mouth of the fast-flowing River Ness that runs out of the north end of Loch Ness, part of Scotland's great geological fault separating the Northern from the Central Highlands, is Inverness, the Highland capital. Seven miles to the east, at Culloden Moor, as the day dawned on 15 April 1746, the 5000 Highlanders, ill armed and hungry, led by Bonnie Prince Charlie, faced 9000 trained soldiers of the British Government. In the ensuing battle, only seventy-six of the Government troops fell, while the battle count of Highland dead reached 1200. As the fighting lapsed, the Duke of Cumberland, third son of George II, gave the order that no enemy wounded were to be spared. For days after clansmen were hunted out and slaughtered. Even some spectators from Inverness were cut down where they stood, and Cumberland's general ordered that the provost of that city should be kicked downstairs for protesting against the inhumanity of it all.

CHAPTER FOUR: THE WESTERN HIGHLANDS

Evening mist settles over Loch Tulla

The scenery of Argyll, with sweeping vistas of mountains, lochs and sea, instantly captures the imagination. Washed by the Gulf Stream, this coast has a higher rainfall than that of the east. Mountain and moorland, lit by shafts of sunlight or enveloped in Scottish mist, wrinkle with rivulets, streams and waterfalls, the vegetation lush and, in places, tropical. Imported palm trees and rhododendrons flourish.

The distant past is inescapable. Here is Dalriada, ancient kingdom of the Scots, those itinerant colonisers who migrated across the Irish sea in the early centuries of the second millennium. Between Kilmartin and the Crinan Canal, across low fields, there is a small hill called Dunaad, and this is where the Scots set up their capital and crowned their early kings on the sacred *Lia-Fail*, the Stone of Destiny, transported from Ireland and said to have originated in ancient Egypt. To this day evidence exists of that early ritual: the image of a wild boar is etched into the rock with, nearby, a footprint, believed by some to be that of the Witch of Cruachan.

Officially recognised as part of the vast Strathclyde Region, Argyll will always have an identity of its own. Once a rich man's playground, with great estates bought and houses built on the proceeds of the Industrial Revolution, some of the sons settled to the farming life but there is yet truth in the saying that the area is full of people looking after

Above: Inveraray Castle, ancestral home of the Dukes of Argyll

Facing: the harbour front at Oban with the Oban Distillery nestling amongst the buildings and McCaig's folly hovering above to the right

other people's land. In recent years there has nevertheless been a change. Tourism has increased and also the influx of young families searching for an escape from city life and creating a quasi-commercial culture of craft industry, fish farming and boats.

West Highland scenery is as refreshing as it is physically unchanging. Evocative with louring clouds, it is manifestly damp, and yet miraculously transformed within seconds should the sun cast light on the hills, especially in September, when the entire panorama blushes purple.

From Oban, gateway to the islands, Caledonian MacBrayne run ferries to Salen and Tobermory on Mull, and on to Iona, Tiree, South Uist and Colonsay. Sheltered from the Atlantic gusts by the island of Kerrera, which lies across the bay in front of Mull, Oban sparkles, and every other building seems to offer accommodation. Above the town, resembling a stone tiara, sits McCaig's Folly, a great, unfinished replica of the Colosseum in Rome, funded in the 1890s by an unusually benign, if somewhat egotistical, local banker to provide work for the town's unemployed.

When Dr Samuel Johnson visited Oban in 1773, it was a tiny fishing village with but a few cottages and an inn. Twenty one years later, the family of Stevenson, slate quarriers, house and shipbuilders, founders of the town of Oban as we know it, built a brewery which was soon converted into a distillery. The House of Commons Committee on Distilleries in Scotland observed, in the years 1798 and 1799 that the situation in Oban was much better than elsewhere in the Highlands. The distillery had been fitted up for a brewery, the barns were large and the granary ample. The person in charge of the work had been bred a distiller in the Lowlands.

Oban Distillery, situated in the town centre against a hill and overlooking the waterfront, remained under the ownership of the Stevenson family until 1866. Hugh Stevenson of Belnahua had become Oban's second provost in 1819, passing his business interests on to his son, Thomas, who, lacking his father's entrepreneurial sense, had his

The Duke and Duchess of Argyll at Inveraray Castle

assets sequestered in 1829. These assets included the distillery (valued at £2,700), farms, house, property, a hotel 'in part erected', the island of Belnahua and its slate quarries, two steam boats and a sloop.

'That neat and compact distillery situated at Oban', containing 'an engine for grinding malt, with ample malting premises, bonding warehouse, feeding house for thirty cattle', was bought by Thomas's nephew, John Stevenson, returned from South America. Three years prior to John's death in 1869 the distillery was sold to Peter Cumstie, a local merchant.

By the mid nineteenth century Oban was established as a major resort with steamships sailing to

and from Glasgow and Fort William twice a week in season. The first scheduled passenger train steamed into Oban station on 1 July 1880, commencing a new era of accessibility to the west coast and islands of Scotland.

In 1883 Cumstie sold Oban Distillery to Walter Higgin, who was the owner at the time of Alfred Barnard's visit described in his 1887 survey of *The Distilleries of the United Kingdom*. In Barnard's words it was ' a quaint old-fashioned work, and dates back prior to the existence of the town . . . built under a rock, which rises 400 feet high, and is festooned with creepers and ivy'. Between 1890 and 1894 Higgins rebuilt the distillery in the form that exists today.

Oban Distillery passed to Aultmore Glenlivet Distilleries then, in 1923, to a consortium which included John Dewar & Sons, James Buchanan & Co, and White Horse Distillers. In 1930 it was acquired by the Distillers Company and has only recently been refurbished with a visitor centre.

Prior to the Scottish Wars of Independence and the arrival of King Robert Bruce, the MacDougalls of Lorn, descendants of the mighty Somerled, twelfth-century Lord of Argyll, held sway over this region from their formidable stronghold of Dunollie Castle, north of the town, the ruins of which can still be seen.

Clan Donald, indisputably the largest of the Highland clans, at one time controlling virtually the whole of the western seaboard from the Butt

Facing: Loch Fyne looking south across Inveraray

of Lewis in the north to the Mull of Kintyre in the south, not to mention possessions in Ireland and the Isle of Man, dominated Gaelic culture until 1493. An inter-family civil war culminated with Crown intervention and, in 1496, the Lordship of the Isles was forfeited by the Crown. This most evocative and romantic of Scotland's great titles has remained ever since with the dukedom of Rothesay, retained and occasionally used by the eldest son of the reigning British monarch. As Macdonald power diminished in the isles there was a Highland mainland clan which benefited enormously: Clan Campbell.

In 1871, when Princess Louise, Queen Victoria's daughter, became betrothed to the Marquis of Lorne, heir to the 8th Duke of Argyll, an old lady resident of the town of Inveraray was overheard to comment: 'Och, it's a prood wumman the Queen'll be the day, wi' her dochter gettin' mairrit on the son of Mac Cailein Mor!' The present holder of the ancient Gaelic title Mac Cailein Mor, which translates as 'Son of Colin the Great', denoting the noble progenitor of the mighty Clan Campbell, is the 12th Duke of Argyll. In keeping with the lands and the powers over which his predecessors held sway, the Duke's other titles incorporate his being Marquis of Kintore, Marquis of Lorne, Earl of Campbell, Earl of Cowal, Viscount Lochow, Viscount Glenyla, Lord Inveraray, Lord of Mull, Morvern and Tiree, and Lord Sundridge. In addition, he holds the hereditary posts of Master of the

Loch Cluanie between Glenshiel and Glen Moriston

Left: mountain water cascades towards Loch Cluanie beneath an ancient drovers' bridge

Right: Ben Cruachan rises steeply above Loch Awe and the rich pastureland of Argyll

Celebrated in song, thirty distilleries once stood on the shores of Campbeltown Loch on the Mull of Kintyre

Royal Household in Scotland, Admiral of the Western Coasts and Isles, and Keeper of the Royal Castle of Dunstaffnage.

Reminiscent of a French château, Inveraray Castle, one of Scotland's most elegant and spectacularly situated clan seats, rises from the northwest shore of Loch Fyne. Most of the present-day building was completed by the 5th Duke in 1773. Ravaged by fire in 1975, it has since been extensively repaired.

To the southwest is the Crinan Canal which cuts across Knapdale and links Loch Fyne with the Sound of Jura. Built by John Rennie and opened in 1801, the canal was designed to provide an alternative to the long sail around the Mull of Kintyre.

All along the road south from Crinan the rhododendrons and wild flowers splash their colours.

With so many inlets from the sea, with continual comings and goings from the Hebrides and Western Isles, this coastline was, for centuries, a smuggler's haven. When President Ronald Reagan, 40th President of the USA, attended the 1991 Autumn Banquet of The Keepers of the Quaich, it was discovered that the President had a link with the Mull of Kintyre. In the last century there had lived in Kintyre a family of the name of Blue and one of the daughters was the President's great-grandmother. Her cousin was one Johnny Blue, a lobster fisherman and a well-known character on the west coast. He was also a distiller, in partner-

ship with a blacksmith and cooper called Donald Mackinlay. Blue soon became famous for his two grades of distillation – moonlight and daylight – the difference being that the former was twice as strong as the latter.

Donald Mackinlay, a particularly ingenious individual, had devised specialised barrels for salted butter which had an inner compartment for the whisky, thus enabling them to evade the attention of the exciseman. This cargo was shipped regularly through Grogport on the Mull of Kintyre to Saltcoats in Ayrshire where it was much enjoyed by the local miners.

_____

Facing: a dawn mist rises over Rannoch Moor

The River Lochy flows silently towards Loch Eil

The popular song about about Campbeltown Loch, on the tip of the Mull of Kintyre, recalls that once there were thirty distilleries in this small Argyllshire town. Surviving is Springbank Distillery, founded in 1828 by the Mitchell family. A Mitchell heiress married a Mr Wright and the present managing director, Hedley Wright, is a great-great-grandson. The Springbank Distillery retains its old-world charm and keeps a measured distance from its competitors.

Something of the character of the west coast and the people, descendants of the Gael, can be gleaned at the various Highland games and gatherings which take place in the summer and autumn. At these – Inveraray, Taynuilt, Arisaig, Glenfinnan – the athletes of the games circuit gather to test their prowess at tossing the caber, putting the shot, throwing the hammer, and other competitive sports associated with an ancient way of life. Highland dancing and piping competitions nowadays keep company with cycle racing, sheep-dog trials, and the recently introduced haggis hurling.

———

Facing: evening light on Loch Tulla

The deceptive allure of Glencoe

Best known of the traditional sports is probably tossing the caber, otherwise known as 'ye casting of ye bar'. The practice is said to derive from the time when woodmen cast their logs into the deepest part of a river so that the current would carry them swiftly downstream. Whatever the true origin, the practice of caber tossing is recorded as far back as the sixteenth century, not only in Scotland, but in Germany, Sweden, France and Italy. Even the

Facing: the waters of Loch Creran

portly King Henry VIII of England, in his youth considered the finest athlete in his realm, is reputed to have excelled at the sport.

The Cowal Games, held in August at Dunoon, on the Mull of Kintyre, that sliver of land which stretches down the west coast of Argyll with sea on either side, are the largest of their kind in the world. Crowds in excess of 18,000 are expected annually to watch the world championship events and the march of 2000 pipers.

At Mossfield Park in Oban the Argyllshire Gath-

ering, also held in August, dates from 1872 and is followed by balls, major social events in the Scottish calendar. To commence the proceedings, the Duke of Argyll heads a procession of his Campbell chieftains, other local chiefs and hereditary landowners such as the Captain of Dunstaffnage and Malcolm of Poltalloch.

In northern Argyll, as the mountains of Breadalbane in Perthshire spill towards Rannoch Moor, the dramatic mountains which contain Glencoe rise into the skyline. Entering Argyll from Crian-

larich in west Perthshire, through Glen Lochy to
Dalmally, the road travels along a short northern
stretch of Loch Awe towards Oban and passes the
seven peaks of Ben Cruachan, 3695 ft above sea
level. On the northeastern shore of Loch Awe
stands the ruined castle of Kilchurn which dates
from 1440. A Campbell of Glenorchy stronghold
in use until 1740, it was used briefly to garrison
English troops in 1745. In 1879 the hurricane that
caused the Tay Bridge disaster destroyed the castle's
turrets.

North of Oban, on Loch Etive, is Ardchattan Priory, dating from the thirteenth century and today
home of the Campbell-Preston family, descendants
of the last prior of Ardchattan, a Campbell of Cawdor. Set in the bay, perching picturesquely on a
rock between the islands of Lismore and Shuna,
is Castle Stalker, a thirteenth-century MacDougall
fortress, later acquired by the Wolf of Badenoch's
Stewart of Appin descendants. North across the
mouth of Loch Etive, through Benderloch, after
skirting Loch Creran, is Appin, the promontory
fronting Loch Linnhe as it flows deeply inland to
Loch Leven and Loch Eil.

Details of the eighteenth-century *cause célèbre*
known as the Appin Murder were outlined in
Robert Louis Stevenson's novels *Kidnapped* and
Catriona. The mystery surrounding the killing of
Colin Campbell of Glenure, a Hanoverian government official known as 'The Red Fox', by an unknown assailant, has never been resolved.

In the years following 1746 Stewart and Cameron lands were confiscated by the government,

*Looking towards
Glencoe from
Rannoch Moor
(Miles Richardson)*

The ruins of Kilchurn Castle on Loch Awe, originally stronghold of Clan Campbell   Facing: the barren slopes of Ben Odhar

Loch Etive, which meets the Firth of Lorne at the Falls of Lorne

singled out as the scapegoat. Abruptly seized and imprisoned at Fort William, a jury of fifteen, comprising no less than eleven Campbells, sentenced the unfortunate James of the Glens to be hanged on a scaffold at Ballachulish.

A bridge now spans the one-time Ballachulish ferry crossing of Loch Leven, taking traffic north into Lochaber and Locheil. This is Clan Cameron country dominated by Ben Nevis, the highest mountain in the British Isles standing 4406 ft above sea level. Sprawling at its feet, on the eastern tip of Loch Linnhe, is Fort William where, in 1825, 'Long John' Macdonald, who stood 6 ft 4 in tall, built a distillery on the slopes, the first legal distillery in the area. His product was rather colourfully called Long John's Dew of Ben Nevis.

One of the most spectacular rail journeys is on the West Highland Line which runs from Glasgow up to Fort William and Mallaig. Crossing Rannoch Moor, the road is left far behind and the track traverses Britain's 'Empty Quarter' before skirting the hills around Ben Nevis and then snaking into Fort William from the north.

Between Fort William and Mallaig there are breathtaking views of the Inner Hebrides and the white sands of Morar. In summer, steam-hauled services come into use, recalling a more leisurely age when travellers changed to the ferry, originally a paddle-steamer, at Oban bound for the islands. The route from Inverness to Lochalsh cuts right across the backbone of Scotland to run along the bays and promontories of the western shore.

To the north, Morvern, Morar, Moidart,

and Colin Campbell, as government factor in Appin, was in the process of evicting Stewart lairds from their homes and replacing them with members of Clan Campbell. When he was shot on the shores of Loch Linnhe on 14 May 1752 it was seen as a direct act of provocation against George II.

Curiously, Colin Campbell's one-time neighbour and friend, James Stewart of Glen Duror, had been among the few conciliatory voices to be heard in the neighbourhood. He had been virtual leader of the Stewarts of Appin during the exile of his half-brother, Charles Stewart of Ardsheal, and it is particularly ironic that it should have been this gentle, transparently innocent individual who was

Castle Stalker, one time stronghold of the Stewarts of Appin, rises from an island on Loch Linnhe

Knoydart and Glenshiel march to comprise Scotland's greatest wilderness. At Glenfinnan, at the head of Loch Shiel, on 19 August 1745, Bonnie Prince Charlie, watched by 850 Highlanders, raised his standard to commence his campaign to win back the Stuart throne. 'If he succeeds,' commented the 11th Lord Lovat, 'the whole merit will be his own; and if his mad enterprise bring misfortune upon him, he has only himself to blame.'

To the west of Glengarry is Knoydart, most easily accessible from the sea, and Loch Hourn, the 'Loch of Hell' opening out on to the Sound of Sleat. From Invergarry the road traverses Glenshiel, then Mam Rattachan with spectacular views of Loch Duich and the Five Sisters of Kintail and Ben Attow, to Glenelg and the tiny, four-car ferry crossing to Kylerhea on Skye. The community here is spread along Glenelg Bay, Glen More and Glen Beg. There were people here one hundred years before the birth of Christ. Across the salt marsh is Kylerhea where the mountains of Skye drop

Left: Loch Leven from the Pap of Glencoe

Ben Nevis

steeply into the sea, seemingly curtaining the gem-like Glenelg from an outer world. In Gaelic legend a giant warrior of the name of Reidh gave his name to these narrows. His companion had successfully vaulted across the water using spears, but the unfortunate Reidh's spear shaft snapped, plunging him into the torrent to be swept away to his death. In a cottage at Eilean Bhan, on this coastline, Gavin Maxwell wrote *Ring of Bright Water*, his enchanting book on otters.

Before the roads through Glen Carron and Glen Shiel were constructed and improved in the eighteenth century access to Kintail and Lochalsh was easier by boat. At the junction of Loch Duich and Loch Long is the fantasy castle of Eilean Donan, held by Clan MacRae for the powerful Mackenzies of Kintail. Northwards from the Skye crossing at Kyle of Lochalsh the coastline becomes increasingly ragged and rugged. The road, with the pretty holiday village of Plockton on Loch Carron to the west, runs via Stromeferry with its paradoxical notice announcing 'No Ferry' to meet the A896

The Ben Nevis Distillery at Fort William

swinging north towards the Applecross peninsula and Shieldaig on Loch Torridon.

Torridon is the most marvellous rock landscape with incredible mountain ranges of red sandstone topped with sparkling quartz containing intriguing fossils. The peaks of Beinn Eighe (3309 ft) are said to be 750 million years old, and for many, the saw-toothed An Teallach, rising above Dundonnel, is Scotland's finest mountain.

Inland the road winds to meet the A832 which continues west 12 miles along Loch Maree, a rock basin gouged by ice, guarded by the castellated peak of Slioch. Eighty million years ago this area was part of the crust of Greenland and Canada before the formation of the North Atlantic. And once this was a thick headland of forest.

At the head of Loch Ewe, Scotland's earliest iron smelting business, the Red Smiddy, was based at Poolewe in the seventeenth century, raping the landscape of its fine trees for fuel. When the supplies of timber were exhausted and the remoteness of the location made exporting increasingly difficult, the smelter failed.

Osgood Mackenzie, third son of Sir Francis Mackenzie, 12th Laird of Gairloch, was born in 1842, and, for his twentieth birthday, his mother purchased for him the estates of Inverewe and Kernsary, next door to Gairloch. At Inverewe he built himself a house at the landward end of the peninsula, and around this, encouraged by the warmth of the offshore Gulf Stream, he created the

Facing: the Bay of Glenelg from the Isle of Skye

The car ferry from Kylerhea to Glenelg

most remarkable gardens. As there was no suitable soil on the peninsula he transported all that was required from inland on the backs of out-of-work labourers. He waited twenty years for the trees he had planted to grow round the perimeter of the peninsula so as to offer sufficient protection from the winds and then cultivated plants of great rarity, many gathered from his extensive travels overseas.

Osgood Mackenzie lived at Inverewe until his death in 1922, and his evocative memoirs, *A Hundred Years in the Highlands*, were published the year before he died. In them he describes the shooting of golden eagles, which may horrify us today, and the ingenious use of cormorants to collect fish.

Much of the early material is drawn from manuscripts left behind by his uncle who had some acute observations to make on the subject of Highland whisky distillation:

My father never tasted any but smuggled whisky, and when every mortal that called for him – they were legion daily – had a dram instantly poured for him, the ankers of whisky emptied yearly must have been numerous indeed. I don't believe my mother or he ever dreamed that smuggling was a crime. Ere I was twenty he had paid £1000 for the 'superiority' of Platcock, at Fortrose, to make me a commissioner of supply and consequently, a Justice of the Peace and one of about thirty or forty electors of the county of Ross: and before it had occurred to me that smuggling was really a serious breach of the law, I had from the bench fined many a poor smuggler as the law directs. Then I began to see that the 'receiver' – myself for instance, as I drank only 'mountain dew' then – was worse than the smuggler. So ended all my connection with smuggling except in my capacity as magistrate, to the grief of at least one of my old friends and visitors, the Dean of Ross and Argyll, who scoffed at any resolution and looked sorrowfully back on the happy times when he was young and his father distilled every Saturday what was needed for the following week. He was of the same mind as a grocer in Church Street, Inverness, who, though licensed to sell only what was drunk off the premises, notoriously supplied his customers in the back shop. Our Pastor, Donald Fraser,censuring this breach of the law, was told, 'But I never approved of that law!' He and the Dean agreed entirely that the law was iniquitous and should be broken.

When Mackenzie died, Inverewe Gardens were bequeathed to Mrs Robert Sawyer, his only daughter, who continued her father's work until 1953, when she handed them over to the National Trust for Scotland.

The village of Ullapool was founded on a promontory two hundred years ago and the sparkling of today's buildings gives an eternal holiday look to the place. Lobsters, crabs and prawns are still big business, with herring and mackerel sold to the 'Klondyking' factory ships from Eastern Europe. For many, however, this is simply a popular sailing centre with ferry services to Stornoway and cruises to the Summer Isles off Achiltibuie, 25 miles to the north. In 1988 Ullapool celebrated its bicentenary as the largest and busiest centre of population on the northwest coast. Inland from this coastline are located many of the great stalking estates of Scotland. Red deer, wild and alert animals, are a native species in the Highlands and prior to the nineteenth century were regarded as a convenient source of fresh meat in a territory where agriculture was virtually unknown. Existence in this region of hostile mountains, lochs and glens had been isolated and spartan to the extreme, but with the arrival of the Victorian sporting estates came employment. Roads and tracks were made and shooting lodges built in the remotest locations.

Highland sporting estates prospered until the advent of the First World War when venison, not widely considered as a delicacy, became an important commodity for feeding a beleaguered nation and deer stocks were decimated as a result. The large sporting acreages had barely time to revive and restock themselves before the Second World War created a similar demand for meat, with the same decimating results from which they never fully recovered.

In 1965 the Red Deer Commission was instituted as a statutory body 'to conserve and control red deer in Scotland'. Since that time deer stalking has come to be regarded as 'deer-population management' and, in the absence of natural predators, selective stalking has become essential in order to remove the weaker elements of the breed and thereby ensure the survival of the species. Sporting rights on Highland estates rapidly moved into big business and venison, marketed as a quality meat, has found a renewed popularity.

From Achiltibuie on Coigach the view across Badentarbet Bay is breathtaking. The Summer Isles and Tanera Mor loom in the foreground with, beyond, the Cuillins in Skye and An Teallach, Slioch and Torridon on the mainland. To the west lie the looming shadows of Lewis and Harris. In 1985, at Achiltibuie, a thriving community with croftland sloping down to the sea, Robert Irvine, a hotelier, built the Hydroponicum, a space-age garden where plants grow without soil.

With more than forty lochs, Coigach is famous trout and Atlantic salmon fishing country. Whether in search of the elusive brown trout of the mountain pools or the sea trout of the River Garvie which drains Loch Osgaig, fishermen consider this a true paradise.

The roads from Achiltibuie and from Loch Shin and Lairg meet at Laxford. Northwards and to the east stretch the empty lands of Sutherland comprising giant mountains, rocky torrents and barren moorlands. Bypassing stormy Cape Wrath, which juts into the sea at Scotland's northwest corner, the route curls east to wriggle across the very top of Scotland. East of Cape Wrath, it touches Durness and skirts Loch Eriboll, once seriously mooted, because of its deep water anchorage, as the ideal site for a Highland city and port. In effect, this vast expanse of wild, unmanageable landscape is largely inhabited by sheep.

———————

Facing: the road to Skye between Glensheil and Loch Duich

Facing: a scene in the Grampians, The Drover's Departure *(Edwin Landseer)*   *Above: the Macduff Distillery on the River Deveron*

The Grampian Region encompasses the old counties of Kincardine, Aberdeen, Banff and Moray. From Dundee the coastal road north is dramatic, bypassing Montrose and Stonehaven, where the conspicuous ruin of Dunottar Castle, stronghold of Clan Keith, dominates the seascape. A Pictish fort stood here in the Dark Ages, and during the Civil War in the seventeenth century the Scottish regalia was brought here for safekeeping.

The castle was besieged by Oliver Cromwell's Commonwealth troops in 1652, determined to seize these Honours of Scotland, but George Ogilvie of Barras, the noble governor, refused to surrender. The regalia, in the meantime, was smuggled out of the castle in the apron of a servant girl and taken to the nearby church of Kinneff where it lay hidden under the pulpit until the Restoration in 1660. Thereafter it was taken to Edinburgh Castle where the items – the ancient Scottish crown, one of the oldest in Europe, the sceptre and sword of state – can now been seen on display in the Crown Room.

Aberdeenshire is the land of castles – Drum, Crathes, Craigievar, Castle Fraser and Fyvie, to name but a few – each a symbol of the achievements of the families of the region, notably Irvines, Burnetts, Forbes, Setons, and, of course, the Gordons. Generally better preserved than many of their southern counterparts, these keeps, fortresses and tower houses survive as a reminder not simply

Highland
Hospitality (*John
Frederick Lewis*): *a
dram of the uisge-
beatha*

The Glenglassaugh Distillery near Portsoy

The southern coastline of the Moray Firth gives constant reminder that to the north, on the other side of the water, the Breidafiord, the 'broad firth of the Vikings', lie the Caithness hills, once a Norse province from whence, up until the twelfth century, came fire and sword to scourge the indigenous Picts. Here is a necklace of coastal fishing villages, notably Portknockie, Cullen, Portsoy, Banff and Buckie, some of which, in medieval times, were trading burghs in the Hanseatic League.

Due south of Portknockie and Cullen, following the discovery of quite a number of springs on the southern slopes of Knock Hill, the Knockdhu Distillery was founded in 1893. The two original pot-stills remain in use and the distillery is owned by Inver House Distillers, based at Airdrie in Lanark-shire.

Portsoy, famed for providing the marble used in the building of the Palace of Versailles in France, boasts the oldest harbour on the Moray Firth. Portsoy's Glenglassaugh Distillery, which dates from 1875, was bought by the Highland Distilleries Company plc in the 1890s and completely rebuilt in 1960. Nowadays it is used for storage only. On a grassy cliff are the ruins of Findlater Castle, built in 1455 by Sir Walter Ogilvie of Deskford. These Ogilvies, who became earls of Findlater, and later in 1701, earls of Seafield, went on to build their infinitely grander Cullen House, tucked into the neighbouring Cullen Bay.

Another great family to stamp its identity on this district was the Duff family. At Banff is Duff House, built by William Duff, a wealthy member

The Glen Garrioch Distillery near Oldmeldrum

of parliament, created Lord Braco in 1735, and Earl of Fife in 1739. From a modestly landed family, his dramatic rise to riches through shrewd financial investment undoubtedly influenced the building of his new house, a fantastic show of opulence intended as a status symbol.

William Adam, father of Robert and James, was the chosen architect, probably the only one of his generation competent to conceive such an elaborate and richly decorated masterpiece. Before long, however, client and architect were quarrelling over costs and a tedious and acrimonious legal fight ensued after which Braco abandoned his plans for the house. The dispute seriously affected Adam's health, and Braco was so disenchanted by

of wealth and privilege but of a time when survival depended on force of arms.

With the granite city of Aberdeen, now Scotland's oil capital, on its lower southeast coast, Grampian is Scotland's eastern shoulder, jutting boldly into the North Sea at Fraserburgh, a town dating from 1576. The creation of Sir Alexander Fraser of Philorth, who dissipated his fortune in the process, Fraserburgh was intended as a university town until its sponsor's funding collapsed. Today, although Scotland's fishing fleets are much depleted, it remains a major fishing port. On the outskirts of Fraserburgh can be seen Cairnbulg Castle, seat of Sir Alexander's descendant, Lady Saltoun, present-day Chief of Clan Fraser.

Left: the Bullers of Buchan much feared by James Boswell

Right: Dunnottar Castle, where the Scottish regalia was taken during Cromwell's invasion of Scotland

his project that he would instruct that the window blinds of his coach be drawn whenever he passed.

Improvements, nevertheless, were made by later generations, and Duff House remained in the family's possession until 1906, when the 1st Earl's great-great-grandson, the 1st Duke of Fife, husband to HRH Princess Louise, daughter of King Edward VII, gifted the building to the adjacent burghs of Banff and Macduff. The town of Macduff, close to where the River Deveron enters the sea, owes its early prosperity to Braco's son, James

Duff, 2nd Earl of Fife, who set in motion a programme of renewals including the harbour construction. The Macduff Distillery, built in 1962, sits across the River Deveron from Duff House.

To the south, at Oldmeldrum, on the Banff to Aberdeen road, is the Glen Garioch Distillery which dates from 1798. Here a display shows the process of producing single malt whisky, and greenhouses grow tomatoes and pot plants fed with hot water from the distillery condensers. To the west, at Kennethmont, William Teacher & Sons

built the Ardmore Distillery in 1897, producing a sweetish whisky for the malty Teacher's blends. In 1960 Teacher's acquired the Glendronach Distillery, east of Huntly, which was erected in 1826. Here much of the whisky is matured in sherry casks and is known as Glendronach 'traditional'.

Over on the east coast, south of Peterhead, a singular natural phenomenon is to be found which much enthralled Dr Johnson and Mr Boswell. This is the Bullers of Buchan, known locally as the Pot, a monstrous rock cauldron into which sea water pounds through a narrow archway. Bullers means 'boilers' and this boiling is the effect given by the waves of the incoming tide as water surges into the chasm. Much to his biographer's horror, Dr Johnson insisted on exploring the cavern by boat, an experience which even today might warrant second thoughts.

Further to the south along the coast, near Cruden Bay, overlooking St Catherine's Bay, are the ruins of two castles, Old Slains and New Slains, homes of the earls of Erroll, chiefs of Clan Hay, and Hereditary Lord High Constables of Scotland.

The 24th Earl of Erroll, a patron of The Keepers of the Quaich, inherited the earldom in 1978 from his mother, countess in her own right. His father was Sir Iain Moncreiffe of that Ilk, one of the most distinguished heraldic experts of this century, not to mention raconteur, historian and wit. Although largely resident in the south of England, Lord Erroll retains the clifftop timber-frame house built by his mother at Old Slains, just yards from the remains of the old castle which

The Earl and Countess of Erroll

was blown up by James VI in 1594 to punish the 9th Earl for supporting a Catholic revolt. The precipitously situated New Slains, built by the 9th Earl as a replacement after his pardon in 1597, was

visited by Johnson and Boswell in 1773.

Old Slains has an interesting association: it was here that Bram Stoker, while staying at Cruden Bay in 1895, first conceived Dracula, emanating from the clifftop ruins of the old castle.

The nearby village of Port Erroll was built by the Hay family. In *A Search for Scotland* R.E. Mackenzie recounts a story told to him by his uncle that took place nearby. A string of fisherwives were one evening tramping along a road with heavy creels on their backs and attracted the attention of a gauger on a visit to the district. On approaching them, one of their number, fleeter on foot than the others, ran off guiltily, hotly pursued by the exciseman. How was he to know that she was the only one with an empty creel, while the other creels were filled to the brim with kegs of whisky?

Inland, to the northeast of Oldmeldrum, at Tarves, and in the care of the National Trust for Scotland, is Haddo House, the magnificent Palladian mansion built by William Adam in the 1730s for William Gordon, 2nd Earl of Aberdeen. In 1778, orphaned at the age of twelve, Lord Haddo, grandson of the 3rd Earl of Aberdeen, found it necessary to turn to his godparents for assistance, which they were only too happy to give. He was particularly fortunate since his godfathers were William Pitt, the British Prime Minister, and Henry Dundas, Viscount Melville, who through his political influence had become known as 'the uncrowned king of Scotland'.

_____

Facing: the Knockdhu Distillery in the village of Knock

Facing: the ruins of Old Slaines Castle, seat of the Earls of Erroll until the late nineteenth century   Above: the harbour at Aberdeen

Both godparents took an interest in the boy's career and saw to it that he was well educated and moved in the 'right circles'. Inheriting his grandfather's title at the age of eighteen, the young 4th Earl travelled to France where he dined with Napoleon at Malmaison, and subsequently became a close friend of the Duke of Wellington and Sir Robert Peel. Soon he embarked upon a political career which culminated in his being created 1st Marquess of Aberdeen, becoming the young Queen Victoria's prime minister and, for a time, her closest adviser.

The city of Aberdeen is mentioned in early Norse chronicles. Snorro's Icelandic *Heimskringla*, of the year 1153, records how Eysteinn, a Norwegian prince, was driven at a winter's end when his girnels were almost empty, to set forth upon a freebooting voyage. Having reached Orkney, spring winds found him 'steering along the eastern shores of Scotland and brought his longboats to the town of Apardian where he killed many people and wasted the city'. No wonder the Aberdonians have a reputation for being tight with their generosity towards strangers.

Aberdeen's charters were granted by William the Lyon in 1179. Two centuries later the town was again virtually destroyed, this time by English invaders, but a new town rose from the devastation, and Aberdeen soon achieved recognition as the main gateway to the northeast for foreign trade. At first, exports were mainly wool, cloth, Dee salmon and trout, and, most likely, whisky. Aberdeen merchants soon established their own staple, or fixed market, at Bruges, where they enjoyed certain customs concessions. In the mid fifteenth century the staple was transferred to the port of Veere on the Dutch island of Walcheren, serving the Low Countries, the Netherlands, Belgium, north France and Germany. Three Scottish houses in the late Gothic style remain at Veere today, one housing a museum recalling this period.

By the end of the sixteenth century Aberdeen was a seat of learning. King's College, named after James IV, had been founded by Bishop Elphinstone in Old Aberdeen in 1494, eighty-four years after the inception of its older university counterpart St Andrews, in the Kingdom of Fife.

From the mid eighteenth century granite became Aberdeen's leading industry and it was

Lochnagar on Royal Deeside

exported throughout the British Empire. Both London Bridge and Waterloo Bridge were constructed of it. Shipbuilding developed alongside fishing; Aberdeen became famous for its sharp-bowed 'clippers' designed specially for the China Seas and for the transportation of emigrants to Australia. A century later in the 1970s, the discovery of oil, deep in the cold, dark waters of the North Sea was to completely regenerate the city which now boasts more two-car families than any comparable centre in Britain. North and south of Aberdeen, the wide-banked rivers Don and Dee flow swiftly into the sea, the latter originating from the Grampian Mountains and forest of Balmoral, where Her Majesty the Queen retains the private Scottish estate purchased by her great-great-grandmother in 1848. Richly forested, this magnificent countryside inspired the impressionable Victoria and her adored German Prince Consort. 'The view from here,' the Queen wrote enthusiastically in her diary, 'looking down upon the house, is charming. To the left you look towards the beautiful hills surrounding Loch-na-gar, and to the right, towards Ballater, to the glen (or valley) along which the Dee winds, with beautiful wooded hills, which remind us very much of Thuringerwald.'

Upper Deeside abounds in tales of whisky smuggling in the early days of the nineteenth century. Great herds of cattle were driven down drove roads to the markets of the south and often, at

---

Facing: the River Dee at Tillycairn

The young Queen Victoria and Prince Albert visit the Lochnagar Distillery (waxwork model at visitors centre)

night along these same pathways, Highlanders, fully armed with pistols and cudgels, would escort convoys of ponies laden with kegs of contraband whisky. Around 1823 James Robertson of Crathie, having taken out a licence, is known to have operated a legal still in Glen Feardan, north of the River Dee. Unlicensed distillers, set on vengeance, it is said, torched it to the ground. Undeterred, Robertson immediately set about building himself another distillery, calling it Lochnagar after the

nearby mountain, which is 3789 ft high. In 1841 this building also caught fire. After this, one suspects, he lost heart.

In 1845 John Begg was granted the long lease of a suitable site on the Abergeldie Estate, belonging to the castle where Queen Victoria's mother, the Duchess of Kent, was soon to take up residence. Three years after Begg built his distillery, which again was called Lochnagar, Queen Victoria and her family moved into Balmoral Castle, half a mile away as the crow flies.

Begg's own diary takes up the story: 'I wrote a note on the 11th September to Mr G.E. Anson [Her Majesty's Private Secretary] stating that the distillery was now in full operation, and would be so until six o'clock next day, and knowing how anxious HRH Prince Albert was to patronise and make himself acquainted with everything of a mechanical nature, I should feel much pleasure in showing him the works ... Next day ... I observed Her Majesty and the Prince Consort approaching. I ran and opened the door, when the Prince said, "We have come to see through your work, Mr Begg".' After all stages in the process of transforming barley into a distilled spirit had been explained to the visitors, Begg asked Prince Albert whether 'he would like to taste the spirit in its matured state, as we had cleared some that day from bond, which I thought was very fine. HRH having agreed to this, I called for a bottle and glasses (which had previously been in readiness) and, presenting one glass to her Majesty, she tasted it, followed by Prince Albert, and their three oldest children.' The visit was obviously deemed a success since, within days, Lochnagar Distillery received the grant of a Royal Warrant of Appointment as supplier to the Queen. Lochnagar Distillery continued to be owned by the Begg family until 1916 when their company and shareholding were acquired by the Distillers Company.

With royalty in residence on Deeside, a new era began for the Highland estates. With the Queen

Reeling at a highland ball during the season

and her family entrenched at Balmoral, worshipping at Crathie Church at Ballater and attending the Braemar Highland Games and Gathering, the Victorians discovered Scotland as a holiday playground – the high mountains, the dark lochs and moody glens supplying every sort of sporting diversion. Autumn in Scotland became an annual fixture in the British social calendar and those endowed with sufficient wealth came swarming north from England to acquire castles, purpose-built mansions and shooting lodges. Thus a Scottish 'season' was created, a sporting interlude with social gatherings and formal balls in the evenings, by invitation only, held across the Highlands, and, in the case of the Northern Meetings, dating back to the late eighteenth century. At these balls held in Inverness, on Deeside and Donside, on Skye, in Lochaber, Angus and Perthshire, Scottish country dances, reels and Strathspeys, revived and formalised in the nineteenth century, are an inimitable feature.

The season for the stalking of red and sika stags runs from July to October and on the great Highland estates is the traditional means by which the survival of the species is ensured. Otherwise seen as a social pastime, stalking has subsequently become big business, so that estates consisting of mountain, moor and little else to sustain employment are today valued on their sporting rights: number of stags, grouse, average annual salmon and sea-trout catch. Many Highland landowners continue to enjoy the sporting privileges of their land, but the large majority depend upon syndicates and lets to provide the much needed income required to sustain their livelihoods.

Stalking, with its accompanying rituals, is one of the great, raw challenges of outdoor Scotland. On an average excursion, with an early start around 8 am, stalkers will possibly divide into two parties, one heading north, the other south. Two members will be chosen as rifles for the day and it is usual for them to be taken off by the head stalker to check that they can zero in on a target, often a cast-iron stag cut-out at 200 yards. Then the ascent into the hills begins.

The first spy point is usually at 1000 ft, the second at 1500 ft, the third at 2000 ft. The course is arduous and testing; waterproof clothing and stout shoes essential. Stalkers may be called upon to lie motionless for hours in damp, midge-infested heather or to immerse themselves in a mountain stream during a downpour of rain. The thrill of sky, mountain and scenic splendour, climaxed by the distant roar of a stag, is nonetheless indescribable. Once the kill is sighted and the shot fired, the deer, if tradition is followed, is brought down the hill on garrons. In Highland lodges, remote and basically furnished, often without electricity, the day's adventure is celebrated with hearty teas and dinners, accompanied, naturally, by generous quantities of the *uisgebeatha*.

A royal stag down from the glens

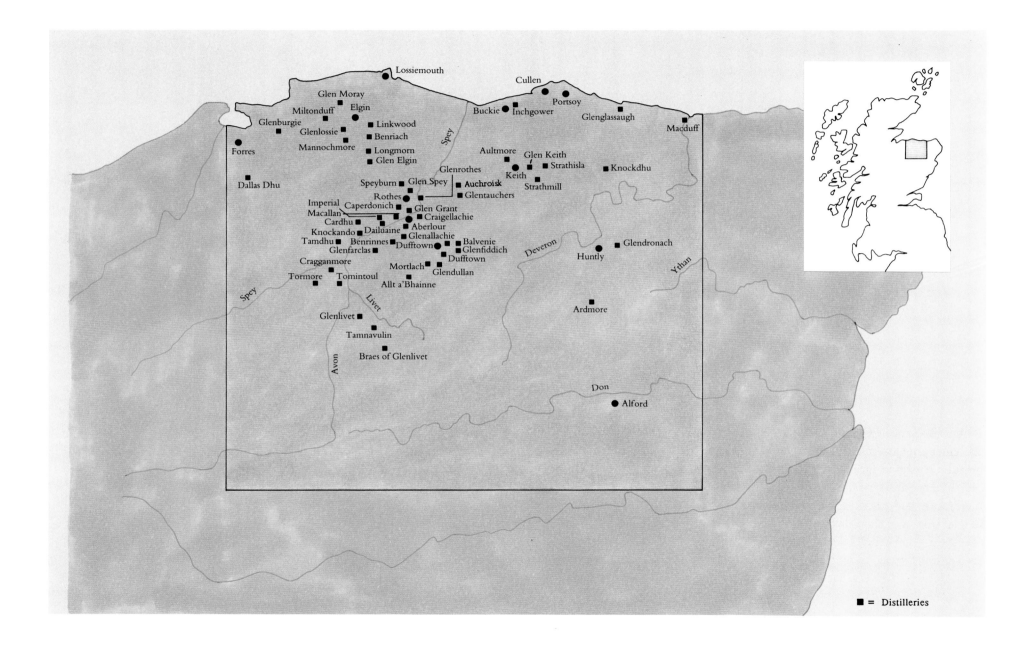

Lossiemouth

Glen Moray
Miltonduff   Elgin
Glenburgie
Glenlossie   Linkwood
Benriach
Forres   Mannochmore   Longmorn
Glen Elgin
Dallas Dhu

Cullen
Buckie   Portsoy
Inchgower
Glenglassaugh
Macduff

Spey

Aultmore   Glen Keith
Glenrothes   Keith   Strathisla   Knockdhu
Speyburn   Glen Spey   Auchroisk   Strathmill
Rothes   Glentauchers
Imperial   Caperdonich   Glen Grant
Macallan   Craigellachie
Cardhu   Aberlour
Knockando   Dailuaine   Glenallachie
Tamdhu   Benrinnes   Balvenie
Glenfarclas   Dufftown   Glenfiddich
Cragganmore   Dufftown
Mortlach   Glendullan
Tormore   Tomintoul
Allt a'Bhainne

Deveron
Huntly   Glendronach
Ythan

Spey

Glenlivet

Livet

Tamnavulin

Ardmore

Avon

Braes of Glenlivet

Don
Alford

■ = Distilleries

CHAPTER SIX: SPEYSIDE

The Auchroisk Distillery situated to the west of Rothes

The sweep of moorland, fern and bracken, ancient pine forest, river and loch – this is the great bowl of rich agricultural land between the Monadhliath and Cairngorm mountains known to the Gaels as Badenoch. Herein lies Speyside, the very heartland of Scotch whisky country.

This region, which stretches between the Highland cities of Inverness and Aberdeen, through the abundance of inland water, is sometimes known as 'the drowned land'. Snow and rain, gathered in the mountains, rising in granite, and soaking through peat, provide the continuous water flow for the rivers of this green landscape: the Spey, the Findhorn, the Lossie, the Avon, the Fiddich and, of course, the Livet.

The great rivers are the life-blood of the Speyside whisky industry, feeding the greatest concentration of distilling expertise and variety to be found anywhere in the world. Fishermen will verify that the Spey is ranked among the finest salmon rivers in Scotland, but equally important is the quality of its water which lends a special individuality to the whiskies produced along its banks.

The earliest known lords of this region were the Comyns who came to Britain with William the Conqueror. Their lust for power, coupled with Norman arrogance, brought them a Celtic heiress, the ancient mormaership (earldom) of Buchan, and the lordship of Badenoch.

After the Battle of Bannockburn, however, Comyn lands were given to Thomas Randolph by King Robert and on the death of John Randolph in 1346, Badenoch returned to the Crown. Robert II

The River Spey, life-blood of the Speyside distilleries

took this opportunity to bestow it upon Alexander, his fourth son by his first wife, Elizabeth Mure, appointing the young man King's Lieutenant in the north. This was a king's way of ensuring a loyal, if unpredictable, representative in an unstable territory, and at the same time removing a troublesome son to a safe distance.

At an early stage in Alexander's marriage to the widowed Countess of Ross it became apparent that they loathed each other. In consequence, she took up residence at Dingwall Castle, while he, with Mariota of Altyn, his mistress, occupied the rather more spartan, and sinister in appearance, island, quarters of Lochindorb on the border of Cromdale and Edinkillie. Known to the Highlanders as Alasdair mor Macan Righ, meaning 'Big Alexander: the King's son', he is probably best remembered in Scotland's history as the 'Wolf of Badenoch'.

Surprisingly, through imposing a reign of terror, Alexander Stewart brought a level of order to a region where, despite the endless beauty of the countryside, there had hitherto been little tranquillity. Perhaps the savage Highlanders understood the ruthless justice of this King's Lieutenant. Removed first from his father's court, then from that of his brother, he was free to do much as he pleased, adopting many of the rough, primitive ways of those over whom he ruled. Like all the Stewarts he proved immensely prolific, and his many natural sons by Mariota were to found the Highland

Stewart clans, thus enabling him to command what ultimately amounted to his own family army.

Tradition gives us the story that four hundred years later, after that dreadful spring day on Culloden Moor, there lived in a cave in the Cairngorms a clansman, possibly of Clan Grant, who was known as An 'Gobha (Gow) the Smith. For the down-trodden Highlanders survival was everything and An Gobha was known to shoe horses for the Hanoverian soldiers of 'Butcher' Cumberland.

Not surprisingly, even An Gobha's closest friends, many of whom had fought for the Stuart cause, were appalled at his behaviour. One night, in fear of his life, An Gobha fled into the hills and over to Speyside where he found himself in Glenlivet – 'that beautiful, lonely glen, some fourteen miles long and six miles broad, which lies thirty-five miles from the sea'.

Once safe and established, An Gobha changed his name to Smith, the English interpretation of the trade he practised, and with much enthusiasm set about establishing himself as a farmer, which, for the majority of his compatriots, also involved his becoming a distiller. The proceeds from the distillation of whisky enabled the farmers of the glen to pay their rents, although distilling remained illegal for a further seventy years. Evading the tax laws enforced largely by patrolling English excise officers became a way of life.

These were troubled times for the folk of the Highlands, struggling to reassert their self-confidence and to make ends meet. Highlanders, by act of parliament in 1746, were even forbidden

Conglass Water, northwest of Tomintoul on the Glenlivet estate

to wear their own, traditional clothing, tartan being seen as the uniform of rebellion.

The belted plaid, subsequently Victorianised into the kilt we know today, had become the universal costume of the Highlander. Although dress for the ancient Scot and Irish Gael was a shirt or tunic known as the leine, and a mantle known as the brat, the belted plaid was widely in use in the Highlands by the seventeenth century. After Culloden, Highlanders were henceforth expected to

wear the hodden grey trews of the Lowlands.

The first recognisable reference to tartan cloth, in fact, appears in the sixteenth century. Contrary to popular belief, early tartan cloth worn in the Highlands did not have any specific clan significance, apart from the fact that people from the same clan area tended to wear the cloth woven locally. The colours of this local cloth would reflect the plant dyes most abundant in that area, In fact, one suspects that tartan cloth was worn in much the same way as a decorative fabric or tweed would be chosen by a person today for a suit or jacket. To endorse this argument, the late Sir Iain Moncreiffe of that Ilk would often draw attention to the famous series of portraits of retainers at Castle Grant by Richard Waitt, in which each subject is wearing differing tartan patterns, in some cases, more than one.

No contemporary account, prior to the Battle of Culloden, makes reference to 'clan' tartans. It was, indeed, apart from the Duke of Cumberland's redcoats, difficult for both sides in that battle to distinguish Jacobite supporters from Highland loyalists. The main difference was that the Jacobites wore a white cockade in their bonnets, whereas their opponents wore red or yellow crosses of ribbon. Traditionally, sprigs of plant worn in bonnets were the usual means of identifying a clan allegiance.

In the second half of the eighteenth century the Hanoverian Whig government took every opportunity to pour scorn on the disgraced and down-trodden Highlanders, who took solace only in

Lochindorb Castle, stronghold of the Wolf of Badenoch

by formal balls to be held in autumn and winter, and which came to be known collectively as the Northern Meeting. These private subscription balls, held at various locations in and around the Highland capital of Inverness, have taken place ever since, providing an opportunity for the more privileged Highland families to socialise with one another and to entertain guests from far and wide.

With the more relaxed atmosphere in the Highlands came a return of confidence and a greater sociability towards the outside world. For the agricultural worker, however, times continued to be hard. Although abuse of the law was impossible

The Dallas Dhu Distillery, a Scottish heritage museum

their own everyday ability to survive off the land, and even this was exacerbated by a grain shortage.

In 1778 the Highland Society of London was formed under the chieftainship of Simon Fraser of Lovat, whose Lovat peerage had, for the time being, been forfeited owing to his family's involvement in the 1745 uprising. One of the objectives of this society was the repeal of the absurd Dekilting Act of 1746, and, with the parliamentary efforts of the Marquess of Graham (later to become 3rd Duke of Montrose), this was achieved in 1782, thus allowing the development of Highland dress as we know it today.

It is not surprising that by the end of the eighteenth century, after decades of persecution and attempts to retain some of the old traditions, the local lairds and landowners of the Highlands should decide to hold a gathering. This took the form of a piping competition and games, followed

The Glenlivet Distillery

to monitor, legislation had also been introduced forbidding distillation other than on a purely domestic scale. Distilling, however, had become an essential practice for the majority of those involved with earning a living from the land. Reactions ranged from outrage to outright rebellion, and by the early part of the nineteenth century it was obvious that something required to be done about it.

Thus it was that in 1824 the 5th Duke of Gordon personally encouraged one of his tenants, George Smith, An Gobha's grandson, to apply for a licence under the new legislation of that year. George Smith was granted the first government licence to build a distillery, and that distillery, and the product for which it subsequently became famous, was named The Glenlivet.

To give some idea of the state of affairs in the early nineteenth century, in Glenlivet alone there were rumoured to have been one hundred or more illicit stills, all hidden away in the mountainous terrain, impenetrable to the stranger. Almost everybody in the vicinity was involved, in one way or another, with smuggling to the populous centres of Dundee and Perth, and to the south. Understandably George Smith's sudden 'legality' caused great ill-feeling among his more immediate associates, disapprobation not dissimilar to that meted out to his grandfather in the century before.

But, apart from being the first to be publicly recognised, there had to be something special about Glenlivet. From the start the name came to be associated with quality and excellence. More recently over twenty distilleries have used the appellation 'Glenlivet', although only four – Tomintoul, Tamnavulin, Braes of Glenlivet and, of course, The Glenlivet – can claim to be actually located in that glen.

To travel through Speyside nowadays, however, is to explore whisky country. Through the rich farmland, wrinkled with rivers, burns and streams, distilleries pop up around every corner forming, with agriculture, the modern-day foundations of the region's economy.

Although it dates from 1897, a relative latecomer in the chronology of Speyside distilleries, Tomatin, meaning 'Hill of the Bushes', is located south of Inverness near the inner reaches of the River Findhorn. Situated at a height of 1028 ft on the foothills of the Monadhliaths, this mountain fastness can justifiably boast that it is the largest malt whisky distillery in Scotland. With twenty-three stills, this great temple of distilling has not necessarily benefited from its size. Whisky produced in such large quantities requires to be bought accordingly, and the glut of the 1980s inevitably brought about a period of closure, but happily Tomatin is now back in production with whiskies which include their brand Big T.

The River Findhorn winds northeast, reaching the Moray Firth north of the town of Forres. Here another late-built distillery has been rejuvenated into a promising future. Dallas Dhu, taking its name from the Gaelic 'Black Water Valley', was one of several distilleries developed, with the support of Alexander Edward of Sanquhar, on a small estate just outside Forres. With water from the Altyre Burn, proximity to good barley-growing land and, of equal importance, to the old Highland Railway line, it occupies a classic site. One of the original operators was Wright & Greig, a firm from Glasgow, whose best-known blend at the time was Roderick Dhu, named after one of the protagonists in Sir Walter Scott's *The Lady of the Lake*. When, in 1983, under the ownership of United Distillers, Dallas Dhu was closed, it was chosen by the Department of Historic Buildings and Monuments in Scotland, now Historic Scotland, as a classic example of a small, working distillery, and has hence been developed as a museum.

Forres, between the glacial mounds of the Cluny Hills and the fossil cliff which forms the boundary of the raised beach, is associated with the 'blasted heath' of William Shakespeare's *Macbeth*. The Brodies, one of the original Pictish tribes of Moray, were confirmed in their lands at Forres by King Malcolm IV in 1160. Brodie Castle, to the west of Forres, is baronial with conical turrets, the original Z-plan tower embellished by William Burn in 1824. It is approached down a fine avenue of beech trees and is now administered by the National Trust for Scotland.

To the south of Forres is Darnaway Castle, the lands of which were gifted by Robert the Bruce to his nephew Thomas Randolph in gratitude for his support in the great victory at Bannockburn in 1314. The original castle was built by Randolph, but most of the present building dates from 1810, incorporating fragments of the old keeps, also the banqueting hall in which Mary Queen of Scots danced when she visited in 1564. Mary bestowed the Moray earldom on her half-brother James, and the present holder of that title is a direct descendant.

West of Forres, on the road to Inverness, is Nairn, a holiday resort much loved by Charlie Chaplin in his later years. Even William McGonagall, the nineteenth-century Dundee bard renowned for his somewhat unusual verse, was much impressed by Nairn, penning his own idiosyncratic impression in the 1870s:

The town of Nairn is worth a visit, I do confess,
And it's only about fifteen miles from Inverness.
And in the Summer season it's a very popular bathing place
And the visitors from London and Edinburgh find solace,
As they walk along the yellow sand inhaling fresh air.
Besides, there's every accommodation for ladies and
    gentlemen there.

Dr Johnson's response on his 1773 visit was as usual not so favourable. 'At Nairn,' he wrote, 'we may fix the verge of the Highlands, for here I first saw peat fires, and first heard the Erse language.'

The Campbells of Cawdor are still to be found at Cawdor Castle, south of the town. Popular legend has it that an early thane had a dream in which he was instructed to place a treasure chest upon the back of an ass, set the beast free, then to follow whither it led. This he did and, having strolled from thistle to thistle, the exhausted beast eventually sat down under a hawthorn tree. Around this same tree, the thane built his keep and, amazingly, the tree can be seen to this day, sprouting rather stuntedly out of the dungeon floor.

Royal Brackla Distillery is set on this coastal

Sir Iain Tennant at Innes House

plain at Cawdor, between the River Findhorn and the Moray Firth, surrounded by gentle hills and open spaces of heath and pine wood. A map drawn in 1773 for the Cawdor Estate shows a 'malt brewhouse' on the site where the current Brackla Distillery was built by Captain William Fraser of Brackla House in 1812. In 1835 Fraser was the first whisky distiller to be granted a Royal Warrant of Appointment. An advertisement in London's *Morning Chronicle* of 20 January of that year announced that 'Brackla or The King's Own Whisky – His Majesty [King William IV] having been pleased to distinguish "this by his Royal Command to supply his establishment" has placed this whisky first on the List of British Spirits, and when known should be

in truth termed "The Divine Spirit" – only to be had of the Importers, Graham & Co., New Road, facing the Mary-la-bone Workhouse.' The 'Royal' prefix has been employed ever since, and a Royal Warrant of Appointment to Queen Victoria was also granted in 1838. Another great clan house in the neighhbourhood is Kilravock, built on the site of an ancient chapel in which St Columba is said to have preached in AD 565. The oldest building to survive, however, dates from 1460, a century and a half before the Rose family acquired their estate. Like the Brodies, the Roses avoided commitment to Jacobite activities.

The town of Elgin lies east of Forres, on a promontory of higher land extending towards the low-lying, flooded depression of the River Lossie, inland from Lossiemouth. Elgin's most famous son was Ramsay Macdonald, first Labour Prime Minister, who was born there in 1866. Elgin has a cathedral and nine distilleries in its immediate vicinity, and is a major centre for the bottling of single malts.

Sir Iain Tennant, former Chairman of Seagram Distillers and a former Grand Master of The Keepers of the Quaich, administers his business interests from Innes House, the Elgin home bought by his grandfather because he loved to fish on the River Spey. Sir Iain's involvement with the Scotch whisky industry came about through his having been Lord Lieutenant of Morayshire in 1964. Glen Grant and Glenlivet distilleries had been privately owned companies. Glen Grant was run by Douglas Mackessack and Glenlivet by William Smith Grant.

The Telford Bridge crossing the Spey at Craigellachie

Both men were expert distillers and Mackessack was also an accountant. In 1962 their advisers recommended that they form a public company joining together with an independent chairman. They decided to approach the Lord Lieutenant of the county. The first chairman of the Glenlivet and Glen Grant Distillers, therefore, was the Lord Lieutenant, Sir Harry Houldsworth, one of the great figures of Morayshire, who died in 1963. As his successor as Lord Lieutenant, Sir Iain was invited to succeed Sir Harry on the company board.

In 1970 Glenlivet and Glen Grant Distillers joined forces with Hill Thomson and Longmorn Distillers and established a head office in Edinburgh. Sir Iain became chairman of the new company, Glenlivet Distillers. A link with Courage led to the Imperial Group having a significant shareholding before the company was subsequently taken over by Seagram. In 1977 Seagram put all their United Kingdom interests under the control of one company and appointed Sir Iain as chairman.

From Elgin, the River Lossie splits and winds off in different directions through rich barley-growing land, to the west skirting the Glenburgie Distillery, east of Alves, founded in 1829. Although closed for a period, it was revived in 1878 and enlarged in 1958. On another tributary is the Miltonduff-Glenlivet Distillery, on the original site of an illicit still legalised in 1824. The restored ruins of Pluscarden Abbey nearby are said to stand on the distillery's original site. Also to the west of the Lossie is the Glen Moray Distillery, converted from a brewery in 1897.

In the Lossie valley, south of Elgin, the Glenlossie Distillery was built in 1876 by James Duff, tenant of the Fife Arms, Llanbrhyde, Morayshire, a man described in an *Aberdeen Journal* of 1887 as a 'great moving spirit'. He was obviously canny enough to have as his partners Alexander Grigor Allan, Procurator Fiscal of Morayshire, and H.M.S. Mackay, burgh surveyor of Elgin. A feature at Glenlossie is the Shand Mason & Co fire engine which won a prize at the Crystal Palace Exhibition of 1862. Pulled by a pair of horses, it could raise steam in under five minutes, but failed the test in March 1929 when fire damage resulted in distillation ceasing for a season.

In 1971 Mannochmore Distillery was built on part of the Glenlossie Distillery site. Both distilleries draw process water from the Bardon Burn,

which flows from the Mannoch Hills, and cooling water from the Gedloch Burn and the Burn of Foths. Also owned and managed by the company are three farms: Glenlossie, Easterton and Wardend, which produce barley, turnips and beef cattle on a total area of around 500 acres.

George Brown who came to live at Linkwood House, close to Elgin, as factor of the Earl of Findlater's Morayshire estates in 1788, served six times as Provost of Elgin. One of his sons, General Sir George Brown, commanded the Light Division in the Crimean War; another, Peter, became factor of the Seafield Estates in Moray and Banffshire.

It was Peter Brown who built Linkwood Distillery in 1821; he is recognised as one of the foremost nineteenth-century agricultural improvers of the northern counties. His son, William Brown, pulled Linkwood Distillery to the ground in 1872, and rebuilt it with 'spacious new premises'. In April 1874, the *Elgin Courant* was relieved to note that: 'the aqua produced is quite equal in flavour, and in every other respect, to that which attained the celebrity of Linkwood whisky as produced by the older and very much smaller work now superseded'.

This preoccupation with the quality of Linkwood's malt was taken up in the following century when the distillery was reopened after a period of closure and Roderick Mackenzie was appointed manager. For the next eighteen years, he supervised the production with remarkable skill, insisting that the character of a malt whisky depended on, among other factors, a complex relationship

not just with the vessels in which it is made, but with everything in the immediate environment, including the cobwebs. When the distillery was completely rebuilt in 1962 Mackenzie saw to it that the new stills were exact replicas of the original, and that the innovations matched up with the character of the old.

The dam at Linkwood holds cooling water from the Burn of Linkwood, with other water being piped from the Burn of Bogs and from springs near Milbuies Loch. Swans drift easily on the surface of the dammed water, their predecessors brought long ago from Gordon Castle, seat of the dukes of Richmond and Gordon on the Banff-Moray border, to keep down the weeds.

Seagram Distillers, through Chivas Brothers, own both the Longmorn and Benriach distilleries along the Lossie. 'Lhangmorgund' means in Gaelic 'Morgan, The Holy Man', and the distillery, founded in 1894, stands on the site of an ancient chapel. Benriach, with its typical pagoda roof, lies on the main Elgin to Rothes road and boasts one of the few remaining floor maltings in Scotland.

To the south of Elgin, Glen Elgin was one of the last distilleries to be built in the speculative boom of the 1890s. When it was eventually completed it was said locally that none of the contractors and craftsmen was paid in full except the steeplejacks, who had threatened to demolish the chimney-stacks. Such extreme action, however, was avoided. The distillery survived and was extended in 1964.

Rothes, close to the River Spey, is essentially a one-street town, physically disguising the five distilleries in its midst. Inver House Distillers have acquired the elegant Speyburn Distillery, built in 1897 by James Hopkins & Co of London and Glasgow, and known locally as 'The Gibbet' because of its location near the ancient 'Cnock na Croiche', which means 'Hill of the Gibbet'. On the sloping three-acre site, a feature of this Victorian distillery is its two- and three-storey buildings against a rolling and deeply wooded hillside.

Nearby is the Glen Spey Distillery, founded by James Stuart in 1885 and acquired shortly afterwards by Gilbey's. The distillery was entirely rebuilt in 1970 and is owned by Justerini & Brooks.

Founded in 1840 by two brothers, John and James Grant, the Glen Grant Distillery passed through two family generations before being sold in 1931. At Glen Grant a cash safe, installed and used by the Grant Brothers in order to have ready money, is built into the rock walls of the Back Burn River as it rushes through the gorge. Nearby is a park and orchard, inhabited, according to the proprietors, by tiny, beautiful fairies.

Old maps of the area identify a well named Tobardomhnaich, meaning the Sabbath Well, known locally as Caperdonich. A distillery was first built here in 1897, but when the refurbished distillery was reopened in 1965 it used this name, one which Chivas Brothers retain.

For many years one of the features of the town of Rothes was the whisky pipe which ran from the original distillery to Glen Grant, carrying fillings to the casks at the latter's filling store. The pipe ran overhead, crossing the main street at the north end

Craigellachie with a view of the distillery

of the town and, on being dismantled in the 1960s, a number of spiles, plugging holes of various sizes, were found in the pipe. Obviously these had been inserted by 'night raiders' but, alas, they would have been thwarted in their hopes since customs and excise laws insisted that once whisky had been pumped through the pipe, it must immediately be flushed out with water. Besides, all pumping operations were undertaken in daylight hours.

At the Glenrothes Distillery, owned by the Highland Distilleries Company plc, the Cutty Sark Visitor Centre (open by arrangement) tells the story of Berry Brothers & Rudd Ltd and, in particular, the origin of their Cutty Sark name and label. In March

1923 Francis Berry and Major Hugh Rudd invited the celebrated Scottish artist James McBey to lunch at their offices at 3 St James's Street, London. They were looking for a name for their 'new' whisky, and the partners were anxious to select a name which would reflect the different style of the blend. McBey suggested 'Cutty Sark', the name of the fastest of all the Clyde-built clipper ships and headline news at the time because she had recently been bought by a retired British sea captain who intended to renovate her.

The words 'cutty sark', Gaelic for 'short shift or shirt' were immortalised by the witch's garb in Robert Burns' poem *Tam o' Shanter*. Over lunch, McBey offered to sketch the label with its unusual lettering and recommended that it be printed on paper 'yellowed with age'. The printer by mistake used a bright canary yellow, but the effect against the green bottle was so striking that the partners immediately accepted the printer's error. Today Cutty Sark is a brand leader and its distinctive yellow label is to be found in over 130 markets throughout the world.

To the southeast of Rothes, the rock of Craigellachie, denoting the lower limits of the Grant lands of Strathspey, dominates the scenic road as it travels towards Thomas Telford's 1815 single-span iron bridge at Craigellachie. On the spur of a hill, overlooking the rock and the River Spey, is Craigellachie Distillery dating from 1888. From 1900 until his death on 22 September 1924, the distillery was dominated by the larger-than-life personality of its chairman, Sir Peter Mackie. In January

1924 White Horse Distillers was registered in Edinburgh as a public company with the purpose of acquiring the whole interests in, and assets of, distillery establishments and business belonging to Mackie & Co. Distillers Ltd. Three years later, in 1927, White Horse Distillers joined forces with the Distillers Company, now absorbed into United Distillers.

The Macallan Distillery, at Craigellachie, was ûrst licensed in 1824. It was acquired in the 1890s by Roderick Kemp, an Elgin merchant, having sold his share as co-owner of the Talisker Distillery on the Isle of Skye. To this day his family retains a large shareholding, and Allan Shiach, his great-grandson, combines his work as a Hollywood screenwriter under the pen name of Alan Scott with his role as chairman of Macallan-Glenlivet, the holding company. In 1979 Hugh Mitcalfe introduced The Macallan's extremely successful marketing strategy of selective advertisements: 'Scottish, more than a little humorous'. A classic example, a reminiscence donated by Commander Peter Craig, RN (Retd), Curator, Concorde Exhibition at the Fleet Air Arm Museum, Yeovilton, appeared in the autumn of 1985, and began:

> The Recuperative Effects of The Macallan Single Malt Whisky have seldom been more stirringly touched upon than in a letter recently received. It read as follows:

Easter Elchies House, near Craigellachie, headquarters of Macallan-Glenlivet

Facing: the organ room at Easter Elchies House

The Benrinnes Distillery near Ballindalloch in the Spey valley

'As a wee lad, I once accompanied Grandfather, his ghillie, and Ben, the Labrador, to fish for salmon; but disaster struck and I fell into the Spey's icy swirling waters.

Ben leapt in to retrieve me and near death, I and the exhausted dog were hauled to the bank.

"Quick, Hamish! The Macallan!" cried Grandfather.

A large dram was poured down Ben's throat and, in a trice, he was on his feet, licking colour back into my frozen cheeks.

"A near thing!" gasped Grandfather.

"Aye", replied Hamish. "Ah dinna ken where we'd ha' found anither dog like Ben." '

Easter Elchies House, dating from 1700, once owned by Seafield estates and lived in by the Player tobacco family, stands within the distillery grounds, and has been restored and refurbished as corporate headquarters. With crow-stepped gables, turret stair and round watch-chamber, it is a distinctive example of a laird's house, and the restoration has won the company a Scottish Civic Trust commendation. The centrepiece is an old-style fairground organ, performing on the principle of the pianola, and designed by an eminent film production designer. The associations of Easter Elchies with today's Keepers of the Quaich are strong. Lord Elgin recalls that, for over a period of twenty-six years, his grandfather was in the habit of renting Easter Elchies for family holidays. It was here, in the summer of 1893, that the postman arrived on a pony to inform the 9th Earl of Elgin that he should contact the Prime Minister immediately since he wanted to appoint him Viceroy of India.

The name Aberlour comes from the Gaelic for the Mouth of the Lour, a stream flowing into the Spey and passing the distillery which has taken that name, southwest of Craigellachie. The first reference to a settlement in the area is in the accounts of early Christian missionaries. Within the grounds of the distillery is a well named after St Drostan, a one-time Archbishop of Canterbury. Legend has it that water from this well was used to baptise converts from the local Highland clans. Aberlour's first purpose-built distillery dates from 1826, but it was rebuilt after a fire in 1879. Today it is owned by Campbell Distillers.

Glenallachie Distillery, built in 1967, a near neighbour of Aberlour, was also acquired and re-opened by Campbell Distillers in 1989, effectively doubling the company's production capacity. A small waterfall and dam add character to otherwise functional buildings. Closer to the Lower Spey at Carron is the Imperial Distillery, founded in 1897, then extended in 1965, and which boasts the largest pot-stills in Scotland.

Around the year 1810 John Cumming, son of a hill farmer and grazier, took over the tenancy of Cardow Farm in Upper Knockando. As a young man he had helped his parents manage their farm and also, as was common practice in the region, to manufacture whisky. The remote location of Cardow on the uplands, overlooking the River Spey, was ideal, affording a degree of protection from excise officers. The neighbouring Mannoch Hill provided an abundance of spring water and peat. Helen Cumming, the farmer's wife, was apparently a woman of spirit and cunning. With no inns in the immediate vicinity, excise officers visiting the Knockando district would invariably lodge at Cardow. Whereupon, according to local tradition, the comely Helen would prepare them a meal, set them down at table, then steal into the back yard to hoist a red flag over the barn, a warning to smugglers in the area to hide their distilling apparatus. Helen's popularity and the fame of her product was to spread far and wide. On a bitter night one winter there was a knock at the door and a small creature, shivering with cold and thinly clad, stood before the good lady.

'Where have you come from?' she asked.

'Sheean o'Mannoch,' replied the creature, referring to one of a number of fairy hills which are marked on maps of Knockando.

The fairy was given a dram in a wooden quaich and, after draining it, threw the quaich into the fire, saying: 'Brew, wifie, brew, for you and yours will never want.'

John and Helen smuggled their own product over the Mannoch Hill to Elgin and Forres, but after Cumming took out a licence in 1824, much of it was taken by horse and cart to Burghead and shipped south to Leith. The opening of the Strathspey Railway in 1860 provided a fast and economic link with Aberdeen and Perth.

The distillery remained with the Cumming family until 1893, latterly managed by Elizabeth Cumming, the widowed daughter-in-law of John and Helen, who eventually sold the business to John Walker & Sons of Kilmarnock for £20,500. Her son, John P. Cumming, however, remained as

a director of Walker's and, as a farmer, he built up a celebrated herd of Aberdeen Angus cattle. Advertisements of the early 1890s claimed that Cardow was the only distillery in the Speyside district which had never found it necessary to affix the word 'Glenlivet' to the original name of Cardu. The distillery is nowadays known as Cardhu.

Southwest of Craigellachie, the Tamdhu Distillery was founded in 1897 and takes its name from the 'Little Dark Hill'. It was largely rebuilt in the 1970s and draws its water from the Tamdhu Burn which flows into the Spey. There is a maltings of the Saladin box system and the malt produced is a component of The Famous Grouse.

John and George Grant of J. & G. Grant

The neighbouring distillery, Knockando, built a year later, also means 'Little Black Hill', and was built by John Thomson on a steep bank overlooking the Spey. Thomson also acquired the sole water rights for the Cardnach spring. In the village of Knockando about two hundred people inhabit the stone houses clustered around two centres: the parish church and the distillery. This has always been considered a progressive distillery and was the first to be built with electric light.

British law dictates that spirit should mature for at least three years. Like other single malts, Knockando is matured for much longer. Its distillers adopt the policy that it should not automatically be bottled at a certain age. When the master distiller determines that the whisky has reached its peak – usually between twelve and fifteen years (the label gives the season and date of distillation rather than age) – only then is it bottled. On occasion, a few casks stand out as truly superior, and then the master distiller is empowered to reserve these, sometimes for bottling at twenty to twenty-five years.

On the northwestern bank of the River Spey is Dailuaine, in Gaelic the 'Green Vale'. The distillery was founded by one William Mackenzie, a farmer, in this green vale, and the original distillery dates from 1851. When Mackenzie died in 1865, Jane, his widow, leased the distillery to James Fleming of Aberlour, a banker, later to go into partnership with her son Thomas, trading as Mackenzie & Co.

A major reconstruction was effected in 1960 when the floor maltings were converted into a

Saladin box system, pot-stills increased from four to six, and a mechanical coal-stoking system introduced. Dailuaine Distillery occupies a site of 60 acres and draws its process water from the Bailliemullich Burn, cooling water from the Carron Burn, and malting steeping water from the Burn of Derrybeg, all originating from the springs of Ben Rinnes. Ben Rinnes rises to a summit of 2755 ft, and the Benrinnes Distillery was built on the northern shoulder, at a height of almost 700 ft above sea level, commanding a view of nine counties. Both process and cooling waters in this case are drawn from the Scurran and Rowantree burns.

According to local tradition, the original Benrinnes Distillery had been located near Whitehouse Farm, below Ben Rinnes, until it was swept away in the great flood of 1829. In 1864 David Edward, farmer of Cauldwell, took over the lease of the relocated distillery, and it was his son Alexander who formed the company which built Craigellachie and Aultmore Distilleries. This company was bought over by John Dewar & Sons in 1922.

Beneath Ben Rinnes, at Ballindalloch in the Spey Valley itself, stands the Glenfarclas Distillery, which began legal production of whisky in 1836. Starting as a farm distillery, it was acquired on 8 June 1865 by John Grant and his son, George, and has remained under Grant ownership ever since. With five generations, the family understandably places great emphasis on continuity, but has always been innovative.

Glenfarclas, which means 'Glen of the Green Grassland', opened a visitor centre in 1973 and tours conclude in the Ship Room, which features the original oak panelling from the first-class lounge of the SS Empress of Australia, a passenger liner

The Tormore Distillery designed by Sir Albert Richardson in 1958

The Mortlach Distillery at Dufftown

Balvenie Castle, on the River Fiddich on the north side of Dufftown

and larger stones. One of these lintels was engraved with a lion rampant and the words: 'I fear nae foe, 1898. John Smith, Distiller'.

West of Ballindalloch at Advie, is the Tormore Distillery, designed by Sir Albert Richardson, a past president of the Royal Academy, for Long John Distillers in 1958. It was the first completely new distillery to be built in the Highlands in the twentieth century, and, with a hill of thickly wooded fir trees behind, the white buildings with belfry and musical clock, alongside an ornamental curling lake, this is everybody's idea of what a distillery ought to look like.

The Glenlivet Distillery, southeast of Ballindalloch, has pioneered the story of whisky in the Scottish Highlands. Such was the success of The Glenlivet in the nineteenth century that, inevitably,

which plied the famous routes to the Far East and America.

At the foot of Ben Rinnes is Allt a' Bhainne Distillery, erected in 1975. In the eighteenth century this was the area where Robbie MacPherson kept his mobile still, constantly moving the site around Ben Rinnes to avoid discovery. The new split-level building, with dado wall of local red granite, conventional roof and four small pagodas, blends well into the surrounding countryside.

Adjacent to Ballindalloch, the Cragganmore Distillery was founded by John Smith, formerly manager of The Macallan. He started up the new Glenlivet Distillery in 1858, went south to run Wishaw Distillery and returned to Speyside seven years later as lessee of Glenfarclas at Ballindalloch, which he ran from 1865 to 1870. A man of large stature, Smith weighed 22 stone and travelled everywhere by rail, always in the guard's van, supposedly being unable to enter the door of a passenger carriage. In 1869 he persuaded his landlord, Sir George Macpherson-Grant, to allow him to build a new distillery at Ayeon Farm, close to Ballindalloch Station on the Strathspey Railway. Process water is still drawn from springs on Craggan More Hill, with cooling water from the Spey. In the construction, greenstone quarried from the hill of Craggan More was employed for the lintels

The Balvenie Distillery

The Strathisla Distillery

it attracted its imitators. In a test court case of 1880 it was agreed that other distilleries who wished to announce their proximity to Glenlivet, either geographically or in taste, could do so only by adding the appellation in hyphenated form.

Only four distilleries remain in the immediate Glen of Livet. Elsewhere, along the river system which makes up the Livet and the Spey, so many others use the hyphenated form that it merely implies that the product is from Speyside.

High in the valley, on a stream which feeds the River Livet, is the Braes of Glenlivet Distillery, a curiously appealing modern building dating from the 1970s. A short distance to the west, at the foot of Carn Meadhonach, is Tomintoul, the highest village in Banffshire and a one-time haunt for whisky smugglers. Here, on the River Avon, a few miles from the village on the edge of a forest, is located the Tomintoul Distillery built in the 1960s. At Tomnavoulin, to the east, on the steep side of the glen

and on the River Livet, is Tamnavulin Distillery, differently spelt. The name means 'mill on the hill', and part of the building once housed a wool mill. The distillery was opened in 1965 and provides an attractive visitor centre.

Dufftown, to the northeast of Glenlivet, and on the River Fiddich, grew up on its limeworks and distilleries. From the very beginning nothing was sacred in the local population's determination to confound the excisemen. Even the clock tower, which stands to this day at the centre of the town, once concealed distilling apparatus. Although no longer strictly true, the local saying goes that while Rome was built on seven hills, Dufftown stands on seven stills. Of these, Mortlach, Dufftown-Glenlivet, Glenfiddich and Glendullan are still successfully operational, but Convalmore, founded in 1894, has not operated since 1985, and Pittyvaich-Glenlivet was closed in 1993.

Mortlach, however, was the first, licensed in 1823 under the act of that year. Although the original water source is said to have been Highland John's Well, water today is drawn from springs in the Conval Hills, with cooling water from the River Dullan. The first licensee, James Findlater, had acquired land from the Earl of Mac-Duff. He is recorded as having had two partners: Donald McIntosh and Alexander Gordon, both of Dufftown. Around 1837 the *Elgin Courant* announced that Mortlach Distillery had been purchased by Messrs J. & J. Grant of Glengrant, then distillers at Aberlour. Curiously this company took away the distillery apparatus, and the barley

The Dufftown Distillery close to where the rivers Fiddich and Dullan meet on their way to the Spey

granary then served for some years as a Free Church until an alternative was erected in Dufftown.

A brewery owned by John Gordon eventually started production on the site, but gradually began to distil. His product was sold in Leith, Glasgow and locally, under the brand name of The Real John Gordon. In 1853 George Cowie, a land surveyor, became a partner. After Gordon's death, as sole proprietor, he expanded the business, served as Provost of Dufftown, chairman of the School Board of Mortlach, chairman of the Stephen Cottage Hospital, and, as tenant of Pitglassie Farm, bred hornless Aberdeen Angus cattle. His son, Dr Alexander Cowie, having graduated in medicine at Aberdeen University, in 1890 secured a senior medical appointment in Hong Kong. On his brother's death in 1895 he returned to take over Mortlach, establishing himself as one of Speyside's leading distillers. In addition he served as a town councillor, a county councillor, and was appointed Deputy Lieutenant for Banffshire. Tragically, Cowie's only son was killed in action in the First World War, and in 1923 the business was sold to John Walker & Sons of Kilmarnock.

Glendullan, built in 1897, is the last of the seven Dufftown distilleries established in the nineteenth century. The location was not chosen for its obvious beauty, but for practicality, with water being piped from the River Fiddich about half a mile upstream to an overshot waterwheel which drove

_____

Facing: the Glentauchers Distillery between the rivers Spey and Isla

all the machinery. The waterside Dufftown-Glenlivet Distillery, however, does occupy a picturesque location. Converted from a meal mill in 1896, it was bought by Bell's in the 1930s.

William Grant, a one-time cattle herder and shoemaker's apprentice, built his first distillery at Dufftown in 1886 and spent £119 19s 10d on equipment, most of it coming from Cardow then being rebuilt. His seven sons worked with him, and the Glenfiddich Distillery produced its first whisky from the still on Christmas Day 1887. The Glenfiddich wages book of the period illustrates that for four months of the year the entire working of the distillery was in the hands of William Grant, three of his sons, and Benjie Niven, the brewer. Although they worked seven days a week, the boys did not neglect their studies when periods of waiting made this possible. On one occasion, a visiting exciseman of the name of Burnet was forced to comment when he discovered a Latin grammar lying open on a ledge in the malt barn. In another corner of the building he found a book on mathematics, and in the still house, a book of medical anatomy. Burnet was somewhat astounded. 'I have inspected a few distilleries in my time,' he declared, 'but this is the strangest I have ever seen.'

William Grant also converted the nearby New Balvenie Castle, a rather austere mansion house built in 1724 for the 1st Earl of Fife, into a distillery in 1892. It remains the only distillery in the Highlands still to farm its own barley, and to maintain its own cooperage and coppersmiths' shop in the production of The Balvenie. The company has

recently expanded by building Kininvie, the first malt distillery to be opened in Scotland since the 1970s. After five generations, William Grant & Sons remains the largest family-owned distillery company in the Scotch whisky industry. Their Glenfiddich, having pioneered the market for malt whisky outside Scotland, has become the most widely consumed malt whisky in the world.

To the west of Rothes, Justerini & Brooks built their Auchroisk Distillery to meet the growing demand for Scotch whisky in general and in particular their J & B Rare. Production began in January 1974. The distillery's name is taken from that of a nearby farm and means 'the ford of the red stream'.

A couple of miles north of the town of Keith is the Aultmore Distillery, established in 1895 by Alexander Edward, who inherited Benrinnes Distillery at Aberlour from his father, and who had been one of the founders of Craigellachie Distillery. The place name of Aultmore is derived from the Gaelic *allt mhor*, meaning 'big burn', and the combination of springs on the neighbouring hill and peat deposits of the Foggie Moss, naturally, made this area a favourite haunt of illicit distillers, smuggling their product to Keith, Fochabers and Portgordon. Reconstructed in 1971, Aultmore Distillery is now owned by United Distillers.

West of Keith, situated between the rivers Spey and Isla, is the Glentauchers Distillery, at Mulben. Founded in 1898, it was rebuilt in 1965, and, having been mothballed for a few years by United Distillers, was acquired by Allied Distillers in 1989.

The legal title of the Strathisla Distillery dates

from 1785, although it is known that Dominican monks operated a small brewery on this site on the River Isla as far back as the thirteenth century. Strathisla was once known as Milltown and operated as a farm distillery. The one time holy well of 'Fons Bulliens', which supplies the mash water, is said to be guarded by water kelpies. The magic circle around which they dance is faithfully preserved and those travellers who have seen them – one suspects after having enjoyed a quantity of the distillery's product – are sworn to absolute secrecy.

There is some debate as to whether there was a corn mill or distillery first at Strathmill. Whichever, the buildings, also on the River Isla, date from 1823, and now provide a warehousing capacity of 2,500,000 litres of pure alcohol.

In 1957 Chivas Brothers razed the old Keith flour and oatmeal mills to the ground in order to build their Glen Keith Distillery. In the early 1980s the plant was completely modernised, and Glen Keith was probably the first pot distillery in Scotland to be computerised.

Not a great deal has changed since Alfred Barnard visited Fochabers on the Moray Firth coast in 1887:

> Cultivated fields clothed the slopes of the hills which reached the roadside, and a glorious and expansive view of the sea and the hills of Sutherlandshire across the Moray Firth was obtained. Proceeding along we passed broad acres of goldening grain, studded over with gaudy corn flowers, and ornamented with lines of beautiful trees. Here and there were patches of wild flowers, growing in the rose-covered hedges, the yellow, blue and white cups of those humble blossoms upturned to the sun. As we rattled through this rich and fertile country, we now and then caught site of a village or hamlet and presently, on our left, the famous Bin Hill of Cullen, some miles distant, standing out in bold relief from a background of blue sky.

Inchgower Distillery, at Fochabers, a stone's throw from the fishing town of Buckie, dates from 1871, although the original business was established in 1822 at the Tochieneal Distillery, south-east of Cullen, by Alexander Wilson. When Alfred Barnard visited, the Wilson family was still operating Inchgower. Today owned by United Distillers, Inchgower was expanded in 1966.

The most influential family in the neighbourhood was the Gordon Lennox family, descending through the 7th Duke from the 1st Duke of Richmond, son of Charles II by Louise Renée de Penancoet de Kéroualle, created Duchess of Portsmouth. In 1876 the 6th Duke of Richmond and Lennox, one-time ADC to the Duke of Wellington, was given the additional dukedom of Gordon. Gordon Castle, family seat of the dukes of Richmond and Gordon, is now largely a ruin. At the time of the building of Inchgower Distillery, the nearby Bog o' Gight Castle, the ruins of which can be seen to the rear of Gordon Castle, was part of the inheritance of Catherine Gordon of Gight. 'When the heron leaves the tree / The Laird o' Gight will landless be', ran an old prophesy.

In 1786 the herons which had from time immemorial nested by the Hagberry Pot on the River Ythan flew over the Braes o' Gight to settle on the nearby Haddo estate. There the young Lord Haddo, son of the 3rd Earl of Aberdeen, instructed that no harm should befall them since his cousin's land, from whence they came, would soon follow.

Catherine, 13th Laird of Gight, was twenty when she met and married Captain 'Mad Jack' Byron, heir to Lord Byron of Newstead. Their son, George Gordon Byron, was born in London on 22 January 1788, the year after his mother had sold Gight to the Earl of Aberdeen. Catherine's fortune squandered, her husband soon deserted her and news of his death followed in 1791. Catherine, seeking to retain what was left of her inheritance, with three-year-old son, and seven-year-old step-daughter Augusta, found lodgings in Aberdeen. Seven years later, with the death of his grandfather, George Gordon became 6th Lord Byron and Lord of Newstead. Within nine years he had published his first poems; in 1812, *Childe Harold's Pilgrimage* took London society by storm.

Of his mother, Lord Byron was later to reflect that she 'was as haughty as Lucifer, with her descent from the Royal Stuarts and the "old" Gordons, not the Seyton Gordons, as she disdainfully termed the ducal branch'.

Facing: the Knockando Distillery

Facing: pot-stills at the Glenmorangie Distillery, Tain   Above: the Clynelish Distillery at Brora

The superlative Kessock Bridge carries traffic over to the Black Isle, a name that gives rise to much debate. This fine peninsula, washed by the Cromarty, Inverness and Beauly Firths, was once referred to as 'Ardmeanach', meaning 'the Height Between'. Old statistical accounts state that in early times the area was covered by black, uncultivated moor on which snow rarely lay for long. Today's covering of forest, from a distance, often gives a dark appearance. But another suggested origin for the name comes from the Norseman Thorfinn, who conquered Ross in 1033. Ardmeanach was apportioned for his bloodthirsty followers and their territory became known then as 'the Land of the Black Danes'.

Ptolemy, the Egyptian geographer, in AD 120 reported that this region was inhabited by the Dekanti tribe, and to corroborate this there are sixty of their prehistoric sites to be found in the area. Rosemarkie is believed to have been a centre for Druid culture and this might explain why the area was so thickly populated with Christian churches. Fortrose was considered an ideal site for a strategic northerly 'listening' post, to report back to church and monarch on the movements of inland clans and coastal shipping. For this reason a great cathedral was built here in 1240, dedicated to St Boniface and St Peter by Bishop Duthac of Tain.

The Black Isle, 20 miles long and 8 miles wide, survives on farming, fishing and forestry. On the northeastern tip of the peninsula is Cromarty, in its original unspoiled state, a gem of a town from the Georgian era. It is, in fact, the third Cromarty, the original supposedly founded by Greek sailors washed ashore in a storm. What calamity overtook this first town is unknown, but the ruins of a second town, washed over by the sea, can be seen at low tide. The third town of Cromarty owes its form to George Ross who, at his own expense, built the sandstone pier, opened flax, flour and hemp factories, and built a brewery. He also started a trade in pork which brought the then princely sum of £20,000 a year to the town.

In the nineteenth century Cromarty developed into a significant fishing centre. Cromarty's most famous son, Hugh Miller, the geologist, stonemason and author, was born there in 1802. To the west, at Conon Bridge, Gerald Ogilvy Laing, a sculptor of international repute, has imaginatively restored Kinkel Castle, a fifteenth-century Mackenzie stronghold. In an outhouse he has established a forge for his bronze work which is much in demand both at home and in the USA. Two notable commissions have been his memorial to Sir Arthur Conan Doyle, which shows Sherlock Holmes mourning his creator, and stands near the site

The distinctive roof of the Dalmore Distillery

of the author's birthplace in St James Square in Edinburgh, and the statue of Andy Warhol for the Warhol Foundation in New York.

Away from the Black Isle, to the west, is the Victorian spa town of Strathpeffer, below Ben Wyvis, where Clan Mackenzie has a visitor centre at Castle Leod, the home of the 5th Earl of Cromartie. Clan Mackenzie land once included much of mid-Ross, but in the twelfth century they were removed to Wester Ross, the district known as Kintail which embraces the head of Loch Duich, by King William the Lion. Here they were joined by the MacRaes, who became the Mackenzie chief's bodyguard, and the Maclennans, their hereditary standard-bearers.

The New Statistical Account of Scotland recorded in 1840 that 'distilling of aquavitae' was

the sole manufacture in the Ord district. In addition to Ord Distillery, there were nine small stills in the parish, all licensed. All, except one, were worked by a co-operative group of ten or twelve tenant farmers. The entire local barley crop was used for distilling – the fastest way of turning it into cash to pay the rent. The product was sold to 'Highlanders from Lochaber, the extensive west coast of Ross-shire and the Isle of Skye'.

Robert Johnstone and Donald Maclennan were the first licence-holders of the Glen Ord Distillery, in the village of Muir of Ord on the west of the Black Isle. The distillery dates from 1838 when it shared a water supply with an adjacent meal mill. Today, water is taken from Loch nan Eun and Loch nam Bonnach, both approximately 1000 ft above sea level. Both of these lochs are fed by springs rising in the hills that encircle them and which meet to form the Allt Fionnaidh, the 'White Burn', which flows past Muir of Ord to supply the distillery.

Both the distillery and its product have historically varied between being called Ord and Glenordie, but since the substantial modernisation of 1966 they have been known as Glen Ord. Like the barley, the peat for the furnaces is cut locally, from March onwards, or as soon as the weather permits. Cut peats are piled in stacks on the peat moss to allow natural drying by sun and wind. These are generally dry by the late summer ready for transportation to the storage sheds at the distillery's open-sided maltings.

Some idea of what the discovery of North Sea

oil has meant to this area can be seen along the Cromarty Firth coastline. The aluminium smelter at Invergordon is no longer the sole unaesthetic blot on the landscape when compared to the spectacular oil platform yard at Nigg Bay. Technology and the passing of time have inevitably brought change and, more positively, the benefits of employment to the towns of Alness and Tain. Just down the road from the massive Invergordon Grain Distillery, which occupies an 80-acre site, is the Dalmore Distillery, established in 1839 by Alexander Matheson who lived locally. Situated above the Cromarty Firth, it takes its water from the River Alness which flows from the Loch of Gildermory, close to Ben Wyvis. The spirit stills at Dalmore are noted for their unusual shape, each with a flask-like chamber on top.

Also near Alness is the Teaninich Distillery, founded in 1817 by Captain Hugh Munro, owner of the Teaninich estate. Customs and Excise were pursuing a campaign at that time to stamp out illicit distilling which could use up an entire barley crop in many of the Ross-shire parishes, thereby posing a threat of famine. Commissioners of Supply, forerunners of County Councils, urged landowners to set up legitimate distilleries to provide an alternative outlet for farmers and to achieve a better end-product. Three of the four legal distilleries set up in Ross-shire were soon to go out of business through financial pressure, but, as Munro himself told a parliamentary enquiry in the 1830s, 'I continued to struggle on'.

After the Excise Act of 1823 reduced the fiscal

The modern-day Highland seer

burdens of legal distillers, 'an extraordinary change was soon perceived'. Teaninich's output increased thirty to forty times by 1830.

Distilling at Teaninich was continued by Captain Hugh's son, Lieutenant General John Munro, despite his being resident in India for many years. The process and cooling waters for the distillery continue to be drawn from Dairywell Spring, on John Munro's descendant's Novar Estate. The whisky produced is mostly used in the R.H. Thom-son & Co blends such as Robbie Burns.

Along the coast, at Edderton, Balblair Distillery sits high above the Dornoch Firth. Dating from 1790, the present building, with its disused malting tower, dates from 1895. The single malt produced here is an important component of the Ballantine blends.

Water for the Glenmorangie Distillery at Tain originates from the hills of Tarlogie; this is a hard water, rich in minerals, bubbling up in the midst of a forest through layers of lime and sandstone. Glenmorangie is Gaelic for 'the Glen of Great Tranquillity'. The original buildings date back to 1738, and it was then a noted brewery famous for its fine ale until William Matheson turned it into a licensed distillery in 1843. An entry in the 'Tain and Balnagowan Documents' of 1703 records the death of George Ross of Morangie, son of Thomas the Abbot, noting that his possessions include 'one aquae-vitae pott-still, stand, and fleake [worm]'.

The workforce at Glemorangie is traditionally known as the Sixteen Men of Tain. Standing 16 ft 10¼ in high, the unusually shaped copper stills, the tallest in the Highlands, are a significant feature. The taller the neck of a still, the less the heavier elements and grosser oils climb to mingle with the purer vapours. These, as a result, ascend to the top. The bulge in the neck of the still just above the main body catches the crasser elements and returns them to the boiling, thus ensuring the purity of the spirits finally collected. Glenmorangie malt is matured in American oak casks reassembled at the nearby cooperage. When Queen Elizabeth the

Queen Mother officially opened the Dornoch Bridge on 27 August 1991 she was presented with a special edition Dornoch Firth Bridge commemorative bottling from the Glenmorangie Distillery as a souvenir.

At the west end of the shimmering coastline of the Dornoch Firth, at Ardgay, on the slopes of the Struie Hill, Swein Macdonald, a modern-day Highland seer, crofts and foretells the future. Second sight is a feature of Highland life; whether it is the clear air or the often harsh closeness to the land which gives such gifts, will never be known, but the northeast of Scotland has always had its fair share of wise men.

At Bonar Bridge, on the coast route north, the road splits. To the north, the road bisects the remote wilderness passing through Lairg at the end of Loch Shin, then heads to the west of Loch Naver and up to the Kyle of Tongue before pointing east along the coast. The main road, meanwhile, journeys east along the north shore of the Dornoch Firth through Spinningdale and past magnificent Skibo Castle, purchased in 1893 by Andrew Carnegie, one of the richest men in the world, as a Scottish home for Margaret, his greatly loved daughter. The Dunfermline-born son of a hand-loom weaver, Carnegie had amassed a great fortune in America, and in 1914 offered the Kaiser a blank cheque not to go to war. For the twenty years up to his death in 1918 Skibo Castle played host to virtually every great figure of the time: kings, presidents, prime ministers, tycoons, writers, musicians and artists. In the Ross-shire hills on the northern shores of the Dornoch Firth where the castle nestles, the climate is mild, the vegetation lush, encouraging a profusion of wildlife including nesting ospreys.

At Dornoch, on the northeastern tip of the Firth, is a famous golf course with royal patronage. At the Mound, further round the Firth, the River Fleet enters Loch Fleet and there is a grand salmon pool. High on Ben Bhraggie, at 1256 ft, a monument commemorates the 1st Duke of Sutherland who lived at the fairytale castle of Dunrobin at Golspie, a town built solely for the purpose of housing castle employees.

The earldom of Sutherland is one of the seven ancient earldoms of Scotland. The name originates from 'South Land', because it was south of where the invading Norsemen had come from. The inhabitants of Sutherland, from which they took their name collectively, are considered to have been of Celtic origin.

The chiefly family, however, descends from Freskin, a Flemish noble who owned lands in Morayshire and elsewhere, and who is an ancestor of the Murrays of Tullibardine and Atholl. His grandson Hugh, Lord of Duffus, was granted lands in Sutherland by William the Lion in 1197 and, some forty years later, Hugh's son was created 1st Earl of Sutherland by Alexander I.

On the death of the 18th Earl, the title, following the Celtic tradition, passed to his only daughter in the absence of an immediate male heir. She was the wife of George Granville Leveson-Gower, who succeeded his father as Marquess of Stafford in 1803. Created a duke in 1883, the year of his death, he took his wife's name of Sutherland and he is the Sutherland whose name is most intimately associated with the infamy of the Highland Clearances. When the 5th Duke died in 1963, the chiefship and earldom of Sutherland passed to Elizabeth, his niece, the daughter of the second son of the 4th Duke. The Dukedom passed to the 5th Earl of Ellesmere, a grandson of the 2nd Duke, who currently resides at St Boswells in the Scottish Borders.

A section of Dunrobin Castle's medieval tower still stands, but most of the present-day spectacular building at Golspie was rebuilt on the orders of the 2nd Duke in the middle of the nineteenth century. Charles Barry, architect of the Houses of Parliament at Westminster, was commissioned to restyle Dunrobin from its traditional Scottish baronial appearance into a Franco- Scots palace. Much of Barry's work was destroyed by a fire in 1915, after which the distinguished Scottish architect Sir Robert Lorimer was brought in to supervise the repairs. The castle is today open to the public, and while the Countess of Sutherland has a residence to the north at Tongue, Lord Strathnaver, her son and heir, administers the estate, living, with his wife and family, in a converted Victorian dairy on the beach at Dunrobin.

A few miles south of Golspie is Embo where, in 1988, the Community Association took an original initiative to raise funds for a community centre.

_____

Facing: Dunrobin Castle, seat of the Earls of Sutherland

They hit on the idea of declaring independence for a day and accordingly wrote to Her Majesty the Queen for permission to do so. Much to their astonishment a letter arrived from Buckingham Palace granting formal permission on the provision that it would only be for one day per annum.

On Saturday 16 July 1988 the self-styled State of Embo declared independence, mounted Border guards and issued entry visas. The following year, after the state opening of the Embo Parliament, banknotes designated 'The Cuddie' were issued based on 'The Whisky Standard' and a delegation headed by David Ward, Embo's self-styled Prime Minister, officially visited Clynelish Distillery at Brora. Ward announced that the Embo navy would be mounting a submarine display off the coast which, being made up of submarines, would, of course, be invisible. On 10 May 1990, with the necessary funds raised, the Embo Community Centre was opened amid great public rejoicing and the inhabitants of the tiny town reverted to being permanent loyal subjects of the British Crown.

The road via Brora and Helmsdale to Wick provides dramatic vistas of the North Sea, in the distance the occasional dot of an oil rig. The Clynelish Distillery, acquired by DCL in 1925, was established in 1819 by the Marquess of Stafford. In 1820 James Loch, the Marquess's land commissioner, described the project thus: 'The first farm beyond the people's lot [at Brora] is Clynelish, which has recently been let to Mr Harper from the county of Midlothian. Upon this farm also there has just been erected a distillery at an expense of

Highland cattle

£750. This was done ... to afford the smaller tenants upon the estate a steady and ready market for their grain without being obliged to dispose of it to the illegal distiller.' The hope was that the existence of the distillery would put an end to illicit distilling in the area, a practice which, according to Loch, had immersed the people 'in every species of deceit, vice, idleness and dissipation.'

A stone bearing the coats of arms of the 2nd Marquess of Stafford and the Countess of Sutherland, and the date 1820, has been preserved on the gable wall of the original still house, just under the bell-cote. A new distillery was built on the site over 1967 and 1968, taking the same name Clynelish; the original distillery was renamed Brora, and is now closed.

At Helmsdale the Timespan Heritage Centre

offers a surprise, for alongside exhibitions on the Kildonan Gold Rush and the lives of the local fisherfolk, there is a Barbara Cartland Room, celebrating the career of the romantic novelist, self-styled 'Queen of Morality', who first began holidaying at Kilphedir, her family's fishing lodge on the River Helmsdale, in 1927. South of Wick there are Iron Age brochs to be found. On Sinclair's Bay stand the clifftop ruins of Girnigo Castle, once a Sinclair clan stronghold but destroyed in 1679 by the Campbells of Glenorchy. Nearby, also overlooking the bay, is Ackergill Castle, a fifteenth-century fortress once owned by the Dunbars of Hempriggs who commissioned David Bryce to enlarge the castle in the 1850s. With the demise of the last of the family, Ackergill was transformed into a successful conference and business centre.

Pulteney Distillery at Wick sits on the banks of the Wick River, close to the shores of what was once called the German Ocean. It was established in 1826 by James Henderson, who had previously owned a smaller distillery inland. Pulteney was rebuilt in 1958 by the Hiram Walker company as a component for the Ballantine blends.

John O'Groats, named after John de Groot, a Dutchman who came here in the sixteenth century, is well disposed towards the tourist but there is little here other than the view. In summer there are regular trips to Orkney and most days these northern islands across the Pentland Firth can be clearly seen from Duncansby Head or Dunnet Head, the most northerly cape of the mainland. Day trips can be made by boat to Scapa Flow,

Kirkwall and Skara Brae.

Along the north coast is the Castle of Mey, formerly another Sinclair stronghold. Queen Elizabeth the Queen Mother made this her Scottish home following the death of her husband, King George VI, in 1952. After its restoration, against all the climatic odds, she succeeded in creating a spectacular garden, sheltered from the winds and storms of the North Sea.

The lighthouse at Dunnet Head protecting shipping on the Pentland Firth

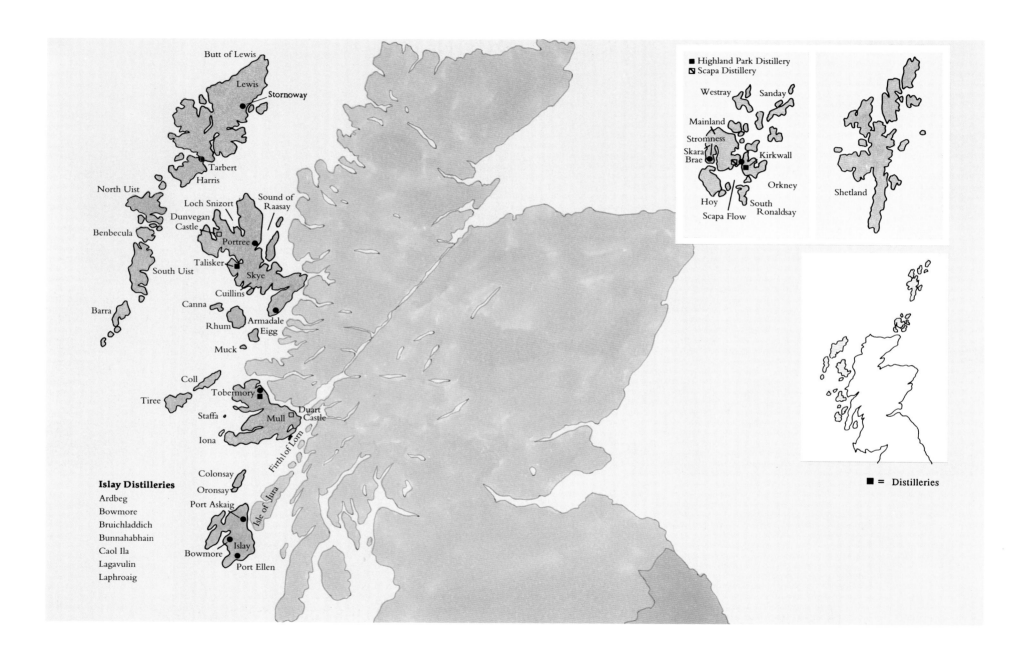

Butt of Lewis

Lewis

Stornoway

Tarbert

Harris

North Uist

Loch Snizort

Sound of
Raasay

Benbecula

Dunvegan
Castle

Portree

Talisker

South Uist

Skye

Cuillins

Barra

Canna

Armadale

Rhum

Eigg

Muck

Coll

Tobermory

Tiree

Staffa

Mull

Duart
Castle

Iona

Firth of Lorn

Islay Distilleries

Colonsay

Oronsay

Ardbeg

Bowmore

Bruichladdich

Port Askaig

Isle of Jura

Bunnahabhain

Caol Ila

Bowmore

Islay

Lagavulin

Laphroaig

Port Ellen

■ Highland Park Distillery

◨ Scapa Distillery

Westray

Sanday

Mainland

Stromness

Skara
Brae

Kirkwall

Orkney

Hoy

Scapa Flow

South
Ronaldsay

Shetland

■ = Distilleries

THE ISLANDS

Gateway to the islands

ISLAY, JURA, MULL AND SKYE – THE ORKNEY ISLANDS

Drovers gathering Sheep in Glen Sligachan, Isle of Skye (*Richard Ansdell*)

THE ISLANDS

Stepping out into the winds of the Atlantic Ocean off the west coast of Scotland, with far flung St Kilda the nearest outpost to North America, are Scotland's Inner and Outer Hebrides. For lovers of islands, these hold their own, incomparable enchantment. With a restless climate – wind, rain, intermittent sun and, always, ever-changing light – there is an old saying that one can experience all the seasons of the year in a day. There is no formula to analyse the appeal of these Hebrides, with their seagull circled ports, gneiss mountains, hearts of emerald green and lonely beaches of pure white sand.

Individually beautiful, they have furnished a harsh living for their sons and daughters. Yet the Gael remains stoical with a philosophy the envy of many a city-dweller trampled by the noise and pressures of compressed existence.

Skye is the main island of the scattered Inner Hebrides. To the south lie the Small Isles: Canna, Sanday, Rhum, Eigg and Muck; further south, off the coast of Argyll, Lismore, Coll, Tiree, Mull, Iona and Staffa, Kerrera, Seil, Eisdale, Luing, Shuna, Torsay, Colonsay, Oronsay, Jura, Islay and Gigha. The Outer Hebrides, sometimes known as the Long Island, comprises a 130-mile-long, jewel-like chain, from Lewis in the north, to Barra in the south. Harris, North Uist, Benbecula, South Uist

and Eriskay are linked in this chain by the thin threads of ferry crossings and causeways. The Hebridean islands number five hundred, of which one fifth are inhabited.

The Hebrides are mentioned by Ptolemy in the first century AD, and marginally earlier by Gaius Pliny, a Roman who made a series of scientific records. Although Pliny almost certainly never visited the islands he heard of them lying far to the north and he gave them the name of Hebudes from which their modern name derives.

In the sixth century came the Scandinavian hordes bringing northern idolatry and a taste for plunder. More Vikings arrived in the centuries that followed, notably in the ninth century to escape from the tyranny of the Norwegian King Henry Fairhair. About the year 1095, Godfrad Crovan, King of Dublin, Man and the Hebrides, died on Islay. Eight years later his son Olaf succeeded him to the government and Olaf's daughter married Somerled, who founded the dynasty of the Macdonald lords of the Isles.

Repeated efforts were made by Scottish kings to displace the Norsemen. In 1263 Haakon IV of Norway sailed with a great fleet to enforce his territorial rule by invading Scotland but was driven back at Largs. Three years later Haakon's son Magnus concluded a peace with Scotland, renouncing all

claim to the Hebrides and other islands with the exception of Orkney and Shetland in return for 4000 merks in four-yearly payments. Part of the bargain was that Magnus's son Eric should marry the Scottish king's daughter, Margaret, thus posing the concept of a northern commonwealth. However this was never to come about because, in 1290, their only child, the Maid of Norway, died.

Remoteness and the rigours of island life meant that from early days the Gaelic-speaking population was poor and badly housed. By the eighteenth century, in common with the mainland Highlands of Scotland, and in the aftermath of the arrival and departure of Bonnie Prince Charlie, times became increasingly oppressive. In 1748, as part of its deliberate programme of reprisals, the British Government, determined to undermine the paternalistic power of the chiefs, struck a crucial blow. The abolition of heritable jurisdiction, and the appointment of sheriffs, at the stroke of a pen stripped the chiefs of their ancestral privileges. A new system of management and high rents was introduced, in consequence of which large numbers of tacksmen or large tenants of the land chose to emigrate to North America. As on the mainland, sheep farming on a large scale was then introduced and the crofters largely relocated in villages or barren corners of the countryside where subsistence was based

almost entirely on potatoes and herrings. Boswell's description of a typical farmhouse on Raasay in 1773 gives some idea of living conditions prevailing throughout the islands:

> It was somewhat circular in shape. At one end sheep and goats were lodged; at the other, the family. The man and his wife had a little bedstead. The place where the servants lay was marked out upon the ground by whinstones and strewed with fern. The fire was towards the upper end of the house. The smoke went out a hole in the roof, at some distance and not directly above it, as rain would hurt it.

Given the promise of wealth and prosperity across the oceans in the New World, it is hardly surprising that thousands should have responded to the incentives and promise of a new beginning.

As early as 1609, island chiefs were concerned about the consumption of alcohol. In the Statutes of Icolmkill it was claimed that the islanders' inordinate love of strong wine and *uisgebeatha* accounted for much of their poverty and for the cruelty and inhuman barbarity practised in their feuds. In consequence, the import of strong wine and aquavitae was banned, but it still remained lawful for individuals to distil their own, although only as much as they and their families might require. Remote from the centres of government, home distillation was considered a right, much the same as an Englishman might brew his own ale. Eighteenth-century legislation to curtail the manufacture and distillation of whisky was received with much the same level of contempt among the island communities as with those on the mainland.

One great lover of the islands was the writer Sir Compton Mackenzie. While resident on Barra he wrote the story of the 12,000-ton cargo ship *SS Politician*, wrecked offshore on Hartamul Rock in the Eriskay Sound in 1941. On board were 24,000 cases of whisky – 288,000 bottles – en route for America. On the evening after the ship came to grief, the three Chiefs of Armed Forces in Scotland were dining at Broomhall with the 10th Earl of Elgin. Just as dinner finished the Admiral received an urgent telephone message and departed at once. Soon after the Air Marshal was similarly summoned and hurriedly left. A little while later the General received his call, from which he returned calmly to drink his port. 'There is a ship,' he said, 'about to be wrecked off Barra. It is full of whisky. The Admiral thinks he could just get a tug there in time; the RAF have sent a fast Air/Sea Rescue launch and I have ordered all my road blocks to seize any whisky sent south by land.' Mackenzie's novel *Whisky Galore*, published in 1947 and based on the fictitious Todday islanders' response to this magnificent, unexpected windfall, proved an international bestseller. This and the subsequent film starring many of the best-known British actors and actressses of the time – Joan Greenwood, Duncan MacRae, Gordon Jackson, Basil Radford – served as one of the most effective post-war, world-wide marketing and public relations initiatives for Scotch whisky that has ever been known.

Facing: the hills of Arran seen from the Isle of Bute

Facing: the Laphroaig Distillery, Islay, originally built on the shoreline for easy access to coastal vessels   Above: wild geese take off from Islay

A thousand years ago a kingdom was created out of the Inner and Outer Hebrides, from the Butt of Lewis in the north, to the Isle of Man off the coast of England in the south. Incorporated also were the mainland seaboards of Argyll and Northern Ireland. The centre of this kingdom became the Island of Islay, medieval seat of the all-powerful Lords of the Isles.

Somerled, Lord of Argyll and the Isles in the twelfth century, unable to meet the constant threat of Norse invasion, married Ragnhildis, daughter of King Olave the Red of Norway. Through marriage and conquest this warrior chief acquired supreme power throughout a seascape region of scattered island communities. After his death his territories were dispersed among his sons, and through them descend the MacDougalls of Argyll and Lorne, and Clan Donald, otherwise known as the MacDonalds of Islay.

Over the centuries Islay has been occupied by Picts, Vikings and Gaels. The ruins of Finlaggan,

179

Facing: the Caol Ila Distillery close to Port Askaig, Islay   Above: the fishing village of Portnahaven on Islay

Clan Donald's once palatial residence, and Dunny-veg Castle, seat of the MacDonalds of Islay and Kintyre, are reminders of a turbulent past when seafaring, plunder and internecine struggle were an everyday reality. The very remoteness of these islands made it impossible for a centralised government to wield control, although following the collapse of the Lordship of the Isles in 1493 Islay was acquired by the Campbells of Cawdor who held relatively peaceful tenure until their finances were undermined by the potato blight of the 1850s. At that time much of the island was acquired by the Morrison family, ennobled to the peerage in the present generation with Baron Margadale.

Fertile fields, deep reserves of blue-black peat, soft water, seaweed on the shores and the sea-enriched Atlantic air, all help to create the distinctive tastes, heavy and smoky, of the Islay malts which have contributed to the island's fame. There are seven distilleries on Islay: Ardbeg, Bowmore, Bruichladdich, Bunnahabhain, Caol Ila, Lagavulin and Laphroaig, all built on the shoreline to make possible the dispatch and receipt of goods by means of the small coastal vessels.

Close to Port Askaig is Caol Ila (the Gaelic name for the strait or kyle which separates Islay from

Jura, otherwise known as the Sound of Islay). On this remote and beautiful site, in 1846, the year he withdrew from the Littlemill Distillery partnership in Dunbartonshire, Hector Henderson built his Caol Ila Distillery. Before the arrival of steam, the islanders had to rely on sail or oar to cross the often treacherous seas to keep them from total isolation. From the nineteenth century steamers plied the waters between the islands and the mainland, often battered by storms or lost in mist, offering the only lifeline available to these Scottish island communities.

From 1923 the SS *Pibroch*, a Clyde 'puffer', would bring malting barley, coal and empty casks to the piers at Lagavulin and Caol Ila through the island waters from Glasgow, returning with filled casks. Clyde 'puffers' acquired their name from the type of engine used in the early vessels which punched out smoke like a steam locomotive. A second *Pibroch*, a motor vessel, replaced the first in 1956, and after 1972 distillery supplies arrived on roll-on, roll-off vehicular ferries at Port Ellen and were then carried to the distilleries by road in Crown-locked vans.

On the south of Islay, close by Port Ellen, the Ardbeg Distillery dates from 1815. Nearby is the Laphroaig Distillery in beautifully landscaped environs, with its own floor maltings. At one time the proprietor of Laphroaig was Ian Hunter, who had employed Mackie & Co, owners of the neighbouring Lagavulin Distillery, as agents. When Hunter

Deep reserves of blue-black peat and soft water abound in the moorland landscape of Islay

Ardbeg Distillery near Port Ellen, Islay

withdrew the agency the Glasgow businessman swore he would have his revenge by building his own distillery only a short distance away in the grounds of Lagavulin and naming it Malt Mill. Equipped with pot-stills of an identical character, he would copy all the manufacturing processes to produce an identical whisky. By selling this to the blending firms on the mainland he would surely undermine Hunter's business.

Peter Mackie carried out his threat, but when

Facing: Lagavulin Distillery, Islay

the first spirit flowed, indisputably a good whisky, it was found to be entirely different from Laphroaig and Lagavulin. The reason, of course, was the source of water: although drawn from the same hills, the water did not issue from the same spring. In the manufacture of Scotch whisky that is what, in every case, makes the difference.

Originally there were two legal distilleries based at Lagavulin, also close to Port Ellen. One was founded in 1816 by John Johnston, the other, a year later, by Archibald Campbell. By 1837, following Johnston's death a year earlier, there was

only one distillery, and this was acquired by Graham's, a spirit merchant in Glasgow.

The ruins of Dunnyveg Castle stand at the entrance to Lagavulin Bay, denoting ancient strategic significance. The reputation of the Lagavulin Distillery, however, really took off in 1878 under the ownership of Sir Peter Mackie, senior partner in Mackie & Co, who launched White Horse as a blended Scotch label. On his death, the Times obituary observed that Sir Peter had possessed 'the restlessness of a vigorous mind, constantly planning fresh enterprises. most of which he suc-

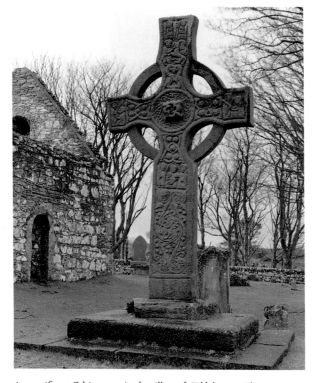

A magnificent Celtic cross, in the village of Kildalton on Islay

ceeded in carrying out'.

Islay's capital, north of Port Ellen, on the eastern shore of Lochindaal, is Bowmore, a 'planned' village built in 1768, notable for its round church, one of several in Scotland designed so that the devil should find no corner in which to hide. The Bowmore Distillery stands on the edge of the sea loch known as 'Lovely Lochindaal'. Erected in 1779, taking water from the Laggan River, Bowmore Distillery retains the traditional method of

turning the barley on the malting floor by hand. It is then dried in kilns fired by the local blue-black peat, creating the finished malt's strong flavour and aroma, heavy and smoky. Maturation in American oak bourbon or Spanish sherry casks, stored in warehouses on the shore, completes the process.

The story goes that in 1951 Stanley P. Morrison, a whisky broker, was dining at Malmaison, his favourite Glasgow restaurant (alas no longer in existence), when he overheard a conversation in which it was said that, with the death of Mr Grigor, the owner, Bowmore Distillery was to be sold to a foreign investor. In an instant Morrison was on the telephone to Grigor's widow and a deal was struck. It is now owned by Morrison Bowmore, the Glasgow-based holding company which is chaired by Brian Morrison, Stanley's son.

One outstanding feature of the Bowmore Distillery is the waste energy retrieval system which makes a major contribution to the local community. Hot air from this system is used to heat the island's first swimming pool, housed in the old distillery building which was given to the town.

Across the bay from Bowmore, on the western shore of Lochindaal, is the white-washed Bruichladdich Distillery, founded in 1881 and the most westerly of Islay's distilleries. The elongated necks of the stills at Bruichladdich produce a light spirit.

The château-like Bunnahabhain Distillery, with its pear-shaped stills, is located on the north coast of the island where the River Margadale flows into

Port Ellen, Islay, from where ferries carry whisky to the mainland

the Sound of Islay. Founded in 1881 by William Robertson, of Robertson & Baxter in Glasgow, the company, along with houses for employees, also built a school, a library and 'villas' for the excise officers. Half a mile across the sound from Islay is Jura, which was given its name of 'Dyr-er', Deer Island, by the Vikings. Even today, red deer heavily outnumber the human population. The famous Paps of Jura, the highest peak of which is 2751 ft, are an unmistakable landmark on the horizon seen from the Kintyre Peninsula. Eight miles long at its broadest, Jura has one road. Between its most northerly point and the island of Scarba beyond, lies Corryvreckan, the whirlpool whose roaring

sound can be heard on the wind twenty miles away. Tradition has it that this treacherous stretch of water took its name from the unfortunate Prince Breachan, son of the Scandinavian King of Lochlin, who fell in love with a princess of the isles. The lady's father would only consent to the match on the provision that Breachan anchored for three days and nights in the whirlpool.

Accepting the challenge, the young prince hastened back to Lochlin to consult his sages, who directed him to equip himself with three ropes, one

Above: a ferry plies its way through the Sound of Jura
Left: Bunnahabhain Distillery   Facing: Bowmore Distillery

of hemp, one of wool, the third to be twined from the maiden's hair. Thus armed, he returned to anchor in the whirlpool. First the hemp rope broke; on the second day the wool rope snapped. The third day dawned and Prince Breachan remained confident. Alas, the hair rope also broke and Breachan and his craft were sucked into the void. His body is said to have been recovered by his faithful dog and a little cairn marks the spot where he is buried.

The strait between the two islands is known as the Gulf of Corryvreckan. Craighouse, on Small Isles Bay, is the capital of Jura, and it is here that the Isle of Jura Distillery is located, drawing water from the spring of Bhaille Mharghadh which runs through a cave once used by smugglers on to quartzite and over peat and heather. A distillery on this spot was part of island life as early as 1810, but was closed during the First World War. In 1985, through popular demand, Charles Mackinlay & Co, then part of Scottish & Newcastle Breweries, decided to reintroduce the island's only single malt.

To the northeast, shortly before the road ends, is a farmhouse cottage at Barnhill, where the writer George Orwell came in the late 1940s to write his last novel, 1984, his disturbing vision of the future. Nearer to Craighouse is Tarbert, an estate purchased in 1920 by the 2nd Viscount Astor, whose American wife Nancy was Britain's first woman member of parliament. Although not

---

The Talisker Distillery, Skye and waterfall. Facing: the River Laggan, Islay

overimpressed by the wilderness of the west coast, she built herself a quaint windowed summerhouse on a knoll in front of the lodge overlooking Tarbat Bay. Here she would read and paint as she looked across at the great wash of silent Hebridean water.

North across the Firth of Lorne, offshore from Oban and beyond Kerrera, lies Mull, the largest of the Small Isles situated in the Inner Hebrides, with its daily ferry service from Oban. The ferry, having crossed the firth, enters the Sound of Mull, guarded by the formidable fortress of Duart Castle which dates from the thirteenth century, and is today the home of Sir Lachlan Maclean of Duart, 28th Chief of Clan Maclean. A short distance from here is Craignure, the first port of call on the ferry's tour of the Hebrides.

On the eastern edge of Tobermory Harbour is the Ledaig Distillery, established in 1823 by John Sinclair and closed from 1928 to 1972. It was then reopened by the Distillers Company passing later to the owner of a Yorkshire-based property company. In July 1993 Ledaig was bought by the Barrhead-based Burn Stewart Distillers. The transaction included rights for the Ledaig, and Tobermory malt whiskies.

Tobermory, however, is best known for the events of almost four hundred years ago, following the fiasco of the Spanish Armada in 1588. Straying, storm-battered, up the west coast of Britain, the *Florencia*, a Spanish galleon, arrived at the Bay of Tobermory. To begin with the crew was welcomed

Left: Ben Beinn Bhreac, Skye   Facing: Paps of Jura

192

A drover's halt, with the island of Mull in the background (Richard Ansdell)

by the locals, but when it transpired that the men planned to depart without paying their bills, a group of townsfolk clambered on board and planted sufficient dynamite to blast the ship to the bottom of the bay.

There is another version of this story which involves a passenger on the galleon, a Spanish princess of great beauty who, it is said, had become obsessed by a man in her dreams. To search for her hero she stowed away on the *Florencia* and was undiscovered until it found anchorage in Tobermory Bay. Shortly after its arrival the lady caught sight of the handsome Lachlan Maclean of Duart, ancestor of the present chief, and realised that her search was at an end. Not unexpectedly, the Lady of Duart thought differently, and it was she who took it upon herself to encourage Donald Maclean to dynamite the ship with the princess aboard. The princess's remains, it is said, were laid to rest at Colum-kill in a stone coffin.

Off the western toe of Mull lies Iona, the holy island where St Columba founded his abbey in AD 563. Early Scottish kings were laid to rest here, including both Macbeth and Duncan I. In 1938 a Church of Scotland minister, with faith and determination, founded the Iona Community, for which he was later honoured as the Very Reverend Lord Macleod of Fuinary. The sanctuary he created, with the restored abbey at its heart, remains a renowned retreat for prayer and worship.

The best-known of the Hebridean islands is

The Talisker Distillery on Skye

Skye, the 'Island of Mists', mostly moorland and mountains. Of the mountains, the Cuillins, in the southwest, are the most famous and most inhospitable. The highest summit is Sgurr Alasdair, 3309 ft, but the best-known is Sgurr-nan-Gillean, 3167 ft, overlooking wild Glen Sligachan. Although dangerous and bleak, and with a nasty habit of playing tricks with compasses because of magnetic rock, the Cuillins are favourites with rock climbers and contain fifteen summits over 3000 ft. Another mountain system on Skye is the spine of swart basalt forming the backbone of Trotternish, rising into the pinnacles of Storr and Quiraing. In Duirinish stand the two flat-top basalt tubs known as Macleod's Tables.

Some historians suggest that Clan Donald descends from Conn of the Thousand Battles, Ard Righ of Ireland in the first century AD. Today the three million descendants of Clan Donald have their shrine at the former stable block of Armadale Castle, which lies between Ardvasar and Armadale village, just where the ferry arrives after plying across the Sound of Sleat from Mallaig. Administered by the Clan Donald Trust, largely funded by the American Glencoe Foundation, the former family home of Lord Macdonald has been transformed and restored.

In 1815, at the end of the Napoleonic wars, with his wealth enhanced by a sudden upsurge in the kelp trade, the 2nd Lord Macdonald of Macdonald commissioned James Gillespie Graham to convert one of the Macdonald homes into a mansion fit for the chief of a great clan. It was in this house, prior to its refurbishment, that Flora Macdonald spent some of her childhood, and the castle today, with restaurant, and apartments available for let to visitors, is filled with reminders of great Clan Donald figures from the past. The 8th Lord Macdonald lives with his family at nearby Kinloch Lodge, the hotel which he and Lady Macdonald, well known as a cookery writer, have been running since he inherited the title in 1970.

Flora Macdonald, whose brief escapade with the fugitive Bonnie Prince Charlie enabled him to escape from Benbecula to Skye, became the heroine of the '45. The outcome was her imprisonment in the Tower of London. Returning to Skye on her release in 1747 she married her cousin Allan Macdonald of Kingsburgh, a farmer on the shores of Loch Snizort on the Trotternish Peninsula. Times were becoming increasingly hard for the Highland farmer and Kingsburgh found himself falling into debt. In 1772, accompanied by one daughter and four sons, leaving two children behind to be cared for by friends, he and Flora sailed for America, a classic example of the Scottish emigrant family of the time.

Visiting Kingsburgh House with Dr Johnson, shortly before the Macdonalds' departure, Boswell was much taken with Allan Macdonald: 'He had his tartan plaid thrown about him, a large blue bonnet with a knot of black ribbon like a cockade, a brown short coat of a kind of duffle, a tartan vest with gold buttonholes, a bluish filibeg, and tartan hose. He had jet-black hair tied behind and with screwed ringlets on each side, and was a large stately man with a steady sensible countenance.' Flora was 'a little woman of a mild and genteel appearance, mighty soft and well-bred'.

In 1980, having purchased a large parcel of the Macdonald estates, Sir Iain Noble, the Scottish merchant banker, founded Sabhal Mor Ostaig, a school for the Gaelic language, at Teangue. Full time higher Gaelic education and a range of summer courses attract students from far afield. Sir Iain, with entrepreneurial flair, has since launched two old-style brands of Gaelic whisky from his headquarters at Eilean Iarmain, each containing some Talisker, but also with a discernible input from Speyside: a twelve-years-old named Poit Dhubh, the Gaelic for 'Illicit Still', and a blend called Te Bheag nan Eilean, which means 'Little Lady of the Islands'.

To the very northwest of the island is Skye's other great clan house, that of Dunvegan Castle, historic stonghold of the MacLeods. The earliest part dates from the ninth century and stands on a rock crag facing the sea. Most of the present structure dates from the fourteenth century, but as was the way with families of fluctuating wealth, it was modified from time to time until the nineteenth century. Dunvegan Castle is the home of John MacLeod of MacLeod, 29th Chief of MacLeod, who is an opera singer and who organises the annual Dunvegan Castle Arts Festival. Among the treasures displayed in his home is the Fairy Flag, supposedly given to an early chief by a fairy well-

Facing: a lonely shieling in an island landscape

wisher. Should the flag be waved in battle, then the MacLeods would surely triumph. Through the centuries what remains of this faded flag has proved startlingly effective. During the Second World War, MacLeod pilots serving in the British Airforce carried photographs of it when embarking upon hazardous missions.

Across to the east and facing into the Sound of Raasay is Portree, essentially the 'capital' of Skye, which derived its name in the sixteenth century from Port Righ, meaning 'King's Harbour', when James V landed here to mediate between the feuding MacLeods and MacDonalds. A town very much geared to the summer holidaymakers, there has been a tradition since 1879 for local landowners in Ross and Cromarty, Skye and Lochalsh, to hold formal September balls in the Gathering Hall, built for that purpose by a Lord MacDonald.

In 1880 Robert Louis Stevenson, author of *Treasure Island*, paid tribute to Skye and Scotch whisky in 'The Scotsman's Return from Abroad':

> The King o' drinks, as I conceive it,
> Talisker, Isla or Glenlivet.

Talisker Distillery is situated on the southwest of the island on the shore of Loch Harport, within sight of the Cuillins. The MacLeod chief of the day, a benign landlord, had been desperate to help the impoverished crofting community on his land and by subsidising them had run into serious financial problems. MacLeod had taken a job in London to try and meet his debts but this was not enough to make any dramatic difference. In 1825, therefore, he was obliged to sell a portion of his clan land to Hugh MacAskill, who had originated from Eigg, where his father was a tacksman and doctor for the Small Isles. Hugh was following in his father's footsteps by holding and subletting leases of land, and had acquired the tack of Talisker House and the north end of the Minginish Peninsula.

MacLeod possibly assumed that the old tenant-crofter way of life would continue, but the discovery that the Cheviot breed of sheep could survive the Hebridean winter changed everything. First and foremost a businessman, MacAskill, with the aid of government incentives, immediately cleared out the crofters to make way for the infinitely more profitable prospect of sheep farming.

Five years later, with his brother Kenneth, bank agent in Portree, MacAskill obtained a lease of 21 acres at Carbost to build a distillery. Bearing in mind MacAskill's treatment of the crofters and perhaps the local attitude to alcohol, the Rev Roderick MacLeod, former minister of the parish, condemned the distillery's erection at Carbost as 'one of the greatest curses that, in the ordinary course of Providence, could befall it or any other place'.

Hugh MacAskill, having inherited Calgary Castle and the estate of Mornish on Mull, died in 1863, predeceased by Kenneth. In the years that followed the Talisker Distillery was bought and sold several times and in 1901 the premises were extended and a pier built by Thomas Mackenzie DL, JP, managing director. Following his death in 1916, Talisker Distillery was absorbed by a consortium and eventually acquired by United Distillers.

There is, indeed, another drink with which the Island of Skye is associated. Having found refuge on the island, Bonnie Prince Charlie at one point enjoyed the protection and hospitality of the Laird of MacKinnon at Strath, who then helped him escape to Morar. Legend has it that, in the Prince's honour, a sweet cordial was served consisting of whisky, heather honey, herbs and spices. Another version of this story attributes the recipe, very much of a type popular in continental Europe, to Prince Charles himself, a gift to the MacKinnons from a grateful sovereign-never-to-be. Herein lies the origin of Drambuie, 'the drink that satisfies', which was registered by the MacKinnon Family in 1892. Basing their headquarters in Edinburgh, they began commercial production in 1906, and Drambuie now ranks as one of the best-known liqueurs in the world.

CHAPTER NINE: THE ORKNEY ISLANDS

Remnants of the German fleet in Scapa Flow

North from the Caithness coast, across the Pentland Firth, lies green and fertile Orkney, a chain of seventy islands, thirty of which are inhabited, all of which furnish changing moods and constant sea vistas. The largest of the islands is known as 'the Mainland', wherein lies Kirkwall, the capital, and the smaller, picturesque town of Stromness.

'When the first settlers came to Orkney, over 500 years ago,' reads a display panel in the Tankerness Museum in Kirkwall, 'they found a landscape much like the one we see today – land and loch, sand, cliff and sea. And above – wind, weather and sky.'

For five hundred years these islands were part of Viking Norway and Denmark, passing to Scotland in the dowry of Queen Margaret, the Danish bride of James III. Orkney was formally annexed in 1472. Orkney's story is splendidly displayed in Kirkwall's Tankerness Museum, opened in 1968, originally a sixteenth-century merchant laird's house. Fifty yards away is the striking red-sandstone St Magnus Cathedral which predates it by some five hundred years.

Facing: St Magnus Cathedral, Kirkwall, Orkney   Above: the Highland Park Distillery, Kirkwall   Below: Stromness harbour

The most profound social influence on these islands in recent centuries has been war. A relatively short excursion by car takes the visitor along the coast of Scapa Flow, over the Churchill Barriers to the islands of Burray and South Ronaldsay. The rusted remains of sunken First World War German battleships provide a melancholy reminder of those dark days, as do the Churchill Barriers themselves. In 1939 Scapa Flow was considered strategically crucial for the British Fleet, but after the sinking of the battleship *Royal Oak* by a German submarine in October of that year, it became clear that the eastern approaches to the islands were desperately vulnerable. Italian prisoners-of-war were em-

ployed to create massive concrete blocks, each between five and ten tons, and these were dropped into the water to block off the channels.

Using two Nissen huts, the prisoners built a small chapel of worship on nearby Lamb Holm. The chapel is still used, and visited by thousands. The interior was decorated by Domenico Chiochetti, one of the prisoners.

The economy of the Orkney Islands is based primarily on agriculture and the sea. While the North Sea oil boom dominated the Shetland Islands to the north, it passed Orkney by. However, local enterprise is far from lacking. Orcadian jewellery and the traditional round-backed Orkney

The windswept landscape of Mainland Orkney embraces Scapa Flow

chairs have found markets all over the world.

There are two distilleries on Orkney, both highly individual, producing much sought-after single malts. The Highland Park Distillery at Kirkwall was founded in 1798, on the site of a smuggler's bothy. The smuggler, Magnus Eunson, was also an elder of the Kirk, which meant that he could hide his illicit distillations under the pulpit where the excisemen were unlikely to find them.

For today's Highland Park Distillery, peat, saturated by the salt spray of centuries, is dug from Hobbister Moor on the shores of Scapa Flow, and a measured amount is used to fire the kilns for each malting.

Situated less than half a mile to the south is the small Scapa Distillery which takes its name from the nearby Flow. This distillery dates from 1885 but was rebuilt in 1959.

Above: the Italian chapel, Orkney   Facing: interior of the chapel

To the west, at Stromness, the Pier Art Gallery provides a focal point for the annual May Festival based on the town. A permanent exhibition, presented by Margaret Gardiner, includes examples of the work of Ben Nicholson, Barbara Hepworth, Naum Gabo and Eduardo Paolozzi. This public gallery is in a charming setting on the waterfront and throughout the year shows stimulating exhibitions of contemporary painting, drawing and photography.

Nobody should visit Orkney without a pilgrimage – for that is what it amounts to – to Skara Brae, the best preserved prehistoric village in northern Europe; to Maes Howe and Midhowe, the supreme examples of Neolithic chambered tombs in Great Britain; and to the Ring of Brogar, ritual monuments to a time which defies our understanding. But relics of the past are not what the Orkney

Islands are about. Far from it. For the sportsman there is fishing, climbing, walking and sailing. For the naturalist there is a profusion of flora, and the bird life is enthralling. Island hopping is easy, but you have to make arrangements in advance. Orkney enjoys the shortest scheduled flights in the world.

Hoy, the Vikings' 'High Island', features the Old Man of Hoy, a 450-ft high stack. Some say that Papa Westray, off its larger namesake to the north, is the most beautiful small island in the world.

No wonder these islands inspired such Scottish writers as Edwin Muir and Eric Linklater, and, more recently, George Mackay Brown, the true Orcadian bard steeped in Orcadian lore, who has never chosen to move away. And for musicians too there is a special enchantment: Sir Peter Maxwell Davies, the composer, has his home on Hoy.

Remoteness has its appeal. Orkney is a place for relaxation and for contemplation, affording the opportunity to gaze out over the ever-changing seascape under an ever-changing sky. It is a place for meditation or solitude or for being with the person of your choice. Fresh air, fine flat land, a sense of being where time began, and where time has never quite managed to keep pace with the rest of the world – this is Orkney.

Highland Park Distillery sihouetted in the setting sun   *Facing: Standing stones of the Ring of Brogar, ritual monument of a distant age*

THE DISTILLERIES

THE DISTILLERIES

These whiskies are described in the regional lists on the following pages

Aberfeldy *Southern Highlands*
Aberlour *Speyside*
An Cnoc *Grampian Region and Eastern Highlands*
Ardbeg *Islay, Jura, Mull and Skye*
Ardmore *Grampian Region and Eastern Highlands*
Auchentoshan *Southwest*
Aultmore *Speyside*
Balblair *Northern Highlands*
The Balvenie *Speyside*
Benriach *Speyside*
Benrinnes *Speyside*
Blair Athol *Southern Highlands*
Bowmore *Islay, Jura, Mull and Skye*
Bruichladdich *Islay, Jura, Mull and Skye*
Bunnahabhain *Islay, Jura, Mull and Skye*
Caol Ila *Islay, Jura, Mull and Skye*
Caperdonich *Speyside*
Cardhu *Speyside*
Clynelish *Northern Highlands*
Cragganmore *Speyside*
Craigellachie *Speyside*
Dailuaine *Speyside*
Dallas Dhu *Speyside*
Dalmore *Northern Highlands*
Dalwhinnie *Southern Highlands*
Deanston *Southern Highlands*
Edradour *Southern Highlands*
Glen Deveron *Grampian Region and Eastern Highlands*
Glen Elgin *Speyside*

Glen Garioch *Grampian Region and Eastern Highlands*
Glen Grant *Speyside*
Glen Keith *Speyside*
Glen Moray *Speyside*
Glen Ord *Northern Highlands*
The Glen Rothes *Speyside*
Glen Spey *Speyside*
Glenburgie *Speyside*
Glencadam *Southern Highlands*
Glendullan *Speyside*
Glenfarclas *Speyside*
Glenfiddich *Speyside*
Glengoyne *Southwest*
Glenkinchie *Borders, Lothians and Fife*
The Glenlivet *Speyside*
Glenlossie *Speyside*
Glenmorangie *Northern Highlands*
Glentauchers *Speyside*
Glentromie *Southern Highlands*
Glenturret *Southern Highlands*
Highland Park *Orkney*
Imperial *Speyside*
Inchgower *Speyside*
Invergordon *Northern Highlands*
Isle of Jura *Islay, Jura, Mull and Skye*
Knockando *Speyside*
Lagavulin *Islay, Jura, Mull and Skye*
Laphroaig *Islay, Jura, Mull and Skye*
Ledaig *Islay, Jura, Mull and Skye*

Linkwood *Speyside*
Lochside *Southern Highlands*
Longmorn *Speyside*
Longrow *Western Highlands*
The Macallan *Speyside*
Miltonduff-Glenlivet *Speyside*
Mortlach *Speyside*
Oban *Western Highlands*
Old Fettercairn *Southern Highlands*
Old Pulteney *Northern Highlands*
Royal Brackla *Speyside*
Royal Lochnagar *Grampian Region and Eastern Highlands*
Scapa *Orkney*
The Singleton of Auchroisk *Speyside*
Speyburn *Speyside*
Speyside Single *Southern Highlands*
Speyside Vatted *Southern Highlands*
Springbank *Western Highlands*
Strathisla *Speyside*
Talisker *Islay, Jura, Mull and Skye*
Tamdhu *Speyside*
Tamnavulin *Glenlivet Speyside*
Teaninich *Northern Highlands*
Tobermory *Islay, Jura, Mull and Skye*
Tomatin *Speyside*
Tomintoul *Glenlivet Speyside*
Tormore *Speyside*
Tullibardine *Southern Highlands*

THE REGIONS AND THEIR WHISKIES

A lifetime could be spent exploring the diversity of tastes among Scotland's malt whiskies. The taste of whisky is shaped by a number of factors: the region where it is made, its age – whether young, middle-aged or mature – and its six main ingredients.

To make a single malt whisky take some pure natural water, some malted barley, peated to your specification, add yeast for a foaming ferment, let the alchemy of the copper pot-still distil its magic, make an oak cask home and leave it to mature for a minimum of three years.

Single malts can be divided by their regions of manufacture into Lowland, Highland, Speyside and Island malts.

Lowland Malts. The identity of the Lowland malts is shaped by the gentle landscapes and the temperate climate of the region. Lowland malts make a good starting point for anyone keen to explore single malts.

Highland Malts. Highland malts owe their diversity to the vast size of the region and to the wildly contrasting landscapes of its east and west coasts.

Speyside Malts. Speyside malts absorb their quality from the clear, pure mountain waters which flow from sources high in the granite massifs of the Cairngorm and Monadhliath mountains, through peat and fertile rolling farmlands. Speyside is known as the Golden Square of malt whisky distillation, and is, some would argue, where it all began.

Island Malts. As diverse as the Speyside malts in their aroma and flavour, the Island malts of Islay, Mull Skye, Jura and the Orkneys have a distinctive character of their own. They may be subdivided into two categories: the big malts renowned the world over and distilled on Islay; and the lighter malts from Mull, Skye, Jura and the Orkneys.

LOWLAND MALTS

BORDERS, THE LOTHIANS AND FIFE

Glenkinchie: United Distillers
Bottled at: 10 years
Round flavour, slightly dry with a lingering smoothness and a light fragrant sweetness on the nose.

THE SOUTHWEST

Auchentoshan: Morrison Bowmore Distillers Ltd
Bottled at: 10 and 21 years
Light with a soft sweetness and a good aftertaste, delicate, slightly sweet nose.

Glengoyne: Lang Brothers Ltd
Bottled at: 10, 12 and 17 years
Light pleasant all-round malt with a fresh aroma. A Southern Highland malt.

HIGHLAND MALTS

THE SOUTHERN HIGHLANDS

Aberfeldy: United Distillers
Bottled at: 15 years
Fresh, clean, lightly peated nose; substantial flavour with a good, round taste.

Blair Athol: United Distillers
Bottled at: 8 and 12 years
Light, fresh, clean aroma; medium hint of peat with a round finish and plenty of flavour.

Dalwhinnie: United Distillers
Bottled at: 15 years
Gentle aromatic bouquet; luscious flavour with a light, honey-sweet finish.

Deanston: Burn Stewart Distillers PLC
Bottled at: 12, 17 and 25 years
Well balanced, medium bodied, fresh, smooth with a sweet, fruit flavour.

Edradour: Campbell Distillers Ltd
Bottled at: 10 years
Strong marzipan taste which comes through smooth, slightly dry and malty with a nutty, almond-like aftertaste.

Glencadam: Allied Distillers Ltd
Bottled at: an undeclared age
Light hint of sweetness on the nose; full, with quite a fruity flavour and a good finish.

Glentromie: Speyside Distillery Co Ltd

Bottled at: 12 years
Well burnished Highland malt, mellow and creamy, with a smooth afterglow.

Glenturret: The Highland Distilleries Co plc (bottled and marketed by Glenturret Distillery Ltd)
Bottled at: 12 and 15 years

Very impressive aromatic nose; full lush body with good depth of flavour and a stimulating finish.

Lochside: MacNab Distilleries Ltd
Bottled at: 10 years
Light to medium bodied with a soft, smooth, malty taste, including a hint of peat, and with a gentle finish.

Old Fettercairn: The Whyte & Mackay Group plc
Bottled at: 10 years
Rich pungent bouquet followed by a round, pleasing aftertaste.

Speyside Single: Speyside Distillery Co Ltd
Came of age: December 1993
Not to be marketed for some years but samples are remarkable for a young single malt. Its smoothness and sweetness belie its age.

Speyside Vatted: Speyside Distillery Co Ltd
Bottled at: 8 years
Embodies all the best qualities of the region; slightly nutty flavour, sharp but sweet nose.

Tullibardine: The Invergordon Distillers Ltd
Bottled at: 10 years and special aged bottlings under the Stillman's Dram label.
Delicate, mellow, sweet aroma of fruit on the nose; full bodied, with a fruity flavour and a good lingering taste.

THE WESTERN HIGHLANDS AND CAMPBELTOWN

Longrow: J & A Mitchell & Co Ltd
Bottled at: 16 years
Well balanced with a hint of sweetness, a succulent malty palate and a lingering aftertaste.

Oban: United Distillers
Bottled at: 14 years
Fresh hint of peat on the nose; firm malty flavour finishing very smoothly.

Springbank: J & A Mitchell & Co Ltd
Bottled at: 15, 21, 25 and 30 years
Positive and rich with a slight sweetness on the nose; well balanced, full of charm and elegance.

GRAMPIAN REGION AND THE EASTERN HIGHLANDS

An Cnoc: Inver House Distillers Ltd
Bottled at: 12 years
Pale, sweet and fruity; the nose has a distinctive soft aroma with a hint of smoke.

Ardmore: Allied Distillers Ltd
Bottled at: 12 and 18 years
Big, sweet and malty on the palate with a good crisp finish.

Glen Deveron: William Lawson Distillers
Bottled at: 5 and 12 years
Nicely aromatic with a very positive nose; mellow, quite substantial spicy flavour with pleasant tongue-biting tang and a good, long aftertaste.

Glen Garioch: Morrison Bowmore Distillers Ltd
Bottled at: 1984, 12, 15 and 21 years
Pronounced, peaty flavour with a pleasant finish; the nose is delicate and smoky.

Royal Lochnagar:
United Distillers
Bottled at: 12 years and special bottlings at an undeclared age
Good body with a full, malt-fruit-like taste and a delicious trace of sweetness.

THE NORTHERN HIGHLANDS

Balblair: Allied Distillers Ltd
Bottled at: 5 and 10 years
Pronounced and distinctive fragrance of smoke and sweetness; good lingering flavour with a slender hint of sweetness.

Clynelish: United Distillers
Bottled at: 14 years
Quite peaty for a northern malt; rich with a slightly dry finish and lots of character.

Dalmore: Whyte & Mackay Group PLC
Bottled at: 12 years
Matured in American white oak casks and a proportion of sherry casks giving rich velvet tones with a hint of sherry wood coming through at the end.

Glen Ord: United Distillers
Bottled at: 12 years
Beautifully deep nose with a tinge of dryness; very smooth with good depth and a long and lasting aftertaste.

Glenmorangie: Macdonald Martin Distilleries plc
Bottled at: 10 and 18 years
Medium bodied with a sweet, fresh finish; the nose has a beautiful aroma with a subtle hint of peat.

Invergordon Grain Whisky: The Invergordon Distillers Ltd
Bottled at: non-aged, 7, 10 and 22 years
Pale straw in colour; delicate, smooth, medium sweet nose; well matured taste of good weight which lingers well and is refreshing to the palate.

Old Pulteney: Allied Distillers Ltd
Bottled at: 8 years
Light, crisp and refreshing with a hint of fullness which gives a positive finish of length.

Teaninich: United Distillers
Bottled at: an undeclared age
Soft and full of flavour; the nose is subtle and fruity with a gentle bouquet.

SPEYSIDE MALTS

Aberlour: Campbell Distillers Ltd
Bottled at: 10 years
Rich, malty aroma with a hint of smoke on the palate and a restrained sweetness.

Aultmore: United Distillers
Bottled at: 12 years
Smooth and well balanced with a mellow, warming finish; the nose is fresh with a hint of sweetness and a touch of peat.

The Balvenie: William Grant & Sons Ltd
Bottled at: Founders Reserve 10 years minimum; The Classic 12 years minimum
Big, distinctive flavour – almost a liqueur – and with a very distinct sweet aftertaste.

Benriach: The Seagram Co Ltd
Bottled at: an undeclared age
Positive taste of sweetness and malt with a gentle mild fruitiness that slowly comes through on the palate.

Benrinnes: United Distillers
Bottled at: 15 years
Firm and positive with a hint of blackberry fruitiness in the nose; a clean fresh taste which lingers.

Caperdonich: The Seagram Co Ltd
Bottled at: an undeclared age
Medium bodied with a slight hint of fruit and a quick smoky finish.

Cardhu: United Distillers
Bottled at: 12 years
Excellent bouquet with a hint of sweetness;

smooth mellow flavour with a delightful long-lasting finish.

Cragganmore: United Distillers
Bottled at: 12 years
Refined, well balanced distillate; quite firm with a malty, smoky taste which finishes quickly.

Craigellachie: United Distillers
Bottled at: 14 years
Pungent, smoky nose; light bodied, smoky flavour with good character. More delicate on the palate than the nose suggests.

Dailuaine: United Distillers
Bottled at: 16 years
Robust, full bodied, fruity sweetness, which really stimulates the taste buds; excellent balance between refinement and positive assertion of malt.

Dallas Dhu: United Distillers
Bottled at: 10 years
Full bodied with a lingering flavour and smooth aftertaste.

Glen Elgin: United Distillers
Bottled at: 12 years (mainly Japanese market)
Medium weight with a touch of sweetness and a smooth finish; the nose has hints of heather and honey.

Glen Grant: The Seagram Co Ltd
Bottled at: 5 and 10 years and at an undeclared age
Dry flavour, light – a good all round malt with a light, dry nose.

Glen Keith: The Seagram Co Ltd
Bottled at: an undeclared age
Light, fruity sweetness resulting in a smooth well balanced palate.

Glen Moray: Macdonald Martin Distilleries plc
Bottled at: 12, 15 years and vintages
Light, pleasant and malty with a clean finish.

The Glen Rothes: The Highland Distilleries Co plc (bottled and marketed by Berry Bros & Rudd Ltd)
Bottled at: 12 years

Good balance of softness and quality with an exquisite long-lasting flavour.

Glen Spey: Justerini & Brooks Ltd
Bottled at: 8 years
Very smooth and fragrant with a delicate nose.

Glenburgie: Allied Distillers Ltd
Bottled at: 8 years
Fragrant, herbal aroma; light, delicate, aromatic flavour with a pleasant finish.

Glendullan: United Distillers
Bottled at: 12 years
Firm and mellow with a delightful finish and a smooth lingering aftertaste.

Glenfarclas: J & G Grant
Bottled at: various ages from 10 to 30 years
Generally amber in colour, full bodied and rich from the sherry wood used for maturation and with the sensation of peat.

Glenfiddich: William Grant & Sons Ltd
Bottled at: 8 years minimum
Well balanced, with an attractive flavour and an after-sweetness; a delicate touch of peat on the nose.

The Glenlivet: The Seagram Co Ltd
Bottled at: 12 and 21 years
Light delicate nose with lots of fruit; medium light trace of sweetness, quite full on the palate.

Glenlossie: United Distillers
Bottled at: 10 years
Mellowed with age and has a long-lasting smoothness with an almond-like finish.

Glentauchers: Allied Distillers Ltd

Bottled at: an undeclared age
Lightly flavoured with a light dry finish and a sweet aroma.

Imperial: Allied Distillers Ltd
Bottled at: an undeclared age
Rich and mellow with a delicious finish and a rich and smoky nose.

Inchgower: United Distillers
Bottled at: 14 years
Well balanced with a good distinctive flavour finishing with a light sweetness.

Knockando: Justerini & Brooks Ltd
Bottled at: season of distillation and year of bottling stated on label
Medium bodied with a pleasant syrupy flavour which finishes quite quickly.

Linkwood: United Distillers
Bottled at: 12 years
Full bodied with a hint of sweetness and a slightly smoky nose.

Longmorn: The Seagram Co Ltd
Bottled at: 15 years
Full bodied, fleshy, nutty and surprisingly refined with a full, fragrant bouquet of spirit.

The Macallan: Macallan-Glenlivet plc
Bottled at: 7, 10, 12, 18 and 25 years
Full, delightful and sherried with a beautiful, lingering aftertaste.

Miltonduff-Glenlivet: Allied Distillers Ltd
Bottled at: 12 years
Medium bodied with a pleasant, well matured, subtle finish.

Mortlach: United Distillers

Bottled at: 16 years
Medium bodied with a well balanced delightful finish and a pleasant, well rounded aroma.

Royal Brackla: United Distillers
Bottled at: 10 years
Peaty smoky nose coming through on the palate with a hint of fruit and a dry finish.

The Singleton of Auchroisk: Justerini & Brooks Ltd
Bottled at: 10 years minimum
Medium weight with a hint of sweetness and a delicious long-lasting flavour.

Speyburn: Inver House Distillers Ltd
Bottled at: 10 years
Heather honey bouquet; big full bodied malty taste with a sweet finish.

Strathisla: The Seagram Co Ltd
Bottled at: 12 years
Good balance with a slender hint of sweetness and an extremely long lingering fullness.

Tamdhu: The Highland Distilleries Co plc (bottled and marketed by Matthew Gloag & Son Ltd)
Bottled at: 8, 10 and 15 years
Medium bodied with a little sweetness and a very mellow finish.

Tamnavulin Glenlivet: The Invergordon Distillers Ltd
Bottled at: 10 years
Light and fragrant, showing great finesse and a delicate aftertaste.

Tomatin: Subsidiary of Takara Shuzo & Okara

& Co Ltd
Bottled at: 10 years
Golden in colour, fresh and sweet with a slight smokiness.
Tomintoul Glenlivet: The Whyte & Mackay

Group plc
Bottled at: 8 and 12 years
Soft rounded tones reward the palate and linger in the mouth with almost a wood, spicy feel.
Tormore: Allied Distillers Ltd

Bottled at: 10 years
Medium bodied with a hint of sweetness and a pleasant, lingering aftertaste.

ISLAND MALTS

ISLAY, JURA, MULL AND SKYE

Ardbeg: Allied Distillers Ltd
Bottled at: 10 years
Full bodied and luscious with an excellent after-taste and a lovely peaty aroma.

Bowmore: Morrison Bowmore Distillers Ltd
Bottled at: 10, 12, 17, 21 and 25 years (Bow-more Legend – undeclared)
Healthy, middle range Islay with a medium weight and smooth finish. The older vintages are outstanding.

Bruichladdich: The Invergordon Distillers Ltd
Bottled at: 10, 15 and 21 years and special bottlings under the Stillman's Dram label.
Lingering flavour giving the expected fullness of Islay character but lacking the heavier tones.

Bunnahabhain: The Highland Distilleries Co plc (bottled and marketed by Matthew Gloag & Son Ltd)
Bottled at: 12 years
Pronounced character with a flowery aroma and a lovely round flavour.

Caol Ila: United Distillers
Bottled at: 15 years
Not a heavy Islay but with a pleasing weight, a fairly round flavour and a smooth finish.

Isle of Jura: The Invergordon Distillers Ltd
Bottled at: 10 years

Well matured, full but delicate flavour with good lingering character.

Lagavulin: United Distillers
Bottled at: 16 years
A typical Islay with a powerful aroma; quite heavy and very full but with a delightful hint of sweetness.

Laphroaig: Allied Distillers Ltd
Bottled at: 10 and 15 years
Full of character; big Islay peaty flavour with a delightful touch of sweetness.

Ledaig: Burn Stewart Distillers PLC
Bottled at: Vintage at 19 years
Peaty, dry, intense; an excellent Island malt.

Talisker: United Distillers
Bottled at: 8 and 10 years
Unique, full flavour which explodes on the pal-ate, lingering with an element of sweetness.

Tobermory: Burn Stewart Distillers PLC
Bottled at: Between 7 and 8 years
Soft, well balanced, smooth, with a slightly sweet edge.

ORKNEY

Highland Park: The Highland Distilleries Co plc
(bottled and marketed by Matthew Gloag &
Son Ltd)
Bottled at: 12 years
Medium, well balanced flavour finishing with a
subtle dryness; full of character, lingering and
smoky on the nose.

Scapa: Allied Distillers Ltd
Bottled at: 8 years
Delightful aromatic bouquet of peat and
heather; medium bodied with a malty, silk-like
finish.

THE KEEPERS OF THE QUAICH AND THEIR WHISKIES

The main blends and malt whisky brands of the Founding Partner and Corporate Member companies

UNITED DISTILLERS plc

Blended Whiskies
Bell's Islander
Bell's Extra Special
Bell's 12 y.o.
Black & White
Dewar's
Haig Gold Label
Johnnie Walker Red Label
Johnnie Walker Blue Label
Johnnie Walker Black Label
Johnnie Walker Premier
White Horse
Ye Monks
Buchanan's De Luxe
Dimple 15 y.o.
Logan De Luxe
Old Parr 12 y.o.
Old Parr Superior
Peter Dawson
President
Swing
Vat 69
Sandy Mac

Malt Whiskies
Dalwhinnie 15 y.o.
Lagavulin 16 y.o.
Cragganmore 12 y.o.
Glenkinchie 10 y.o.
Oban 14 y.o.
Talisker 8 y.o.
Talisker 10 y.o.

Cardhu 12 y.o.
Glen Ord 12 y.o.
Royal Lochnagar 12 y.o. and special
    bottlings at an undeclared age

ALLIED DISTILLERS LTD

Blended Whiskies
Ballantine's Finest
Ballantine's Gold Seal 12 y.o.
Ballantine's 17 y.o.
Ballantine's 30 y.o.
Stewarts Cream of the Barley
Teacher's Highland Cream
Teacher's Royal Highland 12 y.o.
Old Smuggler
Long John Special Reserve
Long John Special Reserve 12 y.o.
Black Bottle

Malt Whiskies
The Glendronach 12 y.o.
Laphroaig 10 y.o.
Laphroaig 15 y.o.
The Tormore 10 y.o.
Miltonduff Glenlivet 12 y.o.

JUSTERINI & BROOKS LTD

Blended Whiskies
J & B Rare
J & B Reserve 15 y.o.
J & B 25 y.o.
J & B Select

J & B Victorian
J & B Jet
J & B Edwardian
Dunhill
Spey Royal

Malt Whiskies
Knockando (bottled in
    selected years)

THE HIGHLAND DISTILLERIES CO plc

Blended Whiskies
The Famous Grouse

Malt Whiskies
Bunnahabhain 12 y.o.
The Glenturret 12 y.o.
The Glenturret 15 y.o.
Highland Park 12 y.o.
Tamdhu 8 y.o.
Tamdhu 12 y.o.
Tamdhu 15 y.o.

ROBERTSON & BAXTER LTD

Blended Whiskies
Langs Supreme
Langs Select 12 y.o.

Malt Whiskies
Glengoyne 10 y.o.

Glengoyne 12 y.o.
Glengoyne 17 y.o.

THE SEAGRAM CO LTD

Blended Whiskies
Royal Salute 21 y.o.
Chivas Imperial 18 y.o.
Chivas Regal 12 y.o.
Royal Citation
Passport
Something Special
100 Pipers
Black Watch
Queen Anne
Prince Charlie

Malt Whiskies
The Glenlivet 12 y.o.
The Glenlivet 18 y.o.
Longmorn 15 y.o.
Strathisla 12 y.o.
Glen Grant

BERRY BROS & RUDD LTD

Blended Whiskies
Cutty Sark
Cutty Sark 12 y.o.
Cutty Sark 18 y.o.
Berry's Best
Blue Hanger
St James's 12 y.o.

Malt Whiskies
Berry's All Malt
The Glen Rothes

BURN STEWART DISTILLERS plc

Blended Whiskies
Scottish Leader
Burn Stewart 12 y.o.
Black Prince
Black Prince 12 y.o.
Burberry's
Burberry's 12 y.o.
Burberry's 15 y.o.
Old Royal 12 y.o.
Old Royal 15 y.o.
Old Royal 21 y.o.

Malt Whiskies
Deanston 12 y.o.
Deanston 17 y.o.
Deanston 25 y.o.
Ledaig
Tobermory
The Glendower

CAMPBELL DISTILLERS LTD

Blended Whiskies
Clan Campbell
Clan Campbell Highlander 12 y.o.

Clan Campbell Legendary 21 y.o.
White Heather
House of Lords
Malt Whiskies
Aberlour 10 y.o.
Edradour 10 y.o.
Glenforres 8 y.o.

J & G GRANT DISTILLERS

Blended Whiskies
Glen Dowan Special Reserve

Malt Whiskies
Glenfarclas 105° Cask Strength
Glenfarclas 1961
Glenfarclas 10 y.o.
Glenfarclas 12 y.o.
Glenfarclas 15 y.o.
Glenfarclas 21 y.o.
Glenfarclas 25 y.o.
Glenfarclas 30 y.o.

WILLIAM GRANT & SONS LTD

Blended Whiskies
Grant's Royal
Clan MacGregor
William Grant's Family Reserve
William Grant's 12 y.o.
William Grant's 21 y.o.
William Grant's Old Gold 12 y.o.
William Grant's Classic 18 y.o.
William Grant's Superior Strength
William Grant's Centenary 8 y.o.

Malt Whiskies
Glenfiddich Special Reserve
Glenfiddich Classic
Glenfiddich Excellence 18 y.o.
Balvenie Founders Reserve 10 y.o.
Balvenie 12 y.o.
Balvenie Classic 18 y.o.
Balvenie Doublewood
Balvenie Single Barrel

THE INVERGORDON DISTILLERS LTD

Blended Whiskies
The Original Mackinlay
Cluny
Findlater's Finest

Grain Whiskies
The Invergordon Single Grain 10 y.o.

Malt Whiskies
Bruichladdich 10 y.o.
Bruichladdich 15 y.o.
Bruichladdich 21 y.o.
Tamnavulin Glenlivet 10 y.o.
Isle of Jura 10 y.o.
Tullibardine 10 y.o.

INVER HOUSE DISTILLERS LTD

Blended Whiskies
Inver House Green Plaid
Inver House Green Plaid 12 y.o.
Hankey Bannister
MacArthur's Select
MacArthur's Select 12 y.o.

Catto's
Catto's 12 y.o.
Pinwhinnie Royale

Malt Whiskies
Blairmhor 8 y.o.
Speyburn 10 y.o.
An Cnoc 12 y.o.

WILLIAM LAWSON DISTILLERS LTD

Blended Whiskies
William Lawson's
William Lawson's Scottish Gold 12 y.o.
King Edward

Malt Whiskies
Glen Deveron 5 y.o.
Glen Deveron 12 y.o.

MACALLAN-GLENLIVET plc

Malt Whiskies
The Macallan 10 y.o.
The Macallan 12 y.o.
The Macallan 18 y.o.
The Macallan 25 y.o.

MACDONALD MARTIN DISTILLERIES plc

Blended Whiskies
Highland Queen
Highland Queen Grand Reserve
    15 y.o.

Highland Queen Supreme 21 y.o.
James Martin's Special
James Martin's VVO
James Martin's De Luxe 12 y.o.
James Martin's 20 y.o.

Malt Whiskies
Glenmorangie 10 y.o.
Glenmorangie 18 y.o.
Glenmorangie Single
    Barrel Vintage
Glen Moray 12 y.o.
Glen Moray 15 y.o.
Glen Moray 17 y.o.
Glen Moray Glenlivet 1964
Glen Moray Glenlivet 1973

MORRISON BOWMORE DISTILLERS LTD

Blended Whiskies
Roy Roy
Clanroy

Malt Whiskies
Bowmore Legend
Bowmore 10 y.o.
Bowmore 12 y.o.
Bowmore 17 y.o.
Bowmore 21 y.o.
Bowmore 25 y.o.
Black Bowmore
30th Anniversary Bowmore
Auchtentoshan Select
Auchtentoshan 10 y.o.
Auchtentoshan 21 y.o.
Glen Garioch 1984

Glen Garioch 12 y.o.
Glen Garioch 15 y.o.
Glen Garioch 21 y.o.

TOMATIN DISTILLERY CO LTD

Blended Whiskies
Big 'T'

Malt Whiskies
Tomatin 10 y.o.

WHYTE & MACKAY GROUP plc

Blended Whiskies
Whyte & Mackay Special Reserve
Whyte & Mackay 12 y.o.
Whyte & Mackay 21 y.o.
The Claymore
Crawford's Three Star
The Real Mackenzie
Old Mull
John Barr
Buchanan Blend
Haig
Stewarts Finest Old

Malt Whiskies
The Dalmore 12 y.o.
Tomintoul-Glenlivet 8 y.o.
Tomintoul-Glenlivet 12 y.o.
Old Fettercairn 10 y.o.

INDEX

Names of whiskies are printed in *italics*. Bold numerals refer to page numbers of illustrations.

Abbey of the Holy Rood, Edinburgh 44
Abbotsford **24–5**, 27
Aberdeen 129, 135–9, **135**, 143, 155
Aberdeen, 1st Marquess of 132–5
Aberfeldy 92
Aberfeldy 208, 210
Aberfeldy Distillery 94, **94**, 95
Aberlour 154, 158
Aberlour 208, 212
Achiltibuie 124
Ackergill Castle 170
Adam, John 50
Adam, Robert 50, 60
Adam, William 31, 50, 129, 132
Adelphi Distillery 10
Advie 157
Airlie, 13th Earl of 88
Airlie, Countess of 88
Airlie Castle 88
Albert, Prince Consort 81, 94, 139, **139**, 140
Alexander I, King 32, 168
Alexander III, King 61
Alexander & Macdonald 64
Alexandra of Kent, HRH Princess 88
Allan, Alexander Grigor 150
Allied Distillers 14, 66, 68, 161, 210, 211, 213, 214, 215, 216
Allied Lyons 85
Alloa 50
Alloway 61
Allt a' Bhainne Distillery 157
Almond, River 49

Alness 167
Alness, River 167
Altrive *see* Edinhope
Alves 150
American Glencoe Foundation 196
An Cnoc 208, 211
An Gobha the Smith 145
An Teallach 123, 124
Anderson & Co, Nicol 47
Annan 56
Ansdell, Richard **174**, **194**
Anstruther 50
Appin Murder, the 114
Applecross 123
Arbroath 85
Arbroath Abbey 85
Ardbeg 208, 214
Ardbeg Distillery 181, 183
Ardblair Castle 90
Ardchattan Priory 114
Ardgay 168
Ardmore 208, 211
Ardmore Distillery 66, 132
Argyll, 12th Duke of 13, 104–8, 113
Arisaig 110
Arkwright, Sir Richard 79
Armadale Castle 196
Armour, Jean 52, 61
Arran 10, **176**
Arthur, King 27
Astor, Viscountess 190–2
Athole brose 27, 54
Atholl, 10th Duke of 13, 96
Atholl Highlanders 96–7, **96**
Atlantic Ocean 57, 102, 123, 175
Auchencairn 56
Auchentoshan 208, 209
Auchentoshan Distillery **2** (frontispiece), 42, **64**, 68

Auchroisk Distillery **143**, 161
Auchterarder 77
Auld Alliance, the 19
Aultmore 208, 212
Aultmore Distillery 161
Aultmore Glenlivet Distilleries 102, 156
Australia 74
Aviemore 98
Avon, River 143, 158
Ayr 61

Bachelors' Club, the 61
Badentarbet Bay 124
Balblair 208, 211
Balblair Distillery 167
Ballachulish 118
Ballantrae 59
Ballindalloch 156, 157
Balmaclellan 23
Balmoral Castle 81, 139–40
Balmoral Forest 139
Balvenie, The 161, 208, 212
Balvenie Castle **157**
Balvenie Distillery 157
Banff 129, 130
Bannockburn, Battle of (1314) 63, 79–80, 143, 147
Barnhill 190
Barra *see* Hebrides (Outer)
Barrie, Sir James 88
Barry, Charles 168
Bass Rock 32
Baxter, John 64
Beauly Firth 165
Bell, A. K. 81
Bell, Arthur 80
Bell & Son, Arthur 80–1, 161
Ben Attow 119
Ben Breac **192**
Ben Chonzie 79

Ben Cruachan **106–7**, 114
Ben Eighe 123
Ben Lomond **65**, 68
Ben Nevis 98, 118, **121**
Ben Nevis Distillery **121**
Ben Odhar **117**
Ben Rinnes 156, 157
Ben Wyvis 166, 167
Benbecula *see* Hebrides (Outer)
Benderloch 114
Bennane Head 59
Benriach 208, 212
Benriach Distillery 150
Benrinnes 208, 212
Benrinnes Distillery 154, 156, 161
Berry, Francis 151
Berry Bros & Rudd 14, 151, 212, 216
Berwick-upon-Tweed **17**, 20, 31, 49
Bin of Cullen 162
Black, James 44
Black Isle 165–6
Blackford 77
Blackfriars' Monastery, Perth 80
Blair Athol 208, 210
Blair Athol Distillery 92, **92**
Blair Castle 13, **14**, **77**, 95–6 **96**, 97
Blairgowrie Highland Games 90
Blane Valley 68
Blue, Johnny 108
Bog of Gight Castle 162
Bonar Bridge 168
Bonnie Prince Charlie *see* Charles Edward, Prince
Borders *see under* Lowlands
Boswell, James 130, 132; *quoted* 74, 177, 196
Bothwell, Earl of 21–2

Bough, Samuel **62**
Bowhill 20
Bowmore 186, **188**
Bowmore 208, 214
Bowmore Distillery 181, 186, **188**, **189**
Braemar 140
Braes of Glenlivet Distillery 147
Brahan Seer, the *quoted* 74
Braw Lads' Gathering (Galashiels) 27
Breadalbane 113
Brechin 88
British Garden Festival (1988) 66
Brodie Castle 147
Broomhall **10**, 50
Brora **165**, 170
Brotherhood of Scotch Whisky Tasters 12
Broughderig 88
Broughty Ferry 85
Brown, George Mackay 204
Brown, Peter 150
Brown, William 150
Brown & Co, John 68
Bruce, Robert the 19, 80, 81, 85, 102, 143, 147
Bruce, Sir William 22, 44, 50
Bruichladdich 208, 214
Bruichladdich Distillery 181, 186
Bruxner, James 49
Bryce, David 170
Buccleuch, 9th Duke of 52
Buchanan, James 64
Buchanan & Co, James 95, 102
Buckie 129, 162
Bullers of Buchan **130**, 132
Bunnahabhain 208, 214
Bunnahabhain Distillery 64, 181
Burghead 155
Burn, William 147

Burn Stewart Distillers 192, 210 214, 216
Burns, Robert 22, 23, 50, 52–6, 56, 61, 151
Burns House Museum, Mauchline 61
Burns Night 54–6
Burray 201
Burrell Collection, Glasgow 66
Bute 61
Byron, Lord 28, 162

Caerlaverock 57
Cairn, River 57
Cairn o'Mount 86
Cairnbulg Castle 129
Cairngorm Mountains 73, 143, 145
Cairngorm Whisky Centre 98
Caithness 32
Calder, Sir James 64
Caledonian Canal 98
Caledonian Distillery 47
Caledonian MacBrayne Ferries 102
Calgary Castle 198
Cam an Tuire **89**
Cambus Grain Distillery 50
Cameron Bridge Distillery 46, 50
Campbell, Archibald 185
Campbell & Co, S. 91
Campbell Distillers 14, 91, 155, 210, 212, 216–17
Campbell of Glenure, Colin 114–18
Campbeltown Loch **108**, 110
Campsie Fells 68, 73
Canada 74
Caol Ila 208, 214
Caol Ila Distillery **180**, 181–3
Cape Wrath 124
Caperdonich 208, 212
Caperdonich Distillery 151, **151**, 156
Cappercleuch 28
Carbost 198
Cardhu 208, 212

Cardhu Distillery 155
Cardow 154, 155, 161
Cardrona 20
Carew, The Hon. Gerald Maitland 22
Carlyle, Thomas 57; *quoted* 23
Carnegie, Alexander 168
Carnoustie 85
Carron 154
Carter Bar 21
Castle Forter 88–90
Castle Fraser 127
Castle Grant 145
Castle Leod 166
Castle Menzies 94, **96**
Castle of Mey 171
Castle Stalker 114, **119**
cattle-drovers *see* drovers
cattle-stealing 52, **53**, 68
Cawdor 148
Cawdor Castle 148
Charles II, King 32, 44, 81
Charles Edward, Prince ('Bonnie Prince Charlie') **12**, 20, 27, 52, 63, 73, 90, 96, 98, 119, 175, 196, 198
Cheviot Hills 21
Children of the Mist 68
Chivas & Glenlivet Group, The 14
Chivas Bros 10, 150, 151, 162
Christie, George 98
Clarke, Frank 98
Clovenfords 28
Clunie Water **91**
Clyde, River **62**, 63, 68
Clydebank **64**, 66–8
Clynelish 208, 211
Clynelish Distillery **165**, 170
Cockburn, John 32
Coffey, Aeneas 46
Coigach 124
Coldingham 31
Coldstream 31
Colonsay *see under* Islands
Common Ridings 22
Comrie 77

Comyn, John 81
Conglass Water **145**
Connacher, Alexander 92
Conon Bridge 166
Conval Hills 158
Corn Laws 50
Corryvreckan 188
Cortachy Castle 88
Cowal 61, 113
Cowie, Dr Alexander 161
Cowie, George 161
Crabbie, John M. 49
Cragganmore 208, 212
Cragganmore Distillery 157
Craig, Charles 48
Craig, James 44
Craigellachie **149**, 151, **151**, 152
Craigellachie 208, 212
Craigellachie Bridge **149**, 151
Craigellachie Distillery 151, **151**, 161
Craighouse 190
Craigievar Castle 127
Craignure 192
Craigroyston 68
Crail 50
Cramond 49
Crathes Castle 127
Crathie 139, 140
Cree, River 57
Crianlarich 113–14
Crieff 77, **78**, 79, **97**, 98
Crinan Canal 99, 108
Crocket, S. S. 56, **59**
Cromartie, 5th Earl of 166
Cromarty 166
Cromarty Firth 48, 165, 167
Cromdale 144
Cromwell, Oliver 32, 127
Crossraguel Abbey 61
Cruden Bay 132
Cuillin Hills 124, 196, 198
Cullen 129
Cullen House 129
Culloden, Battle of (1746) 20, 23, 73, 92, 98, 148

Culloden Moor 98
Culzean Castle 60, **60**, 61
Cumberland, William Augustus, Duke of 92, 98, 145
Cumming, Elizabeth 155
Cumming, Helen 154–5
Cumming, John 154–5
Cumming, John P. 155
Cumstie, Peter 102
Currie, Harold 10
Cutty Sark Visitor Centre 151

Dailuaine 208, 212
Dailuaine Distillery 155–6
Dalkeith 20
Dalkeith Palace 27
Dallas Dhu 208, 212
Dallas Dhu Distillery **146**, 147
Dalmeny House 49
Dalmore 208, 211
Dalmore Distillery 167
Dalrymple, John 92
Dalwhinnie 98
Dalwhinnie 208, 210
Dalwhinnie Distillery 97, **97**, 98
dancing 140, **140**
Darnaway Castle 147
Darnley, Lord 44
David I, King 19, 21, 44, 50
Davies, Sir Peter Maxwell 204
Deanston 208, 210
Deanston Distillery 79
Debatable Land, the 20
Dee, River 136, **138**, 139
deer 88, 124, **141**, 188
deer-stalking 124, 140–1
Department of Historic Buildings and Monuments *see* Historic Scotland
Deveron, River **127**, 130
Devil's Beef Tub 28, 52, **53**
Dewar, John 94
Dewar, John Alexander 94
Dewar, Tommy 94–5
Dewar & Sons, John 92, 94, 95, 102, 156

Dingwall Castle 144
Dirleton Castle 32
distilleries 8–202 *passim*, 207–17
Distillers Company Ltd (DCL) 47, 48, 50, 63, 64, 95, 102, 140, 152, 170, 192
Don, River 139
Dornoch Firth 167, 168
Dornoch Bay 168
Douglas, William 57
Doune 79
Dowally 95
Drambuie 10, 198
drovers and drove roads 73, 76, 79, 97–8, **97**, **106**, **126**, 139, **194**
Drum Castle 127
Drumguish 98
Drumlanrig 20, 52
Drumochter 97
Dryburgh Abbey 27, **30**
Dryhope Tower 28
Drysdale, Andrew 47
Duart Castle 192
Duff, James 150
Duff, William (Lord Braco) 129–30
Duff House 129–30
Dufftown **156**, 158
Dufftown Distillery **158–9**
Dufftown-Glenlivet Distillery 158, 161
Dullan, River 158
Dumbarton **67**, 68, 98
Dumfries 52, 54, **54–5**, 56, **56**, 81
Dumgoyne 68
Dunaad 99
Dunbar 31–2
Duncan I, King 195
Duncansby Head 170
Dundee 84, 88, 127, 147
Dundonnel 123
Dunfermline 44, 49–50
Duirinish 196
Dunnet Head 170, **171**

Dunnottar 23
Dunnottar Castle 127, **131**
Dunnyveg Castle 181, 185
Dunollie Castle 102
Dunoon 61, 113
Dunrobin 168
Dunrobin Castle 73, 168, 169
Duns 31
Duns Castle 31
Duns Scotus 31
Dunslair Heights 28
Dunstaffnage, Captain of 113
Dunvegan Castle 196–8
Dunvegan Castle Arts Festival 196
Durness 124

Earn, River 79
Easter Elchies House **152, 153**, 154
Ecclefechan 57
Edderton 167
Edinburgh 8, 19, 20, **26**, 42–4, **45**, 48, 63
Edinburgh Castle 44, 80, 127
Edinhope 28
Edinkillie 144
Edradour 208, 210
Edradour Distillery **90**, 91
Edward, Alexander 147, 156, 161
Edwin, King 44
Eglinton Castle 61
Eglinton Tournament 61, 97
Eildon Hills 21, **24**, 27, **29**
Eilean Donan Castle 121
Eisenhower, Dwight D. 60
Elderslie 63
Elgin 148, 150, 155
Elgin, 11th Earl of 9, **10**, 11, 13, 50, 154
Elgin, Countess of **10**
Elibank 20
Elie 50
Elizabeth II, HM Queen 44, 139, 170
Elizabeth the Queen Mother, HM 86, 88, 167–8, 171

Ellesmere, 5th Earl of 168–70
Embo 168
emigration 54, 73, 139, 175, 196
Erroll, 24th Earl of 13, 132, **132**
Erroll, Countess of **132**
Eskdalemuir 28
Ettrick 28
Ettrick Forest 28
Ettrick Water 28
Ewbank, John Wilson **26**
excise duty, evasion of *see under* Scotch whisky

Fairbairn, Sir Nicholas *quoted* 10–11
Fairlie, Alex 98
Fairlie, James 79
Falls of Lorne **118**
Farquharson, W. G. 81
Fettercairn Distillery **84**, 86
Fiddich, River 143, **157**, 158, 161
Fife *see under* Lowlands
Findhorn, River 143, 147, 148
Findlater, James 158
Findlater Castle 129
Finlaggan Castle 179–81
Firth of Clyde 60, 61
Firth of Forth 32, 42, 44, 49, 50
Firth of Lorn **118**, 192
Firth of Tay 50
fishing *see* trout-fishing, salmon-fishing *and under* Scotland
Five Sisters of Kintail 119
Fleet, River 168
Fleming, James 155
Flodden 31
Flodden, Battle of (1513) 22
Floors Castle 20, 31
Fochabers 161, 162
Forfar 86
Forres 147, 155
Fort Augustus 98
Fort William 92, 98, 102, 118
Forth Bridge, Forth Road Bridge 50

Fortrose 165–6
Foulshields 22
Fraser, Sir Alexander 129
Fraser, Captain William 148
Fraserburgh 129
Fyvie Castle 127

Gaelic 19
Gairloch 123
Galashiels 27
games *see* Highland Games
Gare Loch 61
Gardiner, Margaret 202
Garrie, River 124
Gatehouse of Fleet 57
gatherings 88, 90, 110, 113, 140, **140**, 146, 198
George IV, King **26**, 27
Girnigo Castle 170
Girvan 59
Glamis Castle **85**, 86–8
Glasgow 19, 20, 44, **61**, 63, 66, 73, 102, 118, 183
Glasgow School of Art 63
Glen Beg 119
Glen Carron 121
Glen Clova 88
Glen Deveron 208, 211
Glen Dochart 68, 98
Glen Elgin 150
Glen Elgin 208, 212
Glen Feardan 139
Glen Garioch 208, 211
Glen Garioch Distillery **129**, 130
Glen Garry 97
Glen Grant 151, 158
Glen Grant 208, 212
Glen Grant Distillery 148
Glen Gyle 68
Glen Keith 208, 212
Glen Keith Distillery 162
Glen Lochy 114
Glen Lyon 68, 98
Glen Mark 88
Glen Moray 208, 212
Glen Moray Distillery 150

Glen Moray-Glenlivet Distillery 47
Glen More 119
Glen Orchy 68
Glen Ord 166, 208, 211
Glen Ord Distillery 166
Glen Prosen 88
Glen Rothes, The 208, 212
Glen Shiel **104–5**, 121, **125**
Glen Sligachan **174**, 196
Glen Spean 98
Glen Spey 208, 213
Glen Spey Distillery 151
Glen Truim 97, 119
Glenallachie Distillery 154
Glenburgie 208, 213
Glenburgie Distillery 150
Glencadam 208, 210
Glencadam Distillery 88, **88**
Glencoe 98, 113, **114–15** *see also* Massacre of Glencoe
Glendronach 132
Glendronach Distillery 132
Glendullan 208, 213
Glendullan Distillery 158, 161
Gleneagles Hotel 77
Glenelg 97, 119, 121, **123**
Glenelg Bay **71**, 119, **122**
Glenesk 88
Glenfarclas 208, 213
Glenfarclas Distillery 156–7
Glenfiddich 208, 213
Glenfiddich Distillery 9, 158, 161
Glenfinnan 110, 119
Glenglassaugh Distillery 129, **129**
Glengoyne 208, 209
Glengoyne Distillery **66**, 68, **68**
Glenhowan 56
Glenisla 88
Glenkinchie 208, 209
Glenkinchie Distillery 33, **33**
Glenlivet 145, 147, 158
Glenlivet, The 27, 28, 198, 208, 213
Glenlivet and Glen Grant Distillers 149
Glenlivet Distillers 149–50
Glenlivet Distillery 27, **146**, 147,

148, 157–8
Glenlossie 208, 213
Glenlossie Distillery 150
Glenmorangie 208, 211
Glenmorangie Distillery 47, **164**, 167–8
Glenmoriston **104–5**
Glenrothes Distillery 151
Glenshee **86–7**, 88, 90
Glentauchers 208, 213
Glentauchers Distillery **160**, 161
Glentromie 208, 210
Glenturret 208, 210
Glenturret Distillery **78**, 79, **79**, 210
Gloag, Matthew 81
Gloag, Matthew I. 81
Gloag, William B. 81
Gloag & Son, Matthew 213
golf 77
golf-courses 77, 85, 168
Golspie 73, 168
Gordon, John 161
Gordon Castle 150, 162
Gorgie 49
Gow the Smith 145
Gowrie Conspiracy 83
Graham, Alexander 68
Graham, Gillespie 31
Graham, James Gillespie 196
Grampian Mountains 73, **77**, 95–6, **126**, 139
Grampian Region *see under* Highlands
Grant, George **155**, 156
Grant, James 151
Grant, John (of Speyside) 151, **155**, 156
Grant, John (of Rothiemurchus) 27
Grant Distillers, J. & G. 10, 14, **155**, 158, 213, 217
Grant, William 161
Grant, William Smith 148–9
Grant & Sons, William 9, 10, 14, 59–60, **60**, 161, 212, 213, 217

Great Glen, the 73, 98
Green Lowther 51
Greenlees Bros 64
Gretna Green 51
Grey Mare's Tail 28
Grogport 108
grouse 32, 88
grouse-shooting 32, 140
Guinness 81
Gulf of Corryvreckan 190
Gulf Stream 99, 123
Gullane 32

Haddington 32
Haddo, Lord (later 1st Marquis of Aberdeen) 132–5, 162
Haddo House 132
Haig, Field Marshal Earl 27
Haig, John 46, 50
Haig & Co, John 47
Haig & Sons, James 8–9
Hamilton, 15th Duke of 32
Hamilton Palace 20
Hanseatic League 129
Harris see Hebrides (Outer)
Hart, Robert 66
Hawick 22
Hawick Museum & Art Gallery 22
Hebrides (Inner) see under Islands
Hebrides (Outer) 61, 97, 108, 175, 179, 192
    Lewis 8, 97, 102–4, 124
    Harris 97, 124
    North Uist 97
    Benbecula 196
    South Uist 97
    Barra 177
Helmsdale 170
Helmsdale, River 170
Henderson, Hector 183
Henderson, James 170
Hermitage Castle 22
Hestan Island 56, **59**
Higgin, Walter 102
Highland cattle **170**
Highland Clearances 73–4, 168

Highland Distilleries Co, The 14, 64–6, 129, 151, 210, 212, 213, 214, 215, 216
Highland Games 88, 90, **92**, 110, 113, 140
Highland Line 73
Highland Park 208, 215
Highland Park Distillery 201, 202
Highland Society of London 146
Highlands, the 9, 19, 20, 61, 63, **70** (map), 71–171, 175, **210** (map)
    Southern Highlands 77–98
    Western Highlands **71**, 99–125
    Grampian Region and Eastern Highlands 127–41
    Speyside **142** (map), 143–63, **212** (map)
    Northern Highlands 164–71
    Highland and Speyside whiskies and their characteristics 210–14
Hiram Walker Co 170
Hirsel, The 31
Historic Scotland 147
Hogg, James 22, 28, **28**; quoted 28–31
Holy Loch 61
Holyroodhouse, Palace of 27, 44, 80
Home, 14th Earl of 31
Home, Patrick 31
Hopetoun House 50
Hornshole Skirmish 22
Horsburgh 20
Houldsworth, Sir Harry 149
Hoy 204
Hume, David 44
Hunter, Ian 183–5
Hunter, John 52
Hunter's Hill 86
Huntly 132
Hydroponicum, The 124

Illicit Distillation (Scotland) Act (1823) 76

illicit stills and distilling see under Scotch whisky
Imperial 208, 213
Imperial Distillery 154
Inchgower 208, 213
Inchgower Distillery 162
Industrial Revolution 9
Inner Hebrides see under Islands
Innerleithen 28
Innes House 148, **148**
Inver House Distillers Ltd 14, 129, 151, 211, 213, 217
Inveraray **103**, 104
Inveraray Castle **101**, 108
Inverewe Gardens 123–4
Invergarry 119
Invergordon 48, 167
Invergordon 208, 211
Invergordon Distillers Ltd 14, **46**, **47**, 48, **48**, 210, 211, 213, 214, 217
Invergordon Grain Distillery 167
Inverkip 61
Inverness 98, 118, 140, 143, 146, 147
Iona see under Islands
Iona Community 195
Ireland 8, 19, 56, 61, 99, 104
Irish Sea 57, 99
Irvine 61
Irvine, Robert 124
Isla, River **160**, 161, 162
Islands, The 20, 102, 108, 118, **172** (map), 173–205, **214** (map)
    Islay 175, **178**, 179–88, **179**, **180**, **181**, **182–3**, **186**, **187**, **188**, **189**, **191** Jura 108, 183, 188–92, **193**
    Scarba 188
    Mull 102, 192–5, **194**
    Colonsay 102
    Iona 102, 195
    Tiree 102
    Kerrera 102
    Skye 97, 119–20, 121, 124,

140, **174**, 175, **190**, **192**, 195–8, **195**, **197**
    Raasay 177
    Orkney Islands 135, 170–1, 175, 199–205, **199**, **200**, **201**, **202**, **205**
    Shetland Islands 175, 201
    Island whiskies and their characteristics 214–15 see also Hebrides (Outer), Summer Isles, Arran, Bute, St Kilda
Islay see under Islands
Isle of Jura 208, 214
Isle of Jura Distillery 190
Isle of Man 61, 104, 179
Italian Chapel, Lamb Holm 201, **202**, **203**

Jacobite Uprising (1745) 8
James I, King 80
James II, King 31
James IV, King 31, 77, 136
James V, King 198
James VI, King 20, 59, 83, 132
James VII & II, King 92
Jed Water 21
Jedburgh 21
Jedburgh Abbey 21
John O'Groats 170
Johnson, Dr Samuel 102, 132, 196; quoted 74, 148
Johnston, John 185
Johnstone, Robert 166
Jura see under Islands
Justerini & Brooks 14, 151, 161, 213, 216

Keepers of the Quaich, The 13–14, 49, 50, **77**, 132, 148, 154, 216–17
    member companies 14
    banquets 13, **14**, 108
    blends and brands of the member companies 216–17
Keith 161, 162
Kelso 31

Kelso Abbey 31
Kemp, Roderick 152
Kenneth MacAlpine, King 81
Kennethmont 130
Kerrera see under Islands
Kessock Bridge 165
Kilchurn Castle 114, **116**
Kildalton **186**
Kildonan Gold Rush 170
Kilmarnock 61
Kilmartin 99
Kilpatrick Hills 68
Kilravock Castle 148
kilts 27, 145, 146
Kingussie 98
Kininvie Distillery 161
Kingsbarns 50
Kinkel Castle 166
Kinloch Lodge 196
Kinneff 127
Kintail 119, 121, 166
Kintyre 104, 108, **108**, 110, 113
Kirkcudbright 56
Kirkliston 46
Kirkoswald 61
Kirkwall 171, 199, 202
Kirriemuir 88
Knapdale 108
Knock **133**
Knockando 155
Knockando 208, 213
Knockando Distillery 155, **163**
Knockdhu Distillery 129, **133**
Knox, John 44
Kyle of Lochalsh 121
Kyle of Tongue 168
Kylerhea 119, **123**

Lagavulin 183
Lagavulin 208, 214
Lagavulin Bay 185
Lagavulin Distillery 63, 183, **184**, 185
Laggan, River 186, **191**
Lairg 124, 168
Lamb Holm 201

Lammermuir Hills 21, **21**, 31, 32, 33
Landseer, Charles **29**
Landseer, Sir Edwin **72**, **126**
Lang Bros 209
Langholm 57
Laphroaig 208, 214
Laphroaig Distillery **178**, 183
Largs 61, 175
Lauder 22
Laurie, Annie 57
Lawson Distillers, William 14, 211, 217
Laxford 124
Ledaig 192, 208, 214
Ledaig Distillery 192
Leith 44, **46**, **47**, **48**, 49, 155
Lennoxlove 32
Leven, River 50
Lewis *see* Hebrides (Outer)
Lewis, John Frederick **128**
Liddesdale 23
Linklater, Eric 204
Linkwood 208, 213
Linkwood Distillery 150
Linlithgow, 4th Marquess of 50
Linlithgow Palace 50
Lismore 114
Littlemill Distillery 183
Livet, River 143, 158
Loch Awe **106–7**, 114, **116**
Loch Carron 121
Loch Cluanie **104–5**, **106**
Loch Clunie **91**
Loch Creran **112**, 114
Loch Duich 119, 121, **125**, 166
Loch Earn 77
Loch Eil **110**, 114, 118
Loch Eriboll 124
Loch Ericht 98
Loch Etive 114, **118**
Loch Ewe 123
Loch Fyne **103**, 108
Loch Harport 198
Loch Hourn 119
Loch Indaal 186

Loch Laggan 98
Loch Leven 114, 118, **120–1**
Loch Linnhe 98, 114, 118, **119**
Loch Lochy 98
Loch Lomond **65**, 68
Loch Long (Highlands) 121
Loch Long (Strathclyde) 61
Loch Maree 123
Loch Naver 168
Loch Ness 98
Loch of the Lowes 28
Loch Oich 98
Loch Osgaig 124
Loch Ryan 59
Loch Shiel 119
Loch Shin 124, 168
Loch Snizort 196
Loch Tay 92, 94, 98
Loch Torridon 123
Loch Tulla **99**, **111**
Loch Tummel **93**
Loch Turret 79, **79**
Lochaber 118, 140
Lochalsh 118, 121, 198
Lochindorb Castle 144, **146**
Lochmaben Castle 52
Lochnagar **136–7**, 139
Lochnagar Distillery 139–40, **139**
Lochside 208, 210
Lochside Distillery 86
Lochy, River **110**
Lockhart, R. H. Bruce *quoted* 11
Long John Distillers 157
Longmorn 208, 213
Longmorn Distillery 150
Longrow 208, 211
Lorimer, Sir Robert 168
Lossie, River 143, 148, 150
Lossiemouth 148
Lothians *see under* Lowlands
Lowlands, The 9, 19, 17–68, 75, 79, **209** (map)
    Borders 21–31
    Lothians 31–3, 42–5, 47–50
    Fife 44, 49–50
    Southwest **18**, 51–68

Lowland whiskies and their characteristics 209
Lowther Hills 28, 51
Luce Bay 57

Macallan, The 208, 213
Macallan Distillery 152, 154
Macallan-Glenlivet 14, 152, **152**, 213, 217
MacAskill, Hugh 198
Macbeth, King 195
McBey, James 151
McCaig's Folly **100**, 102
MacDiarmid, Hugh 22, 57
Macdonald, 8th Baron 196
Macdonald, Allan 196
Macdonald, Angus 98
Macdonald, Daniel 47
Macdonald, David 48, **49**
Macdonald, Edward 47
Macdonald, Flora 196
Macdonald, 'Long John' 118
Macdonald, Ramsay 148
Macdonald, Roderick 47, 48
Macdonald, Swein **167**, 168
Macdonald & Greenlees 47
Macdonald & Muir 47
Macdonald Martin Distilleries 10, 14, 47–8, 211, 212, 217
Macduff 130
Macduff Distillery **127**, 130
Macfarlane, Lady 49
Macfarlane of Bearsden, Baron 13, **49**
McGonagall, William *quoted* 148
Mackay, Charles 66
Mackay, H.M.S. 150
Mackenzie, Sir Compton 177
Mackenzie, Osgood 76, 123
Mackenzie, Roderick 150
Mackenzie, Thomas (of Mull) 198
Mackenzie, Thomas (of Speyside) 155
Mackenzie, William 155
Mackenzie & Co, P. 92
Mackessack, Douglas 148–9

Mackie, James Logan 63
Mackie, Sir Peter 63–4, 151, 185–6
Mackie & Co 152, 155, 183–5
Mackinlay, Donald 108
Mackinlay & Co, Charles 190
Mackintosh, Charles Rennie 63
Maclean of Duart, Sir Lachlan 192
Maclennan, Donald 166
McLennan, James 49
MacLeod of MacLeod, John 196
Macleod's Tables 196
MacNab Distilleries 210
Macphail, John A.R. 49
MacPherson, Robbie 157
MacThomas of Finegand, Andrew 88
Maes Howe 202
Malcolm III, King 44, 49–50
Malcolm IV, King 147
Malcolm of Poltalloch 113
Mallaig 118, 196
Malt Mill Distillery 185
Malt Tax Riots 74
Mam Rattachan 119
Manderston House 31
Mannoch Hills 150
Mannochmore Distillery 150
Mansfield, 8th Earl of 13, 81–3
Mansfield, Countess of 81
Margadale, River 186–8
Margaret, Queen 44, 49–50
Margaret Rose, HRH Princess 88
Martin, James 47
Martin & Co, James 47
Mary, Queen of Scots 21–2, 44, 50, 147–8
Massacre of Glencoe (1692) 20, 94
Matheson, Alexander 167
Matheson, William 167
Mauchline 61
Maxwell, Gavin **51**, 57–9, 121
Maxwelton House 57
Maybole Castle 61
Minginish 198

Megget Reservoir 28
Melrose 27
Mid Howe 202
Miller, Hugh 166
Miltonduff-Glenlivet 208, 213
Miltonduff-Glenlivet Distillery 150
Mitchell & Co, J. & A. 211
Moffat **18**, 28, 52
Monadhliath Mountains 73, 97, 143, 147
Moncreiffe of that Ilk, Sir Iain 132, 145
Moniaive 57
Monreith Bay **51**, 57
Montrose 86, 127
Moorfoot Hills 21, 28
Moorfoot Loch 88
Morar 118, 198
Moray Firth 129, 147, 148, 162
Morrison, Brian 186
Morrison, Stanley P. 186
Morrison Bowmore Distillers 10, 14, 186, 209, 211, 214, 217
Mortlach 208, 213
Mortlach Distillery **156**, 158, 161
Morvern 118
Morville, Hugo de 27
Mound, The 168
Muir, Alexander 47
Muir, Edwin 204
Muir of Ord 166
Muirhead, Charles
Mulben 161
Mull *see under* Islands
Mull of Kintyre 103, **108**, 110, 113
Munro, Captain Hugh 167
Murdoch, Alexander 48
Murray, Sir David 83
Murray, John 28
Museum of Malt Whisky Production 33

Nairn 148
National Trust for Scotland 57,

60, 61, 88, 124, 132, 147
Neidpath 20
Ness, River 98
New Balvenie Castle 161
New Slains Castle 132
New Zealand 74
Newark 20
Newton, Stewart **23**
Newton, Stewart 57
Nigg Bay 167
Nith, River 52, **54–5**
Noble, Sir Iain 10, 196
North Berwick 32
North British Distillery Co 14, 49, 64
North Sea 129, 139, 170, 171
North Sea oil see under Scotland
Northern Ireland 63, 179
Northern Meeting, the 146
Nova Scotia 74

Oban **100**, 102, 113, 114, 118, 192
Oban 208, 211
Oban Distillery **100**, 102
Ochil Hills 73, 77, 79
Ogilvie, George 127
Ogilvy, The Hon. Sir Angus 88
oil see under Scotland
Old Fettercairn 208, 210
Old Man of Hoy 204
Old Pulteney 208, 211
Old Slains Castle 132, 134
Oliphant, Laurence Blair 90, **92**
Oldmeldrum 130
Ord Distillery 166
Orkney Islands see under Islands
Ormiston 32
Orwell, George 190
ospreys 168
Outer Hebrides see Hebrides (Outer)

Paisley 62
Papa Westray 204
Paps of Jura see Jura, under Islands

Park, Mungo 22
Pass of Drumochter 97
Paterson, Robert 23
Paxton House 31
Pentland Firth 170, **171**, 199
Pernod-Ricard 91
Perth 80, 90, 147, 155
Peterhead 132
Pier Art Gallery, Stromness 202
Pitlochry 90, 92, **92**
Pitlochry Hydro-Electric Dam and Fish Ladder 90–1
Pittenweem 50
plaids 145
Playfair, John 44
Playfair, William 31
Plockton 121
Pluscarden Abbey 150
Poolewe 123
Port Dundas 66
Port Ellen 183, 185, **186–7**
Port Erroll 132
Port Glasgow **62**
Port William 59
Porteous Affair 74
Portgordon 161
Portknockie 129
Portnahaven **181**
Portree 198
Portsoy 129
Prestonpans 32
prohibition 81
Pulteney Distillery 170
punch 8

quaichs 12, **12**, **13** see also The Keepers of the Quaich
Queensferry 49–50

Raasay see under Islands
Rannoch Moor 98, **109**, 118
Reagan, Ronald 108
Red Deer Commission 124
Red Smiddy, the 123
Rennie, John 108
Richardson, Sir Albert **156**, 157

Ring of Brogar 202, **205**
Rizzio, David 44
Robert I, King see Bruce, Robert the
Robert II, King 143–4
Robertson, George 49
Robertson, James 139
Robertson, Robert 92
Robertson, William 64, 188
Robertson & Baxter 14, 64, 188, 216
Robertson of Faskally 92, **92**
Rosebery, 7th Earl of 49
Rosemarkie 165
Ross, George 166
Ross, William 47
Rothes 150–1
Rothes-Glenlivet Distillery 64
Roxburghe, 10th Duke of 31
Royal Brackla 208, 213
Royal Brackla Distillery 148
Royal Lochnagar 208, 211
Royal Mile, Edinburgh 44
Rudd, Major Hugh 151
Ruthven, William, Earl of Gowrie 83

St Abbs 31
St Andrew 50
St Andrews 50, 136
St Anthony's Chapel, Holyrood Park, Edinburgh **45**
St Boswells 168
St Catherine's Bay 132
St Columba 8, 148, 195
St Giles, High Kirk of, Edinburgh 44
St Kilda 175
St Magnus Cathedral, Kirkwall 199, **200**
St Margaret see Margaret, Queen
St Mary's Loch and Kirk 28
St Monan's 50
St Ninian 57
St Patrick 8
Salen 102

salmon 91, 136, 143, 168
salmon-fishing **29**, 124, 140–1
Saltcoats 61, 108
Saltoun, Lady 129
Sandeman, Thomas 80
Sanderson, William 49
Sandyknowe 22
Sanquhar 52
Sawney Bean's Cave 59
Scapa 208, 215
Scapa Distillery 202
Scapa Flow 170, 201, 202
Sciennes House, Edinburgh **23**
Scone Abbey 77, 81
Scone Palace 81, 83, 84
Scotch whisky 8–202 passim, 207–17
  origins and development of whisky industry 8–9, 20, 44, 48–9, 63–6
  manufacture of malt whisky 33–43, **35–43**, 209
  manufacture of grain whisky 44–6, **60**
  maturation 42, 155
  blending 9, 46–7, **46**, 69
  bottling **47**, **48**, 148, 155, 209–15
  exports 8, 9, 13, 66, 81, 136
  illicit stills and distilling 8, 20, 76, 97
  smuggling and evasion of excise duty 49, 52, 56–7, **58**, 59, **59**, 61, 74, 75, 79, 108, 123, 132, 139 145, 146–7, 154–5, 157, 158, 161, 167, 190, 202
  regional variations in taste 9, 209–15
  main blends and brands of member companies of The Keepers of the Quaich 216–17
Scotch Whisky Association 8, 49
Scotland
  geography 19

early history 8, 19, 20, 51, 57, 61, 79–80, 81, 99
  agriculture 19, 20, 32, 51, 52
  sea-fishing 124, 129, 139
  industry 19–20, 22, 63, 84, 136–9
  North Sea oil 139, 166–7, 170, 201
  tourism 9, 101
  see also Lowlands, Highlands, Islands
Scott, Mary (the 'Flower of Yarrow') 28
Scott, Michael 27
Scott, Captain Robert 88
Scott, Sir Walter 22–3, **23**, 24, **24–5**, 27, 28, **30**, 44, 50, 57, 147; quoted 31
  see also Abbotsford
Scott, William 66
Scottish & Newcastle Breweries 190
Scottish Civic Trust 154
Scottish dancing see dancing
Scottish Grain Distillers 66
Scottish Malt Distillers 33
sea-trout see trout
Seagram Co, The 148, 150, 212, 213, 216
Selkirk 22
Sgurr Alasdair 196
Sgurr nan Gillean 196
Shakespeare, William 86, 147
Shee Water 90
Shetland Islands see under Islands
Shiach, Allan 152
Shieldaig 123
Shuna 114
Sinclair, John 192
Sinclair's Bay 170
Singleton of Auchroisk, The 203, 213
Skara Brae 171, 202
Skelmorlie 61
Skibo Castle 168
Skye see under Islands
Slioch 123, 124

Slitrig Water 22
Smailholm 20, 22
Small Isles Bay 190
Small Stills Act (1816) 75
Smith, Adam 44
Smith, George 147
Smith, John 157
smuggling see under Scotch whisky
Society of Improvers of
    Knowledge of Agriculture 32
Solway Firth 51, 52, 56, 57, **58,
    59**
Somerville, John 49
Sound of Islay 181–3, 188
Sound of Jura 108, **188**
Sound of Mull 192
Sound of Raasay 198
Sound of Sleat 119, 196
Souter Johnnie's Cottage,
    Kirkoswald 61
South Esk, River 85–6
South Ronaldsay 201
South Uist see under Hebrides
    (Outer)
Spanish Armada 192–5
Spean Bridge 98
Spey, River 98, 143, 148, **149,**
    150, 151, 154, 155, 157, 158,
    160, 161
Spey Valley **154,** 156
Speyburn 208, 213
Speyburn Distillery 151
Speyside see under Highlands
Speyside Aberlour – Glenlivet
    Distillery Co 91
Speyside Distilleries Group 98
Speyside Distillery 98
Speyside Distillery Co 10, 88, 210
Speyside Single 208, 210
Speyside Vatted 208, 210
Speyside Whisky Trail 9
Spinningdale 168
Spittal of Glenshee 88, 90
Springbank 208, 211
Springbank Distillery 108

Stafford, 2nd Marquess of 73–4
stalking see deer-stalking
Stein, Robert 46
Stein & Co, Andrew 46
Stevenson, Hugh 102
Stevenson, John 102
Stevenson, Robert Louis 59, 114,
    198
Stewart, Alexander see Wolf of
    Badenoch
Stewart, Alexander (whisky
    merchant) 84
Stewart, John 92
Stewart, Robert (Duke of Albany)
    79
Stewart & Son 88
Stewart of Glen Duror, James 118
Stirling 79, 98
Stirling Castle **80**
Stoker, Bram 132
Stone of Destiny (coronation
    stone) 81, 85, 99
Stonehaven 127
Stornoway 124
Stranraer 59
Strath 198
Strathallan 77, 79
Strathardle 90
Strathardle Highland Games 88
Strathclyde Grain Distillery 66
Strathearn 77, 98
Strathisla 208, 213
Strathisla Distillery **158,** 161–2
Strathmill Distillery 162
Strathnaver, Lord 168
Strathpeffer 166
Strathspey Railway 155, 157
Strathtay 95
Stromeferry 121
Stromness 199, **201,** 202
Stuart, James 151
Summer Isles 124
Sutherland, Countess of 168

Tain 167

Takara Shuzo & Okara & Co 214
Tala Reservoir 28
Talisker 196, 198, 208, 214
Talisker Distillery 152, **190,** 194,
    198
Tam O'Shanter Museum, Ayr 61
Tamdhu 208, 213
Tamdhu Distillery 158
Tamnavulin Distillery 147, 158
Tamnavulin Glenlivet 208, 213
Tanera Mor 124
Tankerness Museum, Kirkwall 199
Tarbert 190
Tarbert Bay 192–5
Tarbolton 61
tartans 13, 27, 145
Tarves 132
Tay, River 80, 84
Tay Bridge **82–3,** 84
Tay Road Bridge 84
Taymouth Castle 92, 94
Taynuilt 110
Teacher, William 66
Teacher, William Bergius 66
Teacher, William Curtis 66
Teacher & Sons, William 130–2
Teangue 196
Teaninich 208, 211
Teaninich Distillery 167
Teith, River 79
Telford, Thomas 98, **149,** 151
Tennant, Sir Iain 13, 148, **148,**
    149, 150
Teviot, River 22, **22**
Thirlestane Castle 22
Thomson, George 66–8
Thomson, James 66–8
Thomson, John 155
Thomson & Co, R.H. 167
Threave 57
Tibbie Shiel's Inn 28
Tillycairn **138**
Timespan Heritage Centre 170
Tinto Hills 28
Tiree see under Islands

Tobermory 102
Tobermory 192, 208, 214
Tobermory Harbour 192
Tochieneal Distillery 162
toddy 8, 28
Tomatin 208, 214
Tomatin Distillery 147
Tomatin Distillery Co 14, 217
Tomintoul Distillery 147, 158
Tomintoul Glenlivet 208, 214
Tomnavoulin 158
Tormore 208, 214
Tormore Distillery **156,** 157
Torridon 124
Treaty of Union between Scotland
    and England (1707) 74
Tromie, River 98
Trossachs, the 79
Trotternish 196
trout 136
trout-fishing 124, 140
Tullibardine 208, 210
Tullibardine Distillery 77
Tummel, River **95**
Tweed, River **24,** 27–8, 31
Tweedsmuir Hills 28, **53**

Uist, North and South see
    Hebrides (Outer)
Ullapool 124
United Distillers 9, 14, 66, 95,
    147, 152, 161, 162, 198, 209,
    210, 211, 212, 213, 214, 216
Usher, Andrew 46, 49

Victoria, Queen 27, 44, 81, **93,**
    94, 97, 135, 139–40, **139,**
    140, 148
Vikings 19, 61

Wade, General George 73, 98
Waitt, Richard 145
Walker, Alexander 63
Walker, Archibald 10

Walker, James 10
Walker, John 63
Walker & Sons, John 95, 155, 161
Walkerburn 28
Wallace, Sir William 27, 63
Walpole, Sir Robert 74
West Highland Line 118
whisky see Scotch whisky
White Cockade Society 90, **92**
White Horse Distillers 47, 102,
    152
Whitesands 52
Whithorn 57, **57**
Whyte, James 66
Whyte & Mackay Group, The 14,
    48, 66, 210, 211, 214, 217
Wick 170
Wick River 170
Wigtown 59
Wigtown Bay 57
Wilkie, David 27
William of Orange 92–4
William the Lion, King 32, 52,
    85, 136, 166, 168
Williams & Son, William 64
Wilson, Alexander 162
Wilson, Edward 88
Wilson, John 61
Wilton Lodge 22
Windygates 50
Wishaw Distillery 157
Witch of Cruachan 99
Wolf of Badenoch 79, 114,
    144–5, **146**
Wright, Hedley 108
Wright & Greig 147

Yarrow Valley 22
Yawkins, Jack 57
Young & Co, William 8
Young Pretender, the see Charles
    Edward, Prince
Ythan, River 162